The PARENTS™ Magazine Baby and Childcare Series combines the most up-to-date medical findings, the advice of doctors and child psychologists, and the actual day-to-day experiences of parents like you. Covering a wide variety of subjects, these books answer all your questions, step-by-important-step, and provide the confidence of knowing you're doing the best for your child—with help from PARENTS™ Magazine.

"Dr. Wessel's book reflects his thorough scientific training in modern pediatrics and his long and varied experience as a hospital physician, teacher, and clinical practitioner in the community. His advice and guidance are realistically practical, based on solid medical facts, yet highly tinged with compassion and sincere affection and genuine concern for parents and children."

> Milton J. E. Senn, M.D.
> Sterling Professor Emeritus
> Pediatrics and Psychiatry
> Yale University

Parents™
Book for
Raising a
Healthy Child

MORRIS A. WESSEL, M.D.

BALLANTINE BOOKS • NEW YORK

Library of Congress Catalog Card Number: 86-91590

ISBN 0-345-31430-1

Manufactured in the United States of America

First Edition: April 1987
Sixth Printing: August 1989

Contents

Expanded Contents

Introduction

A great deal of a practicing pediatrician's time is devoted to explaining to parents why their infant, toddler, or child is acting differently than he or she was a few weeks ago. In many instances, the child's behavior reflects normal growth and development; in other instances, the child is responding to certain stresses; and, of course, sometimes the child is suffering a mild, or at times, a major illness.

Parents™ *Book for Raising a Healthy Child* was written to help answer parents' questions and aid them in understanding their child's behavior so that they can comfort and support the child as necessary. It is intended to supplement the advice of their child's physician.

The book is divided into five main sections. The first section, YOUR CHILD'S DEVELOPMENT, begins with choosing your child's pediatrician, an important step in assuring careful monitoring of health and development. The section goes on to examine the enormous leaps an infant makes as he or she becomes a toddler, as the toddler becomes a preschooler, and as the preschooler enters the school-age years. Although each individual's development is strongly affected by his or her temperament, personality, and environment, human beings also exhibit an orderly pattern of development that is basic for all infants and children, and guidelines on what a parent can expect are set forth here. Each chapter also discusses specific parenting concerns of each age, such as breastfeeding vs. bottlefeeding in the chapter concerning early infancy and toilet teaching in the chapter about toddlers.

The second section, YOUR CHILD'S WELL-BEING, presents a discussion of many common developmental concerns, for example, when and when not to worry about certain developmental lags or a child's reaction to various stresses such as moving or family illness. Many times the child's behavior represents normal reactions to growth and maturation; other times (and we'll discuss when) a parent may want to seek additional guidance. This section also covers sex education, day-care and nursery school experiences, and children's reactions to loss of a loved family member, as well as some special problems inherent in adoption.

The third section, THE HEALTHY CHILD, presents our current knowledge of preventive health care. Working with your doctor, what you need to know about immunizations, dental care, and allergies, how to develop good health habits in your child, and how to prevent household accidents and perform basic first aid are also discussed since these are important subjects for every parent to know about and understand.

The fourth section, ILLNESS, begins with a discussion of fever and continues with a chapter called How to Tell If Your Child Is Sick or Very Sick, which identifies various illnesses by symptom rather than by medical name—a particularly helpful, middle-of-the-night guide for parents who want advice but don't know the name of their child's illness. Hospitalization and chronic illness are also covered.

Section five, the A TO Z GUIDE TO YOUR CHILD'S HEALTH, offers in alphabetical order a long list of common conditions so that parents can read more about specific matters of special concern.

I firmly believe that there is no one best way to care for a child. This book is intended to assist parents in caring for their children in a way that fits each family's individual lifestyle, while still providing parents with the latest health care information possible. If this book helps parents better understand and appreciate their infant, toddler, or child, and enables them to support and encourage their child with as much joy and happiness as possible, I shall be very delighted.

1 Your Child's Development

1. Selecting a Pediatrician

Until relatively recently, most parents waited until after their baby's birth—and many until their child's first illness—to find a pediatrician. Today, more and more couples are recognizing the importance of deciding upon a doctor to care for their infant before the child is born. In fact, it has become common practice to schedule a prenatal pediatric conference with one or more doctors in order to select the pediatrician who is best suited to meet the family's needs.

I consider the prenatal pediatric conference important for several reasons. First, it gives mothers- and fathers-to-be an opportunity to develop a feeling of confidence in the doctor *before* they need him or her. It's reassuring to know that if you have a question the day after you bring your baby home from the hospital (a likely occurrence!), or if the baby suddenly becomes ill, you have someone to whom you can turn with trust. Second, this prebirth meeting gives the pediatrician a chance to find out if there is anything in the parents' medical history that might have a bearing on the child's health. Third, it gives the parents a chance to

3

discuss in advance their concerns about such matters as feeding, dressing, and taking care of a newborn.

How should parents go about choosing a doctor for their infant? First, seek a physician who is well trained in the care of infants and children. Other parents whose opinions you value are usually a good source of referral, since they can most directly address your concerns. The local medical society, the chief of staff of a hospital, the head of the pediatrics department of the nearest medical school, or your obstetrician can also provide names of qualified physicians in your community.

Once you have a half-dozen names, it is a good idea to narrow the list by calling each doctor's office and chatting briefly with the nurse or receptionist. Ask what the doctor's hours are, how you can reach the doctor when you have concerns about your baby, and what provisions are made for night, weekend, and vacation coverage. Will you be able to talk with the doctor or one of his or her colleagues at any time of the day or night, if necessary? What hospital does the doctor usually use when a child needs inpatient care? Is the office open on Saturdays and Sundays? What is the fee structure? Where do patients park?

If you are satisfied with the answers you receive, arrange for a prenatal conference. Most doctors like to meet with prospective parents (some may suggest a phone interview instead). Be sure to ask in advance about a charge for this visit, since policies vary regarding fees.

During this first meeting, you will want to share with the doctor your own medical history as well as that of any close relatives. The presence of metabolic, neurologic, or allergic disease in the family can be important information for your child's physician. For example, a formula-fed baby might be experiencing diarrhea and cramps during the first few weeks of life. If the pediatrician knows that many members of the family have allergies, he or she is more likely to suspect a sensitivity to cow's milk than if there were no known history of allergies. (Recent studies suggest that even a breast-fed baby with a milk sensitivity may have cramps when his or her nursing mother drinks cow's milk or eats other dairy products.)

Anemia, hypertension, thyroid disease, viral infections,

bleeding during pregnancy, previous history of miscarriage, or difficulty in becoming pregnant may also have a bearing on the health of the baby. The mother's and father's blood types should be mentioned since an incompatibility between the mother's and the baby's blood, which may cause serious and significant jaundice and anemia in the early days of life, must be treated promptly.

This is also a good time to discuss feeding plans for your baby. If you plan to nurse, be sure the doctor supports breastfeeding, since the interest and advice of a concerned physician can contribute significantly to the ultimate success of the experience. If you plan to bottle feed, ask for the pediatrician's recommendations on formula type and brand, equipment needed, and sterilization procedures.

The pediatrician's opinion on circumcision, the removal of the foreskin of the penis, will also be of significance. The procedure is usually performed immediately after birth by the obstetrician who delivers the baby. (Of course, if the baby is premature or has been ill, the circumcision is postponed.) In the first weeks of life, circumcision is a minor procedure and is not believed to be disturbing to the infant.

Most male children born in the United States are circumcised, although it is not a routine procedure in many other parts of the world. For some families, the decision is a religious one. For most parents, however, the decision is based primarily on personal preference. For example, if the father has been circumcised, he often prefers that his son be circumcised, too.

Whether any medical reason exists for routine circumcision is debatable. Those in favor of the practice note some chance of irritation or infection when the foreskin remains, and there are rare circumstances (for example, when there is an unusually tight foreskin) that suggest that retraction of the foreskin later on will be difficult. If the foreskin is removed in early infancy, the possibility of these problems and the necessity of circumcision at a later date, when it would be far more traumatic, are avoided. Ultimately, however, you must make the decision with which you are most comfortable.

You will also want to talk about when and how often the doctor will see your baby during the early months. The first examination generally takes place in the hospital, shortly after birth. Usually, the pediatrician you have selected will perform the examination. However, if you plan to deliver at a hospital some distance from your home or at a hospital at which your pediatrician does not have admitting privileges, the doctor may arrange for a hospital-based pediatrician or a colleague to care for the baby during the hospital stay. The first office visit is usually at about two weeks. After that, there is much variation in the frequency and timing of well-baby visits. Ask your doctor for his or her preferred schedule.

Equipment and clothing needs might also be discussed. The doctor will be able to advise you regarding car seats, first aid supplies, powders or lotions, and other necessary equipment.

Finally, all expectant parents experience some concern about the health of their child, and many find that sharing these feelings with the pediatrician helps to alleviate some of this very natural anxiety.

Following the conference, you will want to consider: Do you feel confidence in the doctor's medical judgment? Does the doctor answer your questions thoughtfully, or does he or she project an air of boredom and irritation? Do you feel that the doctor is interested in you as well as the baby?

You might ask why it's so important that the *parents* feel comfortable when it is the baby the doctor will be caring for. The answer is simple. The physician who cares for an infant or child provides service largely by advising parents on how to care for their child in times of sickness and health. If you feel uncomfortable with the doctor, this may impede communication between you. In that case, it would be wise to continue your search for the right physician.

Once you have chosen your pediatrician, you should feel that you have found a physician whose skill and interest will provide the family with the best care available. You and the doctor will be entering into a very important relationship dedicated to preserving the health of your child in the days, months, and years ahead.

2. The Newborn

Not so long ago, a baby's birth was relatively impersonal. A new mother often did not get a first glimpse of her infant until several hours after the birth when she had recovered from general anesthesia, and a new father, relegated to the hospital waiting room during delivery, was allowed a first peek at his son or daughter only through the barrier of the nursery window.

Luckily, at present there is a widespread trend toward a more family-centered birth experience. Today both parents usually have the opportunity to see or touch the baby the instant he or she is born, and if the birth is uncomplicated, the family may be permitted to remain together for the first hour or more after the baby's birth. Many mothers also choose to keep the baby in the same room with them during much of the hospital stay—another practice virtually unheard of a few decades ago.

In addition to cuddling and inspecting your baby from head to toe, you may want to try feeding him or her in the delivery room or a few hours later, once both of you are settled in the lying-in unit. Although some babies are very

Newborn, mother & father

active and alert right after birth and ready to nurse or take a bottle, others are exhausted and need a few hours of sleep before they are ready to eat. Yet others may not be interested in food for several days. Whenever the first feeding does take place be prepared for hiccups, spitting up, and crying—all common and perfectly normal behavior during a newborn's early feedings.

A First Look at Your Baby

Shortly after birth, your pediatrician, or a hospital staff physician, midwife, or nurse, will examine your baby. I examine babies, whenever possible, in the presence of the mother and father in order to share my findings with them.

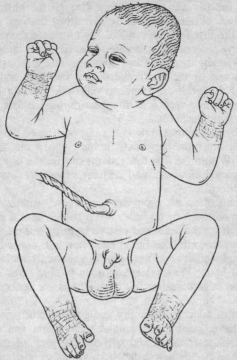

Newborn

This also provides an opportunity for the parents to ask questions—and most of them have many!

Most parents first want to know whether their baby is healthy. Fortunately, in most cases, the findings on examination are reassuring. On the other hand, the initial appearance of even a healthy baby may be quite a surprise to new parents.

A newborn usually bears little resemblance to the rosy-cheeked cherubs pictured in baby magazines. A newborn's skin is covered with a protective cheesy substance called vernix caseosa. The baby's head is often elongated and pointed at the top, the result of the molding that takes place during the passage of the infant through the birth canal. The silver nitrate or antibiotic eye drops that are applied within the first few moments of life to reduce the possibility of eye infection can irritate the eyelids and the eye tissues, leaving them red and swollen. The arteries of the eyelids and of the midforehead over the nose and at the nape of the neck are frequently dilated, creating reddish blotches. These spots will disappear during the first year of life, in most instances.

Because the lower jaw is the last portion of the face to grow, a newborn baby may remind you a bit of Andy Gump. Within the first few months of life, the jaw growth is completed, however, and the baby's face takes on a more defined form.

Parents often ask about the baby's hair, wondering why there is so much or so little. Some babies have a mass of thick hair on the scalp and often a layer of hair on the legs and arms as well. This initial hair often falls out in the first few weeks of life and new growth eventually replaces the original hair. Other babies are quite bald at birth and for many months thereafter. Both conditions are perfectly normal.

Also of concern is the dry and peeling skin some newborns have, particularly around their wrists and ankles. This, too, is common and will usually peel off in a few days. And if, when your newborn yawns or cries, you observe a white spot on the hard palate inside the mouth, rest assured that this, too, will soon disappear.

Enlargement of the breasts and genitalia is also quite common in newborns of both sexes. This is attributable to the passage of female hormones through the placenta to the baby. Sometimes the baby's breasts secrete colostrum, and an occasional female infant will have something like a very light menstrual period. No treatment is necessary. Within a few weeks, the hormone levels will decrease, the breasts and genitalia will reduce to an infantile size, and the secretion of colostrum will cease.

Parents commonly find the baby's color worrisome, too. It is perfectly normal for a tiny baby's hands and feet to have a blue tinge, due to a poor blood supply to these areas during the first weeks of life. And when a baby cries, it is normal for his or her face to become livid red or purplish. Breathing patterns may also cause concern. Some infants breathe rapidly for fifteen or twenty seconds, then slow down and appear not to be breathing at all. Then suddenly, they take a big breath and start over again, only to repeat the entire cycle a few minutes later. This pattern reflects the general immaturity of the newborn infant's respiratory system and is perfectly normal.

Early Bowel Movements

Parents are often surprised at the consistency of their baby's bowel movements. An infant's first bowel movement occurs within thirty-six hours after delivery. Initially, the movements are composed of meconium, a greenish-black, sticky substance produced in the infant's intestinal tract while in the womb. Subsequent bowel movements are usually greenish-yellow and a bit watery at first. As the baby takes nourishment, the bowel movements develop a firmer consistency, comparable to mustard or a little firmer. There is great variation in the frequency of bowel movements in the newborn period. Some infants produce one at every feeding; others may go several days without a bowel movement. As long as the baby has had one bowel movement in the first few days of life, you can assume that the intestinal tract is functioning in a normal way, and the frequency of bowel movements should not, therefore, be a matter of any concern.

Nor should you worry if at first your infant loses some weight. It is normal for an infant to lose about ten percent of birth weight during the first three or four days of life. This is largely due to the loss of fluid that has been retained during life in the uterus.

Possibility of Jaundice

Yet another common phenomenon that surprises parents is the jaundice that many healthy infants experience, beginning on the second or third day of life and lasting for a few days. This yellowish discoloration, which is observable first in the whites of the eyes and later in the skin, is usually a normal physiological event resulting from the destruction of an excess number of red blood cells as an infant adjusts to extrauterine life. The pigment (called bilirubin) released from the red cells is reprocessed and excreted by the liver. However, the immature liver of an infant cannot keep up with the demands to remove the excessive amount of bilirubin produced by the rapid destruction of the red blood cells. The result is a temporary accumulation of bilirubin in the body, which shows up as jaundice. This type of jaundice usually requires no treatment. If the jaundice is prolonged and intense, however, as is common in premature or small babies and other newborn infants suffering from illnesses, the baby is treated by being placed under ultraviolet light. This technique, called phototherapy, hastens the elimination of bilirubin from the body. In rare cases, an exchange transfusion is necessary to remove the excess bilirubin.

Some jaundiced infants, particularly those in whom the yellowish color appears within the first twenty-four hours of life, suffer from a more serious condition known as hemolytic disease of the newborn, caused by an incompatibility between the mother's and the baby's blood cells. A simple laboratory test of the blood obtained from the umbilical cord at birth establishes the presence or absence of this condition. A positive test indicates that the baby's red blood cells are sensitized to maternal antibodies that have crossed the placenta and are circulating in the infant's bloodstream. These antibodies destroy an excessive number of the baby's red blood cells. A few decades ago, babies suffering from hemolytic disease of the newborn were treated exclusively with exchange transfusions. Now this condition is almost always successfully treated with phototherapy. The course of the disease is monitored through repeated measurement of the bilirubin concentration in the blood. In rare cases, the disease fails to respond to this treatment, making a transfusion necessary. (Any infant who experiences hemolytic disease during the first week of life needs to be followed carefully in early infancy.

A blood test may be necessary at the age of four to six weeks to determine if the infant is suffering from significant anemia.)

Special Care

Two other questions to ask before you leave the hospital are how to care for the navel and the penis, if a circumcision has been performed. The umbilical cord, which connects the baby to the placenta, is the route through which nourishment enters the baby's body before birth. The cord is cut by the doctor or nurse shortly after birth, leaving a short stump. The stump is yellow at first and a few days later becomes dark red. Usually a dye is applied to the cord after birth, turning the stump a blackish-blue color. Until the stump falls off (sometime during the first few weeks of life), it is important to keep the area clean and dry. Your doctor may recommend sponge baths until after the stump falls off, and it's a good idea to fold the diaper below the navel to avoid additional irritation. Most doctors also recommend applying alcohol or a similar antibacterial sub-

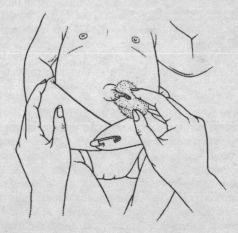

Caring for the Navel

stance to the navel to inhibit the growth of pathogenic germs. If the navel and surrounding area become red, call your doctor, as this suggests the presence of an infection.

The circumcision, too, takes some days to heal. Some doctors recommend putting petroleum jelly on a piece of gauze and applying this to the end of the penis to hasten the healing process.

When you and the baby go home, other questions will undoubtedly arise. Do not hesitate to phone your pediatrician about any of these, and never feel foolish doing so. Your doctor will understand that your questions are prompted by your desire to take the best possible care of your infant.

3. The Early Period: From Birth to Four Months

At no other time in your child's life will the changes he or she undergoes be as vast as during the first year. The infant you bring home from the hospital will primarily eat and sleep, and although newborns see and hear the world around them, they respond only to those activities that directly affect their comfort and survival.

By the age of one year, your baby will likely be crawling or walking and exploring every aspect of the world she can reach. She may be able to use a few words appropri-

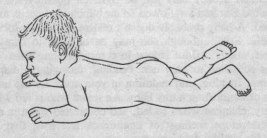

3 or 4 months old

ately, and she is definitely capable of expressing strong likes and dislikes on a variety of topics ranging from food and toys to people. She's hardly a baby anymore!

Because the changes during this first year are so vast, we will consider it in three separate chapters focusing on different phases: from birth to four months, four to eight months, and eight to twelve months.

What to Expect from Your Infant

A baby's ability to move about, use his body, and relate to other human beings is limited in the first weeks of life. He demonstrates little interest in the world about him, devoting most of his waking moments to seeking relief of bodily discomfort. He cries, fusses, and squirms when uncomfortable, obtaining the attention of adults who tend his needs and relieve his distress.

When comfortable, a baby of a few weeks of age can generally be counted upon to sleep quite a bit. Some sleep best on their sides, looking toward a light source; others prefer lying on their backs; still others are happiest on their stomachs. Most babies find it particularly comforting and relaxing to be wrapped snugly in a blanket; some like to be carried on the parent's chest in a front pack.

A baby may remain in a relaxed state for several hours, but periodically discomfort arouses her. This discomfort may be due to hunger, or gas pains, or a wet or soiled diaper. Or a baby may just be cold! Or possibly she has eaten too fast and swallowed an air bubble and needs to be burped. A baby probably doesn't realize the reason for her distress. Still, although she may be helpless to care for herself, she is skillful indeed in communicating when she needs someone to help her. Feeding, changing a diaper, burping, rocking, and cuddling in your arms are the usual ways of comforting a tiny baby. An infant who is fed when hungry, changed when soiled, and comforted when in distress develops feelings of confidence and trust that are basic for healthy development.

All five senses are present and active even in the earliest

days of life. Although an infant spends most of his waking hours gazing vaguely about, without seeming to focus on anything in particular, he will look intently at the face of an adult who is holding and talking to him. He may also focus his eyes on a red object held eight to twelve inches away. If the object is moved from side to side, his eyes will follow it with jerky tracking movements.

A tiny baby can soon distinguish his mother by smell or bodily movements or by the sound of her voice. Hearing is fully developed at birth, and you may notice that your infant stops nursing, briefly, to listen to an unfamiliar sound.

By far the most highly developed of an infant's senses, however, is touch—and it is perhaps the most essential to her survival as well. Babies who are kept clean, safe, and well-fed, but are rarely held and cuddled by their caregivers, fail to achieve optimal growth—emotionally, physically, and behaviorally.

Initially, a baby's movements seem aimless and random. You will notice many automatically coordinated movements known as reflexes, which are responses to stimuli of which a baby may be unaware. These actions are brisk, mechanical, and involuntary. With the rooting reflex, a baby responds to the touch of a nipple or finger against her cheek by turning her head toward it, initiating sucking movements of the tongue and mouth. Present from the moment of birth, this important reflex prepares a baby for nursing at the breast or sucking from the bottle.

The startle, or Moro, reflex is an infant's normal response to a sudden noise, a loss of support, or a sudden movement of the bassinet or crib. A baby's arms, fingers, and legs extend symmetrically in midair, and the infant may utter a short cry.

There are many other such automatic actions you will observe. Reflex crawling, for example, may occur when an infant is placed on his stomach on a hard surface; holding a baby upright with the soles of his feet against a table or mattress will bring into play the stepping reflex, in which one foot follows the other in an automatic walking pattern. Placing one's finger in the palm of the infant's hand evokes the grasp reflex, in which the baby's fingers—loosely held in a half-open, half-closed position most of the first and second months of life—close tightly around the adult finger. An infant may also hold a rattle in an automatic manner for a short time. When he loosens his fingers and drops the rattle, he doesn't seem to miss it. Such grasping and releasing are involuntary during these early weeks of life.

Day-to-Day Care

There is probably no more unsettling period of life than the first couple of months with a new baby. Parental sleep is at a premium, and there is a whole new way of life to adjust to. What's more, your baby may mistake day for night and sleep his best stretches during the daylight hours, leaving it up to his parents to figure out what to do with him during the night! Or she may seem especially fussy at various times, leaving the adults to wonder what they can do to make her happy. Family members, well-wishers, and even the babysitter sometimes add to the confusion of the household at this time.

If you are experiencing this chaos right now, you will be relieved to know that family life will almost surely settle down within the next two to three months. Part of the problem will be solved by time—as babies grow older, they are better able to adjust to the world around them. The rest of the problem must be solved by developing a pattern of day-to-day care that works for you.

Of primary importance in making this adjustment is learning how to satisfy your baby at feeding time—a well-fed baby is likely to be much easier to live with!

For the first four to six months of life, breast milk (supplemented with vitamins A, D, and C, and possibly fluoride) or a commercial milk mixture will provide all an infant needs at this age.

Whether to breast or bottle feed is an individual decision that parents must make for themselves. Although many mothers find breastfeeding emotionally satisfying, it is, of course, perfectly possible to have an entirely satisfactory experience bottlefeeding, too. Nevertheless, there is no question that breast milk has many advantages over formula. Not only is nursing a convenient way to feed a baby —no formula to prepare, no equipment to sterilize, no bottles to warm—but it provides an infant with protection against disease. Infants are unable to make many of their own antibodies in the early months of life, so they benefit from antibodies they receive from their mother's milk. This is why breast-fed infants are likely to experience fewer infections during the first year than are formula-fed babies.

If You Decide to Breast Feed...

Although breastfeeding is, indeed, the most natural way to feed your child, chances are that you will be a bit surprised by the challenge that the initial feedings present. First of all, a newborn's mouth is so small that latching on to the breast may be difficult at first. You can aid your

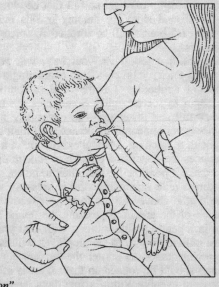

"Latching on"

baby during the early weeks by compressing the entire areola (the darkened area surrounding the nipple) between your fingers and placing it in her mouth. She will most likely be able to take over from there. If she loses hold, simply help her latch on again. To take her off the breast, slip your little finger into the corner of her mouth or between the gums to gently break the suction.

You will probably also find that it takes time for your nipples to become accustomed to nursing. To reduce the risk of soreness, your first few days of breastfeeding should consist of nursings lasting only a few minutes per breast. The next series of feedings might last for five minutes. As you feel more comfortable, you can gradually work up to nursing ten to fifteen minutes per side. (Once the baby becomes an efficient nurser, she will get most of the milk during the first five minutes.) Nurse five to ten minutes on the first side, and then as long as she wants on the second side. At the next feeding, simply start on the second side.

The idea is that if a baby nurses ten to fifteen minutes on the first side, he may get so full that he won't nurse at all on the second side. By nursing in this manner, you ensure that each breast will be emptied completely at alternate feedings.

During the first few days, your baby will be ingesting colostrum, a thick, yellowish fluid containing a high concentration of antibodies. On the third or fourth day, the breasts begin to secrete milk. Sometimes the breasts become very full and distended—so engorged, in fact, that the mother is very uncomfortable and the infant may find it very difficult to latch on. Manual expression of a little milk often reduces the distension enough to relieve the discomfort and make it possible for the infant to nurse.

To express milk manually, cup the breast in your hand, with the thumb above and the forefinger below the nipple at the edge of the areola. Squeezing the thumb and finger together in a gentle pulling motion with firm pressure will cause the milk to flow from the nipple. (It will likely take a little experimentation to master the technique.) The hand and thumb should be rotated so that all areas of the breast are expressed evenly. Within a few days, engorgement is

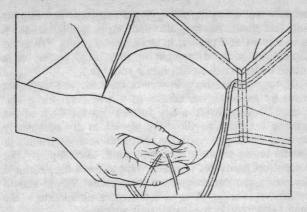

Manually expressing breast milk

usually no longer a problem, and this maneuver will no longer be necessary.

To ensure an adequate milk supply, a nursing mother needs rest and a good diet. Not only will you need to increase your intake of food by about 500 calories a day, but you will also need to increase your intake of fluids—milk, especially. (Of course, if you prefer, you can get the additional calcium needed from other dairy products or tablets rather than from milk.)

If the milk supply appears to be insufficient—that is, if the baby is waking for feedings very frequently and is not gaining well—your doctor may advise you to offer supplementary water for a time. Occasionally, a bottle of formula may be necessary at night so you can get some sleep. However, frequent nursing does stimulate milk production.

For the first few days, you may experience uterine contractions during feedings. These afterpains, which can be quite uncomfortable, are the result of the release of the hormone oxytocin into your bloodstream in response to the baby's sucking. These contractions help your uterus to return to its normal size. Oxytocin also triggers the let-down reflex whereby milk is released from its storage places within the breast and made available to the baby. You may actually feel a tingling or tugging sensation at first as your milk lets down. You may also find that your milk lets down at inconvenient times and in inconvenient places. (To avoid discomfort, wear disposable nursing pads, gauze, or a folded cotton handkerchief inside your bra.)

If your nipples become sore or cracked, you may treat them by exposing the breasts to a heat lamp for a few minutes several times a day and leaving the flaps of the nursing bra open to allow the nipples to dry completely between feedings. Applying ointments such as lanolin or special breast cream to the nipples will also help. If your discomfort is severe, you may want to use a nipple shield (available at most drugstores) temporarily. Its use should be limited to a few days as it decreases stimulation to the breast and may decrease your milk supply.

Also be sure that the baby is sucking on the entire areola, rather than merely sucking or chewing on the nipple. If the baby begins to chew, take her off the breast and help her latch on again, putting the entire areola into her mouth.

Beginning in the second month, it's a good idea to offer a breast-fed baby a bottle on occasion. This will accustom the baby to getting nourishment from a bottle and will make it possible for the father to give some of the feeding or for the mother to leave the house for a few hours.

You may want to use a prepared milk mixture for the relief bottle, or you may find that the baby takes the bottle more willingly if it contains breast milk. Some women can express enough milk manually for a relief bottle, although many find it more convenient to use a breast pump. Several basic types are available. One has a cup to which a bulb is attached. The cup is placed over the areola, and suction is created by squeezing the bulb. An easier, although more expensive, type is made of two plastic cylinders that fit inside each other. A separate cup is placed on the breast, and milk is extracted by moving the outer cylinder in and out, like a trombone. Electric pumps are the easiest to use, but they are also the most costly. You may be able to rent one from a hospital or surgical supply store, however.

One word of caution: A nursing mother should be aware that anything she ingests can be secreted in her milk and thus passed along to the infant. Therefore, before you take

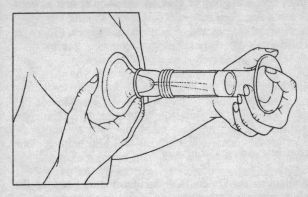

Trombone-style breast pump

any type of drug or medication, discuss its possible effects on the baby with your pediatrician. Nicotine, too, finds its way into the breast milk, so smoking is inadvisable for breast-feeding mothers. Infants may experience abdominal distress if the nursing mother eats spicy foods or such vegetables as cabbage, cauliflower, eggplant, or Brussels sprouts; some infants who are allergic to cow's milk react to their mothers' drinking milk with cramps, fussiness, and explosive bowel movements. If your breast-fed baby develops abdominal discomfort, consult your pediatrician about your own diet. Eliminating specific foods may make a great difference to your baby.

If You Decide to Bottle Feed . . .

If you decide to bottle feed, there are many adequate formulas available, with either a cow's milk, soy, or meat base. All commercial mixtures have vitamins and minerals added, and no other foods or supplements are necessary for the first four to six months of life. It is also possible to make your own formula using evaporated milk, water, and sugar or corn syrup in a ratio recommended by your doctor. (In this case, the infant would need a supplement contain-

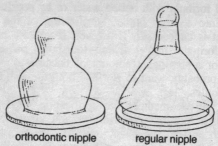

orthodontic nipple   regular nipple

Orthodontic and regular nipples

ing vitamins A, D, and C, and fluoride in parts of the country where the concentration in drinking water is low.

Choosing the right nipple will be mainly a matter of experimenting to find the one your baby prefers. The "preemie" nipple developed for premature and low birth weight babies greatly facilitates feeding the very small infant; but when it comes to regular nipples, I don't see any strong medical reason for choosing one over the other. If your baby is comfortable with the nipple you have bought, fine; if not, try another style.

Begin your first feedings by offering 2–3 ounces per feeding; increase to 4 ounces when the baby polishes off the lesser amount and begins looking for more. In the same way, you'll eventually increase to offering 6–8 ounces per feeding. How much milk should the baby have per day? He'll let you know! But as a general guideline, you might keep in mind that the average baby of two weeks or more can be expected to consume approximately 2.5 ounces per pound during a twenty-four-hour period. For example, the ten-pound baby will likely need about 25 ounces of milk per day, which will likely mean six feedings of approximately 4 ounces each, or seven feedings of 3.5 ounces each. As he grows, his milk intake will increase proportionately. Remember, a baby may eat more one day and less the following. Let him decide how much he needs.

In all likelihood, you will sterilize your baby's bottles, nipples, collars, and caps. Some pediatricians feel that if you are preparing one bottle at feeding time by diluting powdered formula with boiled water or by pouring sterile formula into a clean bottle, sterilization of the feeding equipment is unnecessary. However, if you are preparing enough formula for a twenty-four-hour period (long enough for a significant amount of bacteria to develop), you will probably want to sterilize both the milk mixture and the bottles.

There are two methods for sterilization. In one procedure, called terminal sterilization, you put the formula made with unsterilized water into unsterilized bottles; put the nipples in, upside down; cover with caps or disks; and loosely screw on the collars. The bottles are then placed in a rack and heated in a boiling water bath for twenty-five minutes, cooled to room temperature, tightened, and refrigerated.

The second method involves sterilizing all the equipment in a boiling water bath for five minutes and then filling the bottles with sterile formula, such as ready-to-use formula from a can or concentrated canned formula that is then diluted with boiled water.

Try to avoid a common tendency to coax a bottle-fed

Terminal Sterilization

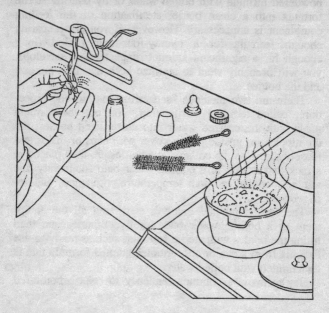

Sterilization of bottles and nipples

infant to eat more than he wants to or than is nutritionally necessary. There is no reason to urge a satiated baby to finish off that last half ounce or ounce. Moreover, this practice may initiate a lifelong problem with obesity. Likewise, it's often tempting to prop the bottle. Don't. A baby needs to be held and cuddled at feeding time. Even when they are able to hold their own bottles, most babies prefer to be held for at least some of their feedings each day.

When can you begin to offer regular milk? The American Academy of Pediatrics recommends waiting until your baby is at least six months of age before offering cow's milk straight from the carton. A number of pediatricians, however, advise waiting until close to the baby's first birthday before starting cow's milk. The reason? Many infants are unable to digest uncooked milk, which can cause gas, abdominal pain, loose explosive bowel movements, and, at times, bleeding from the intestinal tract. Sometimes this bleeding causes reddish or even distinctly bloody bowel movements. This loss of blood can slow a baby's growth and lower resistance to infection. Even when the bleeding is minimal—in which case it may go unnoticed —it is often sufficient to cause anemia. It is also unwise to offer lowfat milk in infancy as babies need the fat that whole milk contains for adequate growth during the first year.

Feeding Styles

Whether you breast or bottle feed, you will notice that your infant has his or her own feeding style:

Barracudas suck vigorously from the start.

Excited ineffectives become excited and active at breast or bottle, grab and then lose the nipple, and begin to scream. It is often necessary to cuddle the babies to quiet them before offering the breast or bottle again.

Procrastinators are late starters. They show no particular interest in sucking at first, but if left alone will usually become interested after a few days.

Gourmets mouth the nipple, get a taste of milk, smack their lips, and stop. If hurried or prodded, they become furious and scream. Usually they settle down after a few minutes and take their feeding quite well.

Resters prefer to eat for a few minutes, rest for a few minutes—even doze off for a time—and then resume sucking. It is best to adapt to their way of doing things; they cannot be hurried.

Burping

Whether breast- or bottle-fed, your infant will need to be burped several times during each feeding to get rid of air that may have accumulated in her stomach, filling her up before she has had enough to eat. It's a good idea to try to get a burp up at least twice—once midway through and once at the end of the feeding.

You may find that rubbing the baby's back is as effective as patting. Otherwise, there are several different positions for burping. One is to sit the baby upright on your lap, supporting her with one hand and patting with the other. Another is putting the baby on her stomach across your lap. And, of course, there is the classic over-the-shoulder position. You will soon learn which one works best for you, and your baby.

Babies frequently spit up and get hiccups after meals, particularly when they have eaten avidly. The hiccups usually stop within a few minutes; or you can try offering some warm water in a bottle or putting the baby back on the breast for a few seconds.

Frequent burping may diminish the tendency to spit up, but only time will relieve the problem altogether. In the first half year or so of life, the muscle at the junction of the

Different Positions For Burping

esophagus and stomach is quite relaxed. When a baby eats too fast and swallows air, his stomach contents are often pushed up into the esophagus and out through the baby's mouth—in some instances, with great force. This is usually an exaggeration of harmless spitting up. However, projectile vomiting (as it is known) that occurs after every feeding suggests the possibility of pyloric stenosis, a condition in which the muscles at the junction of the stomach and the small intestine are too tight and need to be loosened surgically. If your infant vomits consistently after every feeding, you should consult your pediatrician.

Bowel Movements

The normal number, color, and texture of bowel movements vary greatly during infancy. A safe assumption is that if a baby is happy, comfortable, and gaining weight, the frequency, appearance, and consistency of the bowel movements is of little concern.

After the passing of meconium shortly after birth, the subsequent bowel movements, called transitional stools, are firmer and greenish in color. The passage of meconium and transitional stools indicates normal intestinal functioning.

Following the ingestion of significant amounts of breast milk or formula, a baby's stools are usually light yellow and somewhat the consistency of mustard or scrambled eggs. A breast-fed infant may pass six or seven bowel movements a day, or may have only one every three to seven days. Occasionally, a baby will go even longer without a bowel movement with no real difficulties. Frequency is really not an issue if the baby is happy and comfortable and passes his stools with minimal discomfort.

Nursing infants characteristically produce soft, sometimes watery stools. Formula-fed infants usually produce four to six bowel movements daily during the first weeks of life, and a lesser number after the age of a month. The consistency of a formula-fed baby's stool is usually firmer than in the case of the breast-fed infant. Occasionally, the bowel movements are so hard that a baby has difficulty passing them. When this happens, feeding a few teaspoons of diluted prune juice, or a teaspoon of brown sugar or corn syrup in a few ounces of water usually resolves the difficulty. The use of laxatives or rectal suppositories is unwise in infancy because it establishes a pattern of artificial stimulation that is difficult to discontinue.

Changes in bowel patterns may indicate the eruption of a tooth (see Teething in **Part V, The A to Z Guide**) or the onset of an infection. Loose, watery, and explosive bowel movements indicate an irritation of the intestinal tract and often precede the recognizable symptoms of an upper respiratory illness.

Bottle-fed infants who develop loose and watery stools associated with abdominal cramps and gas during their second or third week of life may be reacting to the basic protein in the milk mixture. Substituting a soybean-based formula for a cow's milk formula often relieves a baby's discomfort. However, in some instances infants allergic to cow's milk are also allergic to soybean preparations. In that case, a meat-based or synthetic mixture is necessary.

An infant suffering from loose and frequent bowel movements needs an increased amount of fluid to replace that excreted in his stools. If a baby with loose bowel movements becomes irritable and lethargic, or the stools number twelve to fifteen a day or contain mucous and blood, contact your baby's physician. Diarrhea, an excessive number of loose, watery bowel movements, can be quite serious because a baby may become dehydrated (dried out) and lose fluids containing important salts. Hospitalization for intravenous therapy may be necessary. Associated vomiting, failure to take feedings, fever, and weight loss suggest serious illness and also merit prompt medical attention.

Establishing a Feeding Schedule

One concern shared by all mothers is the issue of scheduling. The eating habits of most babies are very erratic in the first few weeks, but they usually become more predict-able by about one month of age.

It is, of course, unreasonable to expect an infant to ad-here to a strict schedule, but you can help him learn to lengthen the periods between feedings. In general, try not to fall into the trap of feeding your child at the first whimper. Babies cry for many reasons, not just hunger. If it has been less than two hours since the last feeding, first try other methods of comforting him. If he is still crying after five or ten minutes, then try feeding him. If more than two hours have passed since the last feeding, assume that he's hungry and feed him right away. The point is to feed him when he is hungry, but not if he is uncomfortable for other reasons. Rest assured that most babies will eventually arrive at something approximating a four-hour schedule on their own, although they may sometimes demand to be fed at shorter intervals in one part of the day, and sometimes go for longer stretches later on.

Establishing a Sleep Pattern

"How can I get my baby to sleep through the night?" is a question asked by many parents. Some are plagued with a baby who mistakes day for night and sleeps her longest stretches during the daytime; other parents are simply eager to discontinue the middle-of-the-night feedings at the earli-est possible time.

For the first two to three weeks, you'll do best to follow the lead set by your baby. After that, you can begin to try to alter her sleep pattern. If she's sleeping for long stretches during the day and is wakeful at night, you might try letting her sleep no longer than four hours during the day in order to encourage her to take her longer stretches at night. Some families report success with encouraging the baby's wakeful time to be in the evening. Then you can feed her right before your own bedtime, and with luck you both can have a relatively long span of sleep before she calls for her next feeding.

Keep in mind that your initial goal cannot be a twelve-hour night. With a five- or six-week-old, you'll be fortunate if she sleeps a six- or seven-hour stretch. However, for sleep-deprived parents, even six hours at the proper time seem like a real gift!

As the baby gets older, she'll be able to sleep for longer and longer stretches, and soon you'll likely have a baby who really does sleep through the night.

Fussiness and the Highly Perceptive (Colicky) Infant

In all likelihood, your baby has a time of day—usually the evening—when he's especially fussy. He's just eaten, he won't nap, and nothing seems to please him for more than a few minutes. He's just plain fretful. At this point, most parents begin to wonder if they have what is sometimes called a "colicky" baby. Although this sort of behavior is definitely enough to set one's nerves on edge, it is more likely a normal bout of evening fussiness for which holding, rocking, singing, strapping close in a carrier, or going on a car or carriage ride are the best solutions. The fussiness will probably begin to taper off once your baby reaches six weeks of age. However, if his fussy time lasts more than a few hours and is marked by indications of abdominal distress, you may have what I call a highly perceptive (some say colicky) infant.

Most babies—like most adults—have a kind of protective mechanism that allows them to block out noise and other distractions to some degree. However, in some babies, this mechanism is much less effective. As a result, some babies perceive noise, bodily tension in adults who handle them, gas pains, movements of food and waste products through the intestine, and other internal and external stimuli more intensely than do most infants.

Parenting a highly perceptive infant can be very challenging. Such a baby may respond poorly to a scheduled regimen and tends to be difficult to feed. He is likely to work himself up into a frenzy when hungry, suck voraciously, then spit up his feeding. He may then drop off to sleep and awaken ten minutes later, eager to eat again!

His mother may, in turn, become quite frantic, thinking her baby is ill. If she is nursing, she worries that her milk supply is insufficient; if formula-feeding, she wonders if her child might be allergic to cow's milk. If altering the feeding method (offering a bottle of formula, in the case of the nursing infant, or a change in the formula, in the case of a bottle-fed baby) fails to bring relief, the mother can assume that hers is a highly perceptive infant who will, in time, outgrow his sensitivity to his environment.

What can be done to make life easier for a highly perceptive infant and his family? In extreme cases, a doctor might prescribe a mild sedative to help the baby relax so that he can be more comfortable and can rest between feedings. Usually, however, the best course is to try to maintain a calm and peaceful atmosphere in the home. If you are relaxed, your child will tend to be more relaxed. It makes sense, too, to try to minimize household noises, turn down the phone and doorbell, and play TVs and radios at a low volume. On the other hand, some types of sounds can be soothing. Some infants, for example, will quiet when they hear music or even when a vacuum cleaner or blender is turned on. The sound of a ticking clock can also be comforting. Other ways of relaxing a highly perceptive baby—or, in fact, any infant—include rocking, going for a ride in a carriage or car, and cuddling against a lukewarm hot-water bottle. If nothing seems to work, try leaving the baby in the crib, perhaps taking a shower, and then returning when you are more relaxed. You may find that the baby has dozed off on his own during your absence. In any case, you'll be better able to handle another round of rocking and holding if you've had a breather. Does caring for this kind of baby lead to spoiling? I don't think so. There is a significant difference between spoiling a child and giving him the special care and help he may need to overcome specific difficulties that may arise. It's helpful to keep in mind that for the highly perceptive baby, normal stimuli, from within and without, can be very distressing indeed. He is special, and he needs more understanding and comforting than the average infant. But he has many assets, too. Highly perceptive infants are very sociable and they are often aptly

· described as "sparklers." Given the time and the care he requires, he will soon learn to settle down.

Continued Development During the Early Months

Gradually, during the second and third months of life, you will begin to note changes in your baby's ability to move about, use his arms and hands, and relate to adults. Voluntary control evolves, first of his head, then of the arms, hands, and fingers, then a few weeks later of his trunk, the rest of his body, and the lower extremities. Automatic reactions such as grasping, visual following, and rooting, which were fragmented independent responses, become less and less prominent as he begins to be able to control his actions.

By the second or third month, a baby gradually gains sufficient strength and skill to hold her head up quite well when lying against the shoulder of an adult. When lying on her back, she can keep her head centered, instead of turning it to one side or the other as in earlier weeks. She can turn her head, looking to the right and to the left, and follow the movements of adults within her line of vision. She waves her arms and legs and chuckles with glee. She can now lie on her stomach with her head and shoulders raised off the mattress, peering at the world around her. One day in the third or fourth month, she becomes aware of her hands, looking at them as if to say, "Where did these come from?" In a few weeks she gains voluntary control of her arms and hands, responding with great interest and delight when her hands appear in her line of vision.

By about four months, she can voluntarily grasp a rattle and shake it. Likely, she'll study the rattle, drop it, search for it, and pick it up again. Grasping, grabbing, letting go, banging, reaching, and moving occupy much of an infant's waking moments at this age.

A baby's improving vision and memory now enable her to recognize when an adult is preparing to feed her. Of course, she can't wait too long, but she may relax for a few moments as she becomes aware of the adult activities that precede a feeding. A few weeks later she may quiet when she hears familiar footsteps approaching her room or the sound of her mother's or father's voice.

Easy and frequent smiling appears in the second or third month of life, and a baby's language begins to develop at the same time. By three months he coos, gurgles, and sputters in response to being talked to. Soon there are different qualities to his language. He gurgles happily when he feels good. He laughs and coos when tickled. As an adult chuckles, a baby may respond with a broad smile and laughter. He communicates in his own way, but he clearly lets you know when he is comfortable or uncomfortable. As his vision improves, he begins to distinguish familiar adults by sight, reserving his biggest grins and most exuberant vocalizations for those who provide most of his care.

Still, even as babies become increasingly sociable and begin to enjoy the world about them, it is important that they have moments of peace and quiet for resting and sleeping. Although opportunities for social interplay are important, babies also need moments of respite from stimulation. They need time to relax, sleep, and recoup their energies before participating in another round of activity.

Early Visits to the Pediatrician

During this first year, most parents look forward to well-child visits to the pediatrician. It's exciting to get progress reports on the baby's growth, and it's an ideal opportunity to get personalized advice on everything from feeding to infant development.

Your doctor will want to examine your baby during the first month of life and at one or two monthly intervals for the remainder of the first year—somewhat less frequently thereafter. You may wonder what your doctor looks for during these early visits.

First, the doctor will likely ask about your baby's daily waking, sleeping, and eating patterns. How long and how often does your baby nurse, or how much formula does the baby take and at what intervals? How are his nights? How much does he sleep during the day? The doctor may give you the opportunity to ask questions or share any concerns at this time.

Although your baby will probably remain in your lap during the first part of the visit, the doctor will actually have already begun the exam, noting how the baby is responding to you and the new environment. Once the physical examination begins, the doctor will examine your baby's head, feeling the soft spot, and will consider the movements of the eyes and the size of the pupils, check the mouth, gums, tongue, and throat, and look into the ears. Next, he will listen to the heart to determine any disturbances of rate or abnormality of sounds, listen to the lungs to evaluate breath sounds, palpate the abdomen to determine size of liver and spleen or the presence of any unusual masses, extend the legs and hips to rule out any abnormality of the hip joints and examine the genitalia. He will also test your baby's hearing by ringing a bell or utilizing a noisemaker, noting if the baby blinks in response to auditory stimulus. Finally, your doctor will pick up your baby. The general feeling of a baby's muscle tone and the response to being picked up reveal a great deal of information about an infant's general health.

Your doctor or the nurse will also measure your baby's head circumference and record his height and weight. A baby usually regains birth weight by two weeks of age. In addition, most physicians perform a blood test at this initial office visit to rule out the presence of any metabolic abnormality. (In many states, tests for thyroid disease and phenylketonuria, a rare inherited metabolic anomaly, are mandated by law.)

On succeeding visits your doctor will repeat the measurements of height, weight, and head circumference. Although there is considerable variation in normal growth, a full-term healthy infant can be expected to double birth weight in the first half year and triple it by the first birthday. Head circumference increases by slightly less than one-half of an inch per month, and height usually increases by about one inch each month during the first year.

These measurements and also the findings of the physical examination are basic indicators of normal growth. However, there are many other important aspects of a baby's development that your doctor will consider and discuss with you at each visit.

Your doctor will likely ask you to describe how your baby uses his body, and will also observe his behavior during the examination. He will evaluate how the baby reaches, grabs for toys (or his stethoscope), twists, kicks, turns over, squirms on his stomach, and later on, how he sits, crawls, walks, climbs, and runs. Your doctor will evaluate these evolving capacities for movement and use of the body at each visit. He will note whether the baby spontaneously uses these new skills, or whether he needs encouragement and stimulation to show what he can do. A baby developing in a healthy manner will use his evolving motor skills for sheer pleasure. If your infant lags behind in any way, your doctor may suggest ways in which you can stimulate your baby's development. If the delay is significant, your doctor may arrange for further evaluation by a colleague experienced in the field of infant development.

Another important area of development relates to evolving capacities for communication. Cooing, babbling, shrieking, and later using words are important milestones in language development. Delay can be the result of neurologic problems due to congenital deficits, stresses at birth or in the early days of life, or a lack of stimulation. Your doctor will carefully evaluate your baby's hearing if language delay is present. Early detection of hearing problems is important, since the inability to hear limits intellectual development in many spheres.

How a child uses a rattle and other toys is also of significance. Throwing, banging, or reaching for a toy are important indicators of healthy development in the first half year of life. By nine months or earlier, some babies have a treasured blanket or toy to which they cling at bedtime or when tired or lonesome.

A fourth important area is the way in which the baby relates to parents, siblings, and other human beings. Early in life, an infant's social interaction with other human beings usually occurs when others are meeting the baby's physical needs by providing food, changing soiled diapers, or giving comfort. This exchange between caregiver and healthy infant provides a basis for a widening and deepening capacity for relationships, which evolves dramatically in the early months of life. Babies soon demonstrate increasing attachment to the mother or other adults who provide most of their care. They will also begin to develop "stranger anxiety" when approached by someone whom they do not recognize. A child's capacity for social interchange and the establishment of ties to the important adults in the family are indicators of healthy development. Your doctor will observe how your baby is progressing in this area.

These four areas of development, in addition to growth measurements and the findings of the physical examination, indicate to your doctor whether your baby is growing and developing normally. For you, these well-child visits are a prime opportunity to ask any questions you may have and to find out about what to expect in the coming months.

Immunizations

Immunizations are an important part of some of the well-child visits you'll make during this first year. Your baby will be receiving a DTP shot (a vaccine against diptheria, tetanus, and whooping cough, known as pertussis) three times in the first year at one- or two-month intervals. Polio vaccine is usually given orally two or three times in the first year at two-month intervals. Vaccine against measles, mumps, and rubella is not given until the age of fifteen months (see **Chapter 16, Immunizations**, for further information).

4. Your Growing Baby: From Four to Eight Months

By the time your baby is four months old, you will likely be feeling much more confident and more comfortable with the new structure of your family. Your baby's needs and wants almost certainly will have become easier to identify, and most four-month-olds have passed the worst of the fussy stages of infancy and are truly "coming alive." They see and like much of the world around them; smiles come easily and laughter is not far behind.

Growth and maturation from the fourth to the eighth month offer a baby many opportunities to use his body in new ways to express his individuality. He is awake for a much longer portion of the day and is happiest when lying on his back in the kitchen or living room or sitting propped up in an infant seat or on an adult's lap looking at the world about him. Just looking isn't enough, however. A baby who spends long hours in a crib or propped up in an infant seat with little attention from adults tends to be apathetic and limited in his capacity to enjoy life. The loving appreciation of adults, expressed by frequent hugs and attention to and praise of a baby's actions and achievements, encour-

6 or 7 months old

age a child to utilize emerging skills to the fullest extent possible. Attention from the adults around him conveys to a baby a feeling of his own importance and helps him to develop confidence in himself.

At four months a baby has discovered her hands and enjoys watching them—holding them outstretched in order to observe all they can do! Around the fifth month, her skill in eye-hand coordination begins to advance rapidly. She can now spot a toy she wants, pick it up, and bring it to her mouth. In fact, she can now pick up two toys at one time and bang them together.

Dramatic advances in a baby's ability to control her body are also apparent. Sometime around the age of four or five months, she will probably turn over. Usually a baby is first able to turn from back to stomach, then from stomach to back. By seven months, most babies sit easily with support and many without any support. At this age, too, a baby will enjoy standing while being held under the arms by an adult. She may even support her own weight for a few seconds. Bouncing and jumping up and down while in this position are great fun at this age. (There is no danger that this activity will injure a baby's legs or cause her to become bowlegged.) Also fun for a seven- or eight-month-old is her new ability to get her feet into her mouth while lying on her back. A baby often laughs with glee as she accomplishes this maneuver.

Although crawling is still some months in the future, a baby of this age will begin to be able to get around on her own a bit. Babies are very inventive, and if they want to get somewhere badly enough they will usually find a way, whether by belly-flopping, rolling, or squirming. (This is a time for particular caution regarding safety. The infant who used to remain in one spot when lying on a double bed exists no longer—her movements are unpredictable, and she may maneuver in ways that you would never expect. Rolling off the changing table or a bed, or toppling over a lowered crib rail, are particular dangers now.) It is at this age that parents often consider the use of a playpen.

Certainly playpens provide a safe setting for play, and some babies of eight or nine months will enjoy pulling themselves to a standing position and cruising around the edge of the playpen, watching the activities in the kitchen or living room. However, it is a rare baby who is satisfied for more than twenty or thirty minutes in a playpen—and many won't even tolerate it for that long. I suggest that parents try to arrange a room with gates at the foot or top of the stairs and at the entrances to adjoining rooms, thus providing the baby with a large, safe area to explore and enjoy. Of course, care must be taken to remove small items and plants, for everything within reach usually ends up in a baby's mouth. (For information on babyproofing your home, see **Chapter 18, Preventing Accidents.**) Although babyproofing does take time and thought, it is vital to your child's safety, and it will greatly reduce parental stress if you have the confidence of knowing your baby is playing in a safe environment.

One problem that crops up around the middle of the first year is establishing an appropriate balance between time parents spend actively involved with the baby and time when they encourage her to play on her own. Helping a baby develop the capacity to play alone with adults nearby is very important. Most well-rested babies can enjoy periods of solo play: cooing, babbling, and waving their arms and feet and a rattle. A tired baby, however, will usually want to be held and cuddled. This wavering back and forth between mature and immature phases of development is normal. A baby cannot continue to function at her most advanced level for long periods of time. But when you can, encourage your baby to play on her own while you fold laundry, cook, or read the mail. Don't expect to write a novel during this time, but you certainly do not need to constantly entertain your child.

Separation Anxiety

One problem that may crop up during this period concerns a child's anxiety about separation from his parents. Although in the fourth month he already began to distinguish his parents and other familiar adults from strangers, by six or seven months this preference becomes more marked. For example, if a baby is being held in the arms of another person and a parent or other primary caregiver walks into the room, the baby usually reaches toward this adult. He is distressed when this person leaves, and looks longingly at the door through which the trusted adult disappeared. This may be distressing to the parent who is trying to leave for an evening out, but it is an important indication of healthy, normal development, and as you'll see, most babies learn to make the best of the time the parent is away. (Most caregivers report that once the parent is gone, the baby will allow himself to be calmed down and have a relatively good time.) All the same, when he hears a parent's voice or observes his or her return, the baby's face brightens, and his entire body posture and movements express his feelings of happiness.

Sleep Difficulties

Often coinciding with this increased attachment to family members and fear of separation from them are changes in sleeping patterns. In earlier months your infant might have fallen asleep in your arms and allowed you to transfer her to her crib without awakening, but by six months or so this may no longer be the case. For this reason, it's a good idea to begin putting your baby in her crib while she's still awake. Give her a kiss and a firm good-night, and then leave. She may cry for a few moments, even longer, but she will almost certainly go to sleep before ten or fifteen minutes have elapsed. (Although she may let out a full-fledged wail as you leave the room, her cries will almost surely begin to taper off as time passes and she settles down to go to sleep.) For some babies, a period of fussiness is necessary during the transition from waking to sleeping. If crying does continue for more than fifteen minutes, I suggest that a parent return to the bedroom, offer a quick hug, and with a firm tone of voice say good-night, and leave once again. It may be necessary to repeat this process several times. However, in time your baby will learn to fall asleep on her own; this approach will encourage her to develop her own capacity to conquer feelings of loneliness as she goes to sleep. As a parent, you need to communicate to your baby that, although you are available for comfort if necessary, you have a firm expectation that she can and will go to sleep on her own. It is wise to establish this routine early in life, as bedtime-separation difficulties can escalate over time.

Another change in sleep patterns that may occur around this age is night waking. The usual pattern is for a baby to sleep for a few hours and then suddenly awaken with a scream. He may be in a half-asleep, half-awake dazed state, or he may be wide awake. Why this behavior suddenly begins at this age is unclear. Some babies apparently are dreaming. I believe that—like the bedtime struggle discussed above—it is another manifestation of separation anxiety.

When you go to him, be sure he has awakened enough to recognize you and understand that a trusted adult is there. If he remains in a dazed state, when you put him down, his dream is likely to continue, and he will be crying again in a few minutes. Many babies in this condition are difficult to arouse; parents often find that turning on a light, singing a lullaby, washing the baby's face, or offering a drink of water can help a baby to awaken enough to become aware of the parent's presence. Then you can change his diaper, give him a hug, and put him back to bed, and in all likelihood, he'll be able to return to sleep.

Starting Solid Food

A healthy infant who is gaining weight, growing appropriately, and is satisfied with breast- or bottlefeedings rarely needs any additional foods until the fourth, fifth, or sixth month of life.

You may have heard that starting solids is the key to helping your baby sleep through the night. It would be nice if the intake of solids would ensure a longer sleeping period, but, unfortunately, experience fails to support this common belief. The digestive system is inefficient in digesting foods other than milk in early infancy. In addition, the immature functioning of the mouth, tongue, and jaw limits a baby's ability to handle solids with any degree of ease during the first few months. Early feeding of solids often results in abdominal discomfort and the passage of loose, watery bowel movements. Indeed, a baby less than four months of age may resist such offerings by pushing the spoon and food out of his mouth.

The introduction of foods at the age of four or five months is usually an enjoyable experience for a baby. I advise beginning with a tasty food such as applesauce, mashed banana, or other pureed fruit. Offer a few teaspoons of a single food daily at first. This provides ample opportunity to determine whether the appearance of abdominal discomfort or a skin rash suggests a specific food intolerance. You may add mashed fruits, vegetables, meats, and cereals one at a time in any order that is convenient. The important consideration is whether the baby likes the consistency, texture, and taste of the food. No food is worth a battle. However, a baby often rejects a new food on the first day, yet accepts the same food with delight a few days later.

At six or seven months, an infant enjoys sitting in a

feeding table or a high chair close to other members of the family. He likes to participate in feeding by using his hands to pick up food and feel the texture. Any mushy food, such as bits of banana or cooked carrots, bits of cheese or dry cereal, are great finger foods at this age. He'll put some food in his mouth—but far more of his meal ends up on his face, in his ears, and in his hair. Such messiness is quite the norm, and any attempts to instill table manners will be fruitless now and probably for several years to come.

Whether to use commercially available mixtures or prepare foods at home in a blender is a matter of personal choice. However, it's important to bear in mind that a baby who is breast-fed or on cow's milk, as opposed to a formula-fed infant, does need additional iron in the second half of the first year. Therefore, if you decide not to feed your baby commercially prepared foods—many of which have iron added—be sure to include meats and iron-fortified cereals in the diet.

By one year, babies can digest most adult foods if mashed or cut in small pieces. Small portions are advisable. It is preferable to allow a baby to finish what she has in front of her and ask for more than to overwhelm her with huge portions that she cannot possibly finish.

A baby's increasing ability to hold her bottle in the second half year of life enables her to assume increasing responsibility for bottlefeedings. This may tempt parents to offer a baby a bottle of milk or juice in her crib at bedtime or when she awakens in the middle of the night. Although that may help a baby who is having difficulty sleeping, it can also lead to serious dental problems. Nursing-bottle syndrome is a well-recognized condition in which deposits of food on the teeth just before or during sleep increases the tendency for dental decay in cavity-prone individuals. Instead, try offering a bottle of plain water or substituting a pacifier. These alternatives allow a baby's sucking needs to be met without harming the teeth.

Babies vary as to when they are able to wean from the breast or bottle. A healthy baby can usually accomplish this task with minimal difficulties toward the end of the first year or early in the second; however, with breast-fed babies, many mothers are happy to continue nursing beyond this time. Whenever weaning from the breast or bottle does take place, a baby will often be upset for a few days. Yet, once having mastered this challenging task, he will often demonstrate increasing advances in his behavior in many important developmental areas.

With weaning and with all aspects of infant feeding, it's good to remember how important feeding is to an infant—and how easily the dinner table can be transformed into a battleground. So, from the very beginning, try to keep feeding sessions relaxed and enjoyable. A happy, comfortable feeding experience helps create a strong bond between adults in the family and your infant.

5. On the Move: From Eight to Twelve Months

The baby who was content to sit in your lap only a few weeks ago is probably on the move now—creeping, crawling, or perhaps almost walking—exploring the fascinating world around him. For parents, this means a more active vigilance, but also the beginning of an adventure together that will continue for the rest of your life—a joint exploration of the world as your child examines each leaf, each stone, each piece of lint, and eventually poses questions only a child can ask.

But for now, most babies are busy with the primary task of this age: the refining of motor skills. Learning first to crawl, later to cruise, and finally to walk are practically an obsession.

An infant will usually master crawling at around eight to ten months; then toward year's end, he'll pull himself to stand and begin to cruise around, holding on to the furniture. Taking an occasional step usually occurs at about one year, with the capacity to walk alone following in a month or so. There are, however, perfectly normal babies who begin to walk as early as nine months or as late as eighteen

11-month-old picking up cereal

months. During the initial phase of walking, a baby may take a few steps, only to return to crawling, which offers him greater speed at this point.

This new ability to move about brings with it a new freedom, but, as you will realize soon enough, it brings new dangers as well. If you have only partially baby-proofed your home, now is the time to finish the job (see **Chapter 18, Preventing Accidents**). Light cords, plants, cigarettes, pins and needles, thumbtacks, and other potentially dangerous items must be placed out of reach. Your child is an explorer now, and areas such as the cabinet under the sink—where cleaning materials are commonly stored—must be secured with a childpoof latch, or, better still, all cleaning products should be moved to a high shelf in a locked closet or cabinet.

While the baby is practicing his gross motor skills, he is by no means ignoring his fine motor skills. He can now pick up even the tiniest objects, and since everything inevitably ends up in his mouth, this requires increased vigilance on the part of the adults who are watching him. He enjoys his toys more than ever. He may be able to stack two blocks and roll a ball, and he likes to place small objects in a container, crumple paper, bang, pull books from the shelf, play pat-a-cake and peek-a-boo. Other favorite activities for babies of this age include looking at themselves in the mirror and touching, rubbing, and pulling at ears, nose, mouth, feet, and genital area.

It might be a good idea to give over one of your kitchen cabinets to the baby or arrange a large box or shelf as a storage area for his playthings. This way, when he approaches a cabinet, a bookshelf, or whatever, that is off-limits, you can pick him up and place him in front of his own storage area. At the time, this will help to distract him, but in the long run, he will begin to learn that some things are his and some things belong to others.

Dramatically improved hand and finger dexterity also makes it possible for a baby to begin feeding herself. She probably won't be able to drink well from a cup yet, nor can she manage a spoon by herself, but toward the end of the year, she may begin to enjoy feeding herself finger foods, such as slices of banana and small cubes of cheese, and she can hold her own bottle, although she still prefers to be cuddled by a trusted adult while she drinks.

As a baby becomes increasingly adept at using her hands, you may notice that she seems to favor one hand or the other for a time. There is no evidence to suggest that this relates to eventual hand preference in later life. The usual pattern, in fact, is for an infant to seem to prefer one hand for a few weeks, and then to switch to the other for awhile. A child gradually develops right- or left-handedness at some time during the second or third year.

Language Development

Language is advancing now, too. Throughout the day, a year-old baby jabbers away, primarily in an unintelligible jargon with accompanying facial expressions and changes in inflection. Some recognizable words may even emerge —perhaps *mama*, *dada*, *bottle*, and *woof* or *bow wow* for the family dog. His comprehension of language, however, is very advanced indeed. He can probably point to quite a few objects on request, and he understands a number of adult phrases, such as "time to eat," "time to go outside," and "coming."

The Separation Process

The separation process, which began to become evident around the middle of the year, becomes more prominent as the year comes to a close. In fact, the usual pattern is one of independent ventures that physically and psychologically separate a baby from her parents, interspersed with moments when a baby returns and seeks close contact with a trusted adult. And actually, this pattern will continue in some form throughout infancy, childhood, and adolescence. At times, a baby—particularly at the end of the day—appears to be confused as to which phase she's in. When picked up, she demands to be put down; yet when put down, she wants to be picked up again. This vacillation is normal, if exasperating for the adults who care for the baby. Sometimes a hug, a pat on the back, or just a cheery greeting is enough to recharge the infant for another round of independent activity.

As mentioned before, a baby in the second half of the first year of life is very attached to her primary caretakers, and her distress when they leave is very real. It's good to remember that learning to tolerate such losses and to anticipate the return of these beloved caregivers are basic life experiences. You should not feel that you have to "protect" your child from such feelings by never leaving her. On the contrary, you are depriving her of an important opportunity for emotional growth. It is helpful, however, to arrange to have consistent adult care for the baby in your absence. Having many unfamiliar caregivers can be difficult for an infant at this time.

It is reassuring to keep in mind that infants of about a year are already developing ways of coping with separation. Often an infant has a strong attachment to a specific toy or blanket and will carry this item wherever he goes. He considers this object—usually called a "transitional object"—to be a "little bit of mother," and it comforts him to hold it, especially at bedtime and other times of separation from his parents. Moreover, the child of a year or so has usually developed a sense of what is called "object permanence." For example, if a ball rolls behind a piece of furniture, he will now know to look for it, whereas in the past he would simply have thought it ceased to exist when he could no longer see it. Likewise, now when his parents leave, he has a mental image of them that serves to comfort him, and he knows from past experience that they still exist and will return.

As your baby nears that first birthday, it is a good time to reflect upon the past year. Perhaps at no other time will you have to adapt to as many changes as you have during the previous twelve months, and if you have weathered the experience with a fair degree of success, you can look to the future with a great deal of confidence. The relationship you have built and the baby's trust in you will be the groundwork for the life you will share in the years to come.

6. The Toddler: From One to Two and a Half

The toddler years are exciting and strenuous for both the child and the adults who provide care. A toddler's insatiable curiosity, her need for independence, and her rapid advancement in motor skills lead to increasing venturesomeness. During this time, she begins to move beyond babyhood and to become, increasingly, a person in her own right.

She will master many complicated new motor skills during this second year: straddling a kiddy car, pulling a toy, pushing a doll carriage, climbing on the sofa, and going up steps. But by far the most impressive of her accomplishments during this time is progressing from speaking perhaps a few words at twelve months to constructing short sentences at twenty-four months.

Toddler

Language Development

Of course, even though a twelve-month-old may not have much, if any, spoken language, this does not mean she cannot communicate. Nor does it mean she can't be communicated with. In fact, she understands a great deal of what is said and can follow simple directions. She is also very skillful at making herself understood. She points to the refrigerator when hungry or to the door when she wants to go out; or she will simply pull an adult to the appropriate setting to communicate an immediate wish. As adults respond with "Do you want some milk?" or "Do you want to go outside?" the toddler will begin to imitate these words and phrases, thus rapidly building her vocabulary. By the second birthday, a child will generally have an expressive vocabulary of 50 to 100 words, although she'll understand many more and will probably be able to put together two- or three-word sentences such as "I eat supper" and "I go bye-bye."

Play

The interest in imitating adults that helps a toddler master speech also influences his play. Make-believe is a favorite occupation of children this age. A toddler spends a great deal of time in doll play—putting the doll to bed, giving it a bottle, changing its diaper—repeating with extraordinary accuracy the behavior he has observed in the adults who care for him. Pretending to talk on the phone, to cook, to mop the floor, or to drive a car are other favorites. As the year unfolds and his language skills advance, he is likely to describe his activities to you as "I cook," "I drive," "I feed baby."

While children this age enjoy being around one another, parallel play (playing side by side) is the norm. It will be a couple of years before they can join together in the same game. Sharing is also an impossible expectation, because a toddler cannot comprehend what is expected. Letting one child have a toy only after the first child has finished with it is the best solution for settling disputes over possessions.

The Toddler Appetite

A toddler will also become increasingly interested in feeding himself in the second year—and increasingly able to do so as well. This is yet another manifestation of his desire to be like his parents, to eat what they eat, to join the family at the table, and to use the same utensils. Keep in mind, however, that messiness is universal at this age. Almost as much food is likely to end up on the child and on the floor as in the child's mouth. Also, a toddler may start out feeding himself well with a spoon but may grow tired and switch to fingers before the end of the meal; or he may prefer to be helped by an adult.

A lot of parents wonder—and worry—about their children's diets at this time. They may question whether their children are getting enough food to satisfy their energy requirements or enough of one or another specific nutrients.

The National Academy of Sciences recommends an average daily intake of 1,300 calories in the second and third years of life, and 1,700 in the fourth and fifth years to provide for growth and energy needs. A healthy child can usually be counted on to eat enough to supply these needs, particularly when allowed to make her own decisions. But bear in mind that caloric needs vary considerably. An active child will naturally need more calories than a placid one.

There is also a wide variety of normal eating patterns: some toddlers may eat equal amounts at each of the daily meals; other children may have one large meal at breakfast and merely nibble at lunch and dinner. Or your child may eat a great deal one day and hardly anything the next. The point is that the *average* intake should be close to the calorie figures stated above; it is not necessary for the calories to add up to that total every day.

As for other specific nutritional requirements, about one-half ounce of protein for every fifteen pounds of body weight is generally recommended. This requirement can easily be met by two or more daily servings of cheese, meat, eggs, or legumes, plus sixteen to twenty-four ounces of milk. The balance of the diet should consist of a variety of fruits, vegetables, and whole-grain breads and cereals.

Vitamin supplements are not usually necessary at this age since vitamin D is added to milk, fruit juices, and other foods. However, a child whose diet is insufficient in dairy products, citrus fruits or juices, or meats, whose appetite is poor in general, or who suffers from a chronic illness may benefit from supplementary vitamin tablets or drops. In areas where the water supply has not been fluoridated, a pediatrician may prescribe fluoride drops as well.

Are there any forbidden foods? Very few. Nuts, popcorn, and foods with pits should be avoided because of the danger of choking. Otherwise, a child of this age can eat almost anything the rest of the family eats, although some foods may still need to be mashed or cut up.

Toddlers—like older children and adults, too—have food likes and dislikes based on color, texture, taste, and familiarity. These preferences should be respected. Forcing a child to eat is likely to lead to an unproductive power struggle, not to greater consumption. If a child rejects a new food on first offering, back off and try again at another time. You may be surprised to find that he accepts the food with relish when offered a few days later.

Many pediatricians and cardiologists believe that a link may exist between dietary habits established early in life and the development of heart and other cardiovascular disease in adulthood, particularly in families where there is a history of such problems. Therefore, if there is a high incidence of cardiovascular disease in your family, you might consider limiting not only your own but also your child's intake of high cholesterol foods and salt. Limiting eggs to two or three a week; serving chicken, turkey, and veal rather than beef; avoiding fried foods; and substituting margarine for butter and lowfat for whole milk will significantly reduce your family's intake of dietary cholesterol.

Separation Process Toddler Style

Separation behavior in the second year becomes increasingly prominent, and clinging to parents and protesting their departure are the norm. Now your child's language may have developed to the point where he can express his distress, not just with tears, but with comments such as "Mommy, don't go," or "Mommy, stay here."

Of course, parents need to leave—for shopping, for recreation, for work. Learning to tolerate such separations is an important task at this developmental stage, and one with which your toddler needs help. It is never a good idea, for example, to sneak out when your child isn't watching. When he realizes you have left, he will feel doubly deserted and is likely to try to keep his eye on you constantly thereafter, protesting even if you go into another room. Nor is it wise to put the child to bed before the babysitter arrives. If the child awakens later and finds his parents have left, he may fear that they've gone for good. Instead, you should tell the child you are leaving, saying, "I know you will miss me, and I'll miss you, too. But Grandma (or Susan the babysitter, or whoever) will take good care of you, and I'll be back soon and will peek in on you and give you a kiss. In the morning, we'll have breakfast together." It might be reassuring to place some cereal or fruit on the table so the child can visualize sitting together in the morning. He may still cry when you leave, but over the course of time he will learn that you always do return.

Sleep Difficulties

The other type of separation behavior that is common in the second year is difficulty in going to sleep and staying asleep. As in the past, the best approach is to respond to your toddler's calls up to a point, to reassure her that you are still there and can be summoned if needed. However, if the demands for your attention seem endless, you might say firmly, "This is the last time. I expect you to go to sleep now."

An angry response or spanking is never a solution; it will, in fact, probably only make the child more frightened and less able to deal with her loneliness and anxiety at bedtime. Taking the child into your bed may seem like a tempting solution, but it's not likely to help in the long run. On the contrary, it may affirm your child's feelings that somehow her room and her bed are unsafe and scary.

Your child may also awaken at night crying, due to bad dreams. As in earlier months, you should try to awaken her completely or the dream is likely to continue. Although you may feel that a bottle would provide comfort, it is unwise to offer one, as the presence of food in the mouth increases the tendency to develop dental decay. If there appears to be no other solution, however, fill the bottle with plain water rather than milk, juice, or sugar water.

One difference in your child's night waking now, of course, is that she may be able to tell you something about what scared her. Moreover, she is beginning to understand the difference between real and pretend. If you explain to her that she had a "pretend" dream, that there really isn't a monster under her bed, for example, this will ease her distress and help her go back to sleep.

In general, you may find that your toddler needs less sleep than she did last year. She is very likely to be taking only one nap a day—usually right after lunch—and sleeping a ten- to twelve-hour stretch at night. Even though toddlers resist settling in for the night, they can usually be counted on to obtain sufficient hours of sleep to meet their needs.

Toilet Teaching

When it comes to toilet training, or, as it is now often termed, toilet teaching, I believe that a relaxed "wait and see" attitude is the best philosophy. With your first child, there will likely be moments when you are convinced he is going to go to college in diapers, but I can assure you that he won't even enter kindergarten in them. Parents tend to be far more relaxed about toilet teaching a second child, and, in general, the second child masters this difficult task about the same time (and sometimes earlier!) than an older sibling who has received a great deal of attention and encouragement. This leads me to believe that parents could save themselves a great deal of worry by introducing the subject occasionally but allowing the child to determine the timing.

At the end of the second year, or just after the second birthday, a child usually reaches a stage of sufficient nervous and muscular development that he can begin voluntarily to control elimination of his feces and urine. To attempt to teach a child to use a potty before control of the sphincter muscles has developed sufficiently places a heavy burden on him. When a child is ready to achieve this step, it may occur spontaneously; often a child needs only a minimal amount of coaxing.

Keep in mind that psychological factors also influence a

child's readiness to meet this challenge. Before the age of two, the desire to be independent and the need to determine when and how to use one's evolving motor skills are intense. A child is also just learning which activities evoke praise and which evoke the displeasure of his parents. And while rules and demands appear logical and reasonable to adults and are in the child's best interest, the toddler is likely to think of adult demands as unnecessary interference with personal freedom. In due time, however, a toddler modifies his actions mainly because he wishes to behave in a manner that pleases the important adults in his life.

Attempts to toilet teach a child in the midst of this intense phase of independence and desire for autonomy usually fail. He sees no reason to alter his habits of elimination. "You are not going to tell me where to put my BMs," he implies, either in action or at times with a strong no and a determined stamp of his foot.

Just before or shortly after the second birthday, a child usually shows signs of increasing interest in seeking parental approval. He climbs only on appropriate furniture. He begins to show signs of incorporating some of his parents'

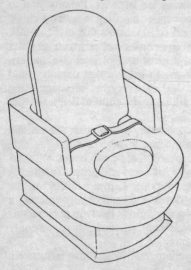

Potty chair

values into his actions. He may prefer to have clean hands and face rather than to be messy. These are all indications of readiness for toilet learning. Once your child begins to show many of these signs of readiness, and perhaps even begins to indicate a desire to have a soiled diaper changed, it's time to introduce the potty.

In general, a potty chair with a removable plastic container underneath has many advantages over using the adult toilet. Having the potty available at the child's own level encourages him to take responsibility for toileting, and it eliminates the need for the child to be lifted on and off the toilet. Moreover, a child will be more comfortable sitting with his feet on the floor. Sitting on an adult toilet, with feet dangling in midair, can be somewhat frightening for a young child. The swirling of the water and disappearance of the feces down the toilet may also be alarming. Children often feel that their feces are a part of them, and to see them being swished down the pipe may cause concern.

On the other hand, sometimes a child sees the potty as demeaning. If he's going to be expected to act like a grown-up, he wants to do it exactly the way they do! In this case, a toidy seat (a plastic seat that rests on top of the adult seat and can be taken on and off as needed) may be useful. Some seats wobble when placed on the toilet, so when shopping, try to ascertain from the label or from the salesclerk whether there is some type of attachment underneath that will help to stabilize it. A stepstool in front of the toilet may eliminate the need for you to lift him up onto it.

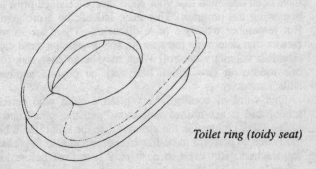

Toilet ring (toidy seat)

Investing in clothing that your child can get in and out of himself, or that come off easily, may also encourage interest in toileting.

Frequently a parent will notice a child squirming and making facial expressions that indicate that he is about to have a bowel movement. This is the moment to suggest using a potty or the toilet. Unfasten the child's pants, remove the diapers, and place him on the seat. If a child responds with a definitive no or fusses, it is better to discontinue efforts and try again in a few weeks. When parents stop making demands, toddlers often take the initiative and master the challenge of using a potty seat or toilet on their own.

Stressful life situations—a move, an illness, absence of a parent, or having a new sibling—may delay complete mastery of this complex psychological and physical task. Any child who is out of diapers is bound to have accidents and at times return to previous patterns of soiling when his mother is away or if he is in any other stressful situation, such as entering a day-care or nursery school setting. A child should not be expected to maintain his highest level of performance during difficult moments of stress. The more matter-of-fact you can be about accidents, the fewer of them there will likely be.

If your child is nearing the age of two and a half or even three and has yet to show any interest in moving beyond diapers, you may be starting to worry because of external demands that you feel are there. You may be investigating nursery schools or day-care programs by now, and you may have been informed that your child must be trained prior to beginning the program. This may, indeed, be a problem. But remember what we have discussed. There are many factors that determine the specific age at which a child can establish voluntary control. What may be an easy task for one toddler at two and a half may be beyond another child's capacity.

One word of comfort: Very often a child who enters school and is not trained will soon "join the gang" upon seeing other children in the group utilize the toilet. He'll be motivated to perform to be like his peers and also to please the teachers. But even then, it may take time before he chooses to continue this mastery at home. I suggest that if you have any concerns, discuss them with your child's doctor or the day-care or nursery school teacher. They should be able to help you arrive at the best way of handling this important issue.

As your child entered the toddler years, she was still very much a baby. She leaves this time with a growing sense of whom she is and an increasing desire to remind you of her independence! It is a time when you can truly appreciate the uniqueness that is hers.

7. The Preschooler:
From Two and a Half
to Five

Around the time your child reaches preschool age, your world and his will be expanding. If he has not been in a school program before, he'll likely be entering one now, and gradually your lives will be enriched by the thoughts and ways of the new friends he makes and the other adults who will provide for his care. It is a time of expansion, and your preschooler is busily preparing to meet the challenge.

Physical growth and intellectual development during the preschool years enable a child to think and act in many new and exciting ways. The rapid increase in the ability to control the body and the capacity to understand language and communicate with others result in greater independence in a variety of areas. Increasing interest in and concern about the world is apparent; and the constant barrage of whys and hows demonstrates a child's intense curiosity. He is ready to move on to a world beyond the home.

Your child is now taking increasing responsibility for himself, his decisions, and actions. Complicated thoughts, worries, and daydreams occupy his daytime hours. This personal life expresses itself in spontaneous play, which

4-year-old

goes on for hours at a time. The manner in which a specific child acts, thinks, plays, and interacts with other human beings distinguishes him as an individual and his interests from those of his parents, siblings, and friends. He is venturesome during playtime, yet he is strongly attached to his parents and usually misses them when separated for more than a few minutes. Initial explorations into the world away from his family are most successful when a parent or trusted adult is readily available when needed.

Dramatic advances occur in a child's ability to use her body during these years. At two and a half she still toddles somewhat when she walks. She manages to hold a crayon effectively, producing horizontal and vertical strokes in imitation of an adult. She scribbles and paints with exuberance, although at this stage, she probably isn't able to portray anything in particular.

By three she is quite nimble on her feet, walking up and down stairs alone; she often jumps down the final step. She can, or soon will be able to, manage a tricycle. Climbing, throwing a ball, and building with blocks are important play activities. She enjoys simple puzzles. She uses crayons and paints to produce pictures that portray her daily life. Her drawings may even begin to bear some resemblance to the people and things they are meant to represent.

By four she can run fast, balance herself on one foot, hop, skip, jump, and climb to the top of the jungle gym. She can catch a ball some of the time. Her drawings reveal her inner thoughts about her daily life experiences. By five she can throw and catch a ball with ease, rollerskate, and perhaps even venture off on an independent jaunt down the street. She can solve complex puzzles and copy numbers and letters. She may be able to recognize her printed name, too.

A child derives great satisfaction as he uses his many new skills. As you admire his achievements, he is stimulated to use his evolving capacities to the fullest, adding new accomplishments daily. Hanging a child's drawing on the kitchen wall or refrigerator door, for example, lets him know that you appreciate his artwork. He develops confidence and pride in his creative abilities and feels good about himself.

Your child will become increasingly responsible for himself during these years. He feeds himself, expressing firmly his likes and dislikes. He brushes his teeth and washes his hands, bathes himself, and assumes responsibility for his own toileting. There are moments, of course, when he slides back to immature behavior, forgetting to brush his teeth or wash his hands; he may also experience bowel and bladder accidents.

A child may be busy all day at school or a day-care setting, using his time and energy to work and play hard.

He is physically able to move away from his mother and home base, yet he may find it difficult to do without her for prolonged periods, even though his inner drive to do so is strong. When he returns home from day-care or nursery school, he is physically worn out and needs a rest and time to recuperate from a busy day. It is at these moments that he may lie on the floor with his favorite toy or ask to be read to or just cuddled quietly against your body. It may be hard to understand why a child who eagerly enters play activity in the morning and during the day is likely to be dependent and clingy when he comes home. This is very normal. A child cannot function at his highest level of achievement all the time. He needs some time to relax and recoup his energies.

Language Development and Comprehension

The rapid development of language skills in the pre-school years enables a child to communicate easily with other human beings. Her vocabulary increases by leaps and bounds during these years. At two and a half she is abandoning jargon; she possesses a vocabulary of 150 words or more. She uses pronouns appropriately and talks in two- to three-word sentences: "I go bye-bye," "I want a cookie," "I go night night," "Ear hurts" are concise comments that convey well-recognized messages. At three she talks end-lessly and with great enthusiasm. She uses plurals, pronouns, present and past tenses, and other grammatical forms with amazing accuracy. Of course, she makes mistakes, for manipulating the tongue and mouth muscles so that words are produced correctly is a complicated task. "Punsorch" for "sunporch" and "pisgatti" for "spaghetti" are examples of common errors.

Language develops during childhood as your child talks with others about daily activities. When you walk down the street or do household chores together, your comments about what you see and are doing become part of the child's vocabulary. "I see the bird," "I go to the store," "I make the beds," "I cook," he says, and in his play he chatters, pretending to help or actually helping with many household chores. Young children enjoy being read to, often preferring the same story repeatedly. Pointing to familiar pictures and retelling the story in his own words are favorite pastimes and also contribute greatly to language development.

One point to keep in mind is that a child's language is often deceptive. Although he may mimic comments such as "Mommy got a job," "We're moving to a new house," "Grandfather is dead," or "Mommy and Daddy are getting a divorce," the real implications of these words are often unclear. You will need to explain repeatedly before a child can grasp the actual meaning of such difficult concepts.

Time, too, is a difficult concept for a young child. When you say "I'll be back in half an hour," this has little meaning to a young child who cannot tell time. In a few minutes he will wonder when you are returning. "I'll be back after Grandma feeds you lunch" is far more meaningful at this age.

You may wonder at times whether your child's language development is lagging. Articulation deficits, failure to combine words into short sentences, and continuation of garbles and jargonlike pronouncements in the third year of life may indicate language delay and merit careful evaluation. Low grade ear infections or the presence of fluid in the middle ear may interfere with a child's hearing. If a child has a hearing deficit, it will be difficult for her to reproduce sounds correctly. In other cases, children have difficulty in processing language—that is, they may know what they want to say, but the words just don't flow easily. A child whose speech remains unintelligible or who is not talking in short sentences by three years of age should have a careful developmental and language evaluation.

Play

A preschool child utilizes all her physical and psychological skills in spontaneous play. It is a very important and satisfying occupation for a young child. A child shouts with glee as she climbs to the top of the slide and surveys the world from its perch, and then slides down. She possesses boundless energy, often playing vigorously for hours at a time.

Whether she plays alone or with friends, a preschool child has an unending capacity for pretending. She assigns roles to furniture, clay, dolls or other items, or to other people. A piece of furniture, a jungle gym, or a few large blocks can serve as a tractor one moment and a boat a few minutes later. Then suddenly it becomes a rocket or her father's car! Sand and water can be a cake, coffee, or dessert at one moment, and face powder and makeup the next. Dolls are often used to play the parts of people, such as a parent, sibling, close relative, teacher, or doctor, or a child may say to her friend, "You be the mommy, I'll be the daddy," or "You be the baby, and I'll be the mommy taking care of you."

A preschool child plays endlessly, singing and talking about important events in her life. Play gives her the opportunity to express her feeling about growing up, about having a sibling, and many other complex issues that may be presenting themselves right now. Her focus often shifts abruptly. At one moment she molds clay and talks about food as she imitates her parents preparing supper. Then all of a sudden, the doll she was preparing to feed becomes a newly arrived sibling and is tossed to the floor in anger. Yet, a few moments later, she will pick up the doll, cover it, and rock it with tenderness, only to throw it on the floor once again. She repeats this cycle, alternately rejecting and caring for the "baby." Playing out such matters provides a child with the opportunity to express her feelings, making them more manageable and tolerable for her to deal with.

A preschool child enjoys taking on some of the adult roles in his family. He likes to set the table, help make cookies, water flowers, and at times he may even rake the lawn! Participating in these and other household activities helps a child feel like a contributing member of the family and the adult world as he temporarily takes on responsibilities for some of these household tasks.

Interest in structured games such as hide-and-seek and follow-the-leader are popular occupations at this age.

These activities offer a child the opportunity to participate with other children and learn the importance of waiting, sharing, and taking turns.

How long a child can participate in a formal, structured activity varies greatly. Swimming, gymnastic, and music lessons are highly structured activities that may demand a longer attention span than many preschool children possess. Too much structure in a preschooler's life limits the time and opportunity to develop his own creativity. A preschool child should not be forced to participate in highly structured activities against his will. If there are activities he doesn't enjoy, it is quite possible that the specific tasks demanded may be inappropriate for him. A few months later he may be ready to meet these challenges.

Television Watching and the Preschooler

Usually about the time their child becomes a preschooler, parents begin to be concerned with how to use television judiciously to allow their youngster to enjoy the stimulation and relaxation that television programs can bring. In most families, watching television is an important daily activity for the children and provides an enormous amount of input as to how a child perceives the world in which we live.

Why does a child watch television? For many reasons. It is readily available; it is easy to turn on; other members of the family are watching; it serves as a relief from boredom; and, the truth is, children enjoy television!

Cartoons, puppet shows, and rhythmical musical presentations are appealing to toddlers and preschoolers. *Sesame Street* and *Mister Rogers' Neighborhood* are well-designed presentations noted for their educational content. These programs enlarge a child's understanding of the world, and also stimulate the development of language and many other intellectual skills.

However, remember that television is a completely passive experience, providing no opportunity for a child to interact with the children and adults he views on the screen. Super heroes also confuse a child as he struggles to distinguish fact from fantasy. This is a particularly difficult task at a time in history when astronauts really do go off into space and float for days on end in limbo! No wonder a child is often confused as to what is real and what is unreal on the television screen.

Commercials, prepared with great thought and skill to stimulate a child to exert pressure on a parent's purchasing habits, are also appealing to young children. The effects of these presentations often lead to dissension between parent and child, frequently observable in the aisles of local supermarkets!

Is watching television harmful to young children? A child who spends endless hours in front of a TV set has little time left to play creatively or interact with siblings, playmates, and caring adults. Long hours of watching television rob a child of important time and the opportunity to play freely and develop his or her own resources in imaginative play and to experience social interaction with peers. There are beneficial aspects of what a child sees on television, but watching it should not be a full-time occupation. Do remember, you have the power to control the amount of television that a child watches. You can always say, "That's it for now," and turn off the switch.

You may also want to consider limiting a child's television watching to moments when you can be present or at least nearby to observe the theme and substance of the program your child is seeing. The constant portrayal of violence on television may affect your child in many different ways. First of all, it can be frightening. The fights, killing, crashes, and other forms of violence bombard a child for hours on end and make it difficult for him to control his own aggressive impulses, such as biting, hitting, and kicking.

When a program extols violence or presents degrading treatment of women, the elderly, or minorities, share your reactions with your child. You can say, "I just don't like solving problems this way," or "I don't like it when I see old people or anybody else treated that way." Express your feelings repeatedly, for only in this way will your child begin to comprehend and adopt your value system.

News presentations of riots and war activities convey the all-too accurate message that violence is, indeed, a common way of life throughout the world. As a child matures and understands what he sees on television, he may develop an overwhelming fear of a nuclear holocaust. We need to sympathize and support a child as he grapples with this realistic fear in a world gone mad with uncontrollable power at the fingertips of the world's leaders.

Television, like reading books aloud and having conversations while taking walks, provides opportunities for family discussions. Do take these opportunities to help your child grow and mature and increase his understanding of the world in which we all live. Watch TV with your child as much as you are able and discuss freely the programs you have been watching together.

Becoming a Separate Person

During these years, a child's concept of himself in relationship to his parents and siblings and other people in the world changes remarkably. Babies and toddlers consider everybody and everything in the world as an extension of themselves. They are unable to distinguish between "what's mine" and "what's not mine." No matter how many toys and playthings he may have, he can be expected from time to time to ransack the kitchen cabinet or his mother's sewing basket or pocketbook. Indeed, many parents report that when they can't find something, they discover it hidden away in a young child's room. A child often picks up a toy at a friend's house or doctor's office, hides it under his clothes, and brings it home, or he may pick up candy from the counter in the supermarket.

When a preschool child appropriates toys or candy, it indicates that he is still struggling with understanding what belongs to him and what belongs to other individuals. It is not a failure on the part of the parents, nor does it mean that the child will become a delinquent. He is not being intentionally bad; he just hasn't yet fully grasped the idea of personal possessions. It takes time and many mistakes before a child can comprehend this important concept and incorporate it into his behavior.

How can you help your child understand and respect the idea of personal property? It is helpful if he has a private shelf, drawer, or box where he can leave his personal belongings and know that these possessions will be there when he returns. When adults he loves and trusts respect *his* personal belongings, he will gradually learn to respect other people's possessions as well. There are always lapses when a child forgets. As a parent, one must be tolerant of these lapses, yet firm in helping a child return the items to the proper owner.

Struggles of the Preschooler

Bedtime and middle-of-the-night fears are still the norm. He may awaken with frightening dreams several times a night. You may be perplexed as to why this difficulty recurs just at the time when your child is more independent than ever during the day. There is a simple explanation. The daytime activities, such as visits to a neighbor or attending nursery school, represent fulfillment of a child's strong inner drive to be independent and venturesome in the world. Although satisfying, this new activity may be overwhelming. At bedtime or in his dreams, a child may worry that his own independence, although exciting, may motivate him to go too far from his parents. He fears that he may not find them when he returns. This prospect frightens him, of course, and it is a perfectly normal reaction at this age.

Spending time with a child at bedtime, returning several times for a good-night kiss, or repeated drinks of water, and attending to him when he wakes with a bad dream usually bring this problem to a conclusion within a few months. Encouraging your child to talk about his "pretend dreams" will often provide opportunity to discuss his worries with him, and you can reassure him that you or some other member of the family or a familiar babysitter will always be there for him.

Other fears are common at this age, too. Fear of the dark, imagining shadows of monsters, fear of loud noises, and fear of certain people are well within normal limits. A child needs support and comfort in her struggle to overcome these common fears; scolding and criticizing accomplish nothing.

This is a confusing time in a child's life. She struggles to achieve control and does, in fact, control many of her activities. She chooses her own foods, often decides what clothes to wear, and she certainly decides how and where to play much of the time. But at the same time many decisions are made for her; she is told which school or day camp to go to and when to eat and when to go to bed. This is difficult for a child whose need for independence is strong and who has an inner drive to be her own person.

Of course, many decisions must be made by parents. It is important to realize, however, that when decisions are made it is natural for a preschool child to resist being told what to do. It is a part of normal psychological growth. You also need to keep in mind that a child's negative reaction does not indicate that you are mistaken in what you have done. Rather, it suggests that she is trying to find out which areas she can be expected to determine for herself and which are still in the area of her parents' responsibility.

By the end of this period, your preschooler will have taken another important step in the separation process, and she'll be more secure in her explorations of the world now that she can communicate with ease and handle feelings and frustrations with reasonable skill. Her enjoyment of life demonstrates her healthy growth and development, and she's now ready for the challenges that school will bring.

8. Entering a New World: The Five- and Six-Year-Old

As your child turns five, you will see that activity is a hallmark of this age. A five-year-old is full of energy and enthusiasm for anything physical. Using his body is almost a full-time occupation. He throws a ball with increasing skill; he can hop, skip, and jump. He may already be able to ride a bicycle and skate, or if not he will soon. His imagination, too, is active and vivid. He enjoys playing for long periods of time while building castles and tunnels and turnpikes in the sand or in the dirt in the backyard. Or he zooms around on his tricycle, pretending he is a fire chief. He chats constantly as he performs these activities and possesses an inner world of imagination that only he may know and understand. Toy cars, dolls, and animals are also favorite play items that a child incorporates into daily activities.

5-year-old

Challenges of School

There are many challenges that face five- and six-year-olds as they leave the informal and flexible experiences of home life and nursery school and enter the more structured activities of an elementary school. It takes time for children to feel comfortable with the demands that come with structure. As they do, however, they find their new environment a fascinating place to be.

Kindergarten and first grade are usually highly structured settings. There is likely to be a high priority on a child's ability to be polite, quiet, cooperative, thoughtful, curious, and attentive. Talking is encouraged, but only when called upon! Rules—such as where to hang your coat, which toys to play with, where to sit, when to go to the bathroom, and where and how to draw with a crayon —are the order of the day.

Just imagine the extent of this change in settings for the young child. Preschool children are largely permitted to play, run, climb, sing, draw, and talk about imaginary events as they see fit. In elementary school, activities are likely to reflect organized lesson plans based on established curriculum. Although children usually do adapt with remarkable skill to the demands of the more structured educational program, it is, indeed, hard work!

Variations in Development

A child of this age is also expected to begin to perform certain tasks with precision. For example, she will be asked to draw within lines, copy letters accurately, and learn to write her own name. These tasks are easier for some children than for others, because there is considerable variation in the rate at which skills for visual-motor and eye-hand coordination evolve. The fingers of some five-year-olds just can't do all that is expected. This variability can make reading, writing, and drawing much more difficult for the child whose maturation proceeds at a slower rate than other children's. Remember, just as it is normal for one child to walk at nine months and another at fifteen months, there is an equal amount of variation in other areas of development. Tying a shoe may be easy for one five-year-old, yet difficult for another child who is almost six. Yet, six months later the latter child's eye-hand and finger coordination has improved sufficiently that she can tie her shoes with ease.

Sometimes teachers fail to recognize this variability in the rate children develop. The quickness with which a child answers questions and remembers yesterday's discussion may lead the teacher to think that she can perform equally well in other areas, but this may not be so. No matter how hard a child struggles to achieve certain tasks, she cannot possibly succeed until her neuromuscular capacities mature. She becomes frustrated and exhausted. Time, patience, and help from adults usually aid a child as her nervous system matures at its own rate. Occasionally, however, when a lag in a certain area persists, a child may need special tutoring to help her overcome a particular difficulty.

Competitive games, particularly those requiring a high level of gross motor skills, may be taxing for some youngsters at this age. A child whose development in this area may be a bit behind other classmates is likely to feel unhappy because he cannot keep up with the other children. Physical education should provide for these differences. Musical activities, free-form dancing, and rhythm bands should be emphasized, while activities such as somersaults or those requiring complicated athletic abilities should be postponed. Activities featuring freedom of movement provide an opportunity for a child to master control of his body and to develop a sense of competence, which should be accomplished prior to beginning organized athletics.

Adapting to Different Rules in Different Places

Other demands in elementary school represent a new experience for a young child. He no longer has the opportunity, as in earlier years, to decide when he does what. To win the teacher's approval, which to the young child is often seen as being loved by the teacher, means adapting to the teacher's wishes, and in many instances different and unfamiliar ways of doing things predominate. How many parents have been told, "But Mrs. Brown, my teacher, says I must do it this way," referring to any one of innumerable aspects of daily life. The broadening of a child's horizons is an important challenge of growing up. And in time the young child learns to adapt his way of doing things to meet the demands of the moment, wherever he might be.

The Importance of Time to Do Nothing

As your child faces all of these challenges, don't be surprised if she comes home from school exhausted, disgruntled, and rebellious. Have patience. A first-grader needs time to rest on the floor, munch crackers, and drink a glass of milk or fruit juice—to do nothing for a short time. Soon she will recuperate and decide to take off down the street or go out in the yard to play with her friends.

Whether a child should participate in after school activities such as dancing, music lessons, swimming, or gymnastics during this first year of elementary school depends on the child. In most instances, a child needs some time to play as he wishes to after the structured hours of school. You may want to postpone these extra activities until later in the year or until the following year when a child has become better adjusted to school life. Certainly organized athletic activities are rarely suitable even for a six-year-old.

A major goal at this time is to help a child develop confidence so that he can meet the demands and challenges of school. A child needs opportunities to talk frequently about his frustrations and difficulties in school and about things that upset him. Then he needs encouragement to return the next day to continue his struggle to adapt, cope, and move ahead.

As a parent, you may disagree with the teacher on a certain issue or may have some reservations about the school program. You should, of course, participate in parents' groups and work toward improving the program. But do remember that changes come about slowly, and your immediate and most important task is to help your child develop confidence and the ability to adapt to challenging situations in the school and in life outside the home. The feeling of confidence that evolves in your child at this early age will become a mainstay throughout his or her life.

II Your Child's Well-Being

9. Developmental Concerns

My two-year-old doesn't speak intelligibly yet . . .
My baby doesn't seem to focus properly . . .
My child seems to be slow in learning certain things . . .
Do you think my child is hyperactive?

These are a few of the more common developmental worries parents ask about. Most likely, your child is perfectly normal, and the problem, whatever it is, will soon be outgrown. However, if you have a continuing concern, the following information about the causes of various developmental delays may be of help. If you remain worried, consult your pediatrician, who may advise a special consultation to clarify your child's developmental status.

Hearing Problems

A child who is profoundly deaf is easy to recognize; however, a moderate hearing loss is often difficult to detect since the child's reaction to loud sounds suggests that his hearing is normal. Whenever a baby fails to turn in the direction of a bell, voice, or other sounds, or when a toddler has little understanding of language by his second birthday, it is important to consider the possibility of a hearing impairment.

A six-month-old baby with normal hearing coos responsively, often initiating a "conversation" with friendly adults. At the end of the first year, a baby babbles for long periods of time, enjoying the sounds of her own voice as well as the echo. A baby with normal hearing turns toward the source of sound. She often looks pleased when a parent calls from another room. By one year, a child has a few distinguishable words, such as *dada*, *mommy*, or the name of a sibling or the family pet. By two, although perhaps still talking in jargon, a child normally has a speaking vocabulary of between 50 and 100 words; she understands several hundred. She also has begun to put words together, such as "me go home?" "daddy home?" "go bye-bye?"

Failure to achieve these language skills at the appropriate ages suggests that a child may have an auditory deficiency. Frequently, the cause is an ear infection, which has continued even after the child has received the recommended course of antibiotics. The hearing impairment itself may indicate the presence of a nonpainful, low-grade infection that has not been completely resolved by the antibiotic treatment. Often, there is an accumulation of fluid in the middle car, which limits movement of the cardrum, resulting in decreased auditory function.

This middle ear condition, known as serous otitis, may respond to repeated courses of antibiotic and decongestant administered orally. In many instances, however, the fluid in the middle ear remains due to a problem with the normal drainage function of the eustachian tube connecting the middle ear and the nasopharynx. This dysfunciton is often caused by swelling of the tissues lining this threadlike tube, due to an allergic sensitivity to ingested food, inhaled pollens, molds, or dust. Enlargement of adenoids, tonsils, and other lymphoid tissue may also obstruct the outlet of this tube in the nasopharynx and interfere with the drainage of fluid from the middle ear.

Recurrent ear infections and accumulation of fluid in the middle ear are common in certain families and suggest the presence of an inherited factor that predisposes a child to develop ear problems. If family members have suffered from chronic ear infections, you will want to be particularly vigilant when your child complains of an earache.

A second type of auditory deficiency experienced by a few infants and children is a hearing loss due to an inherited form of deafness, or as a result of a viral infection in the mother during pregnancy, or stress or illness in the early weeks and months of life.

Luckily, recently developed methods of evaluating auditory function provide a means of accurately determining hearing acuity in babies and toddlers as well as older children.

What degree of hearing loss represents a significant impairment? A bilateral loss of twenty-five decibels or more in both ears endangers the development of language and other intellectual and social skills. It excludes a child from understanding and participating in many of the usual conversations and activities in a day-care center, nursery school, or classroom setting.

Unrecognized auditory dysfunction is a common cause of delay in language development. Early recognition is extremely important. If treated promptly, children suffering from hearing loss caused by fluid in the ear may have their problem corrected with medication. For other children, medical treatment, the use of a hearing aid, and special stimulation of the child's language development are imperative as soon as one becomes aware of the problem. Even a baby who is not yet a year old can be fitted with bilateral hearing aids that can enable him to experience some level of social and language stimulation. With the advances being made in this field, there is great hope that your child with a hearing problem may be among those who can benefit from the many new devices that correct hearing to normal or near-normal levels.

Vision Difficulties

Problems with vision are common during infancy and in the toddler and preschool years. Early recognition and treatment of visual dysfunction are important, since poor vision interferes greatly with a child's growth, maturation, and the educational process.

Lazy Eye

Roving movements of the eyes are normal in the early months of life. However, if one eye predominantly turns inward or outward at six months or after, it suggests a significant dysfunction of the nerves and muscles controlling ocular positioning. This inability to align the eyes can lead to diminished visual acuity in one eye because of disuse. The condition, often termed "lazy eye," may be prevented by intermittent patching of the good eye, thus stimulating the visual function of the weaker eye. Difficulty in aligning the eyes may also be the result of variation of focusing in the two eyes.

Astigmatism

A child with astigmatism (in which the focusing in different directions is uneven, resulting in an imperfect image) may have trouble recognizing letters in a book or on a blackboard because he cannot see horizontal and vertical components with equal sharpness. The problem often goes unrecognized in young children; however, there is a specific test for it. If you notice that your child seems to have difficulty focusing or rubs his eyes and seems to tire easily, ask your doctor about it.

Difficulty Focusing

Many young children who are neither nearsighed nor farsighted are unable to maintain focus of their eyes on a specific point of a printed page for more than a few seconds. The word they are looking at blurs in and out or appears to jump up and down. One moment they see the printed word, the next moment it has disappeared. Synchronizing their eye movement along the line is difficult. Children with these difficulties in visual functioning tire easily and make mistakes inconsistent with their knowledge and intelligence. They may be considered lazy or poorly motivated. However, the real problem is that the deficiency in visual function is tiring and exhausts the most highly motivated child in a few minutes.

Optometrists with special interest and training in the developmental aspects of vision offer special visual training and often prescribe bifocals for children suffering from visual dysfunction due to muscular imbalance and deficit. In many instances, these treatments result in dramatic improvement in a child's ability to meet the demands of reading and writing in the classroom.

Learning Disabilities

If you are concerned about a particular developmental delay and have explored and put to rest the possibility of a problem with the child's hearing or vision, you should consider the possibility of a learning disability—a common condition existing in at least ten percent of all children.

A child suffering a learning disability possesses normal intelligence, yet has difficulty achieving some of the intellectual milestones of the early childhood years. These individuals have a deficit in one or more important psychological processes, which interferes with intellectual growth, particularly in the language area. A child may have difficulty understanding what he hears, or his expressive language skills may be poorly developed. Reading, writing, and spelling are particularly difficult for him. For this reason, early recognition of the problem is important. It is imperative to realize that children with learning disabilities are not dumb, lazy, poorly motivated, or disturbed.

What they need is special educational help to aid them in mastering age-appropriate skills.

Clumsiness may be present in a child with a learning disability. He learns to roller skate or ride a bicycle only with great difficulty; he holds his pencil or crayons in an awkward manner, often writing off the lines onto the edge of the paper and occasionally onto the desk.

What causes a learning disability? Stresses during fetal life are often reported in these children. A viral infection in the mother during pregnancy, bleeding during the first trimester, premature rupture of the membranes prior to delivery, infection of the amniotic fluid, prolonged labor, difficult delivery, and premature birth may produce neurologic damage that predisposes a child to experience learning difficulties.

Illness in the early days of life also places a child at risk. A history of meningitis, serious injury, or seizures of any kind suggests the need for careful observation. Unrecognized elevation of lead levels in the blood, chronic anemia, and malnutrition may also be a cause.

There are also sometimes genetic factors in a child's family history that alert one to the possibility of a significant learning disability. The child with a learning disability often has a parent, sibling, or other close relative who experienced difficulties in reading or other educational tasks.

A stimulating environment and special educational services can improve a young child's skills in the area of deficiency. A child may learn to overcome his difficulty if appropriate help is found. Your pediatrician, local superintendent of schools, or the state commissioner of education at your state capitol can advise you as to how to arrange appropriate evaluation of your child if you have any concerns about his or her development or capacity to learn. Specialized educational programs during the preschool years often will enable children to progress in their cognitive development so that they can effectively meet the challenges of kindergarten and the primary grades. If your school system cannot arrange for this program, most communities have specialized services available in child guidance clinics or in the pediatric clinics of most hospitals or medical centers.

There are, however, some learning disabled children who need special education throughout the school years. How a child responds to appropriate tutoring will demonstrate the extent of his or her disability.

If you have determined that your child is suffering from a learning disability, be sure to arrange for visual and hearing studies. Appropriate glasses and hearing aids are as important for a learning disabled child as they are for any other.

Dyslexia

The tendency to confuse left and right is common during preschool and kindergarten, but by the time a child reaches first grade she should have begun to achieve this capacity. If yours hasn't, she may be dyslexic. These children have a tendency to confuse such betters as *b* and *d*, or *p* and *q*. Reversals in spelling are also common. For example, *was* becomes *saw*, and *but* becomes *tub*.

It is important to identify the problem as soon as possible because a dyslexic child will obviously have difficulties in school with this handicap. As with any learning disability, special tutoring can be very helpful in correcting the problem. For some dyslexic individuals, however, special help may be necessary throughout life.

Handedness

Babies or toddlers often use either hand interchangeably or experience phases of using one hand and then the other. But by the age of three, and certainly by kindergarten, most children are showing a decided preference for either the left or the right hand. This preference should be respected since it represents an expression of dominance in the functioning of one or the other hemispheres of the brain.

A preschool child who has not yet demonstrated a preference for one hand or the other should be encouraged to use the one which seems to be easier for him or her. However, this should not be forced.

A kindergartener who is confused about laterality and uses hands interchangeably may also be experiencing significant delays in the development of other important intellectual skills necessary to achieve normal educational progress.

Hyperactivity, or Attention Deficit Disorder

Parents frequently wonder whether their very active child is suffering from hyperactivity, or, as it has recently been called, attention deficit disorder. The child with attention deficit disorder has a short attention span, difficulty working at any specific task for a prolonged period, and a low tolerance for frustration. In most cases, a parent usually notes that even as an infant, "he was never still for even a moment." Teachers report, "He can't settle down to one task for more than a few moments. He's a bright child. If only I could get him to concentrate for a longer period of time." The condition is four times as common in boys as it is in girls.

Because his developmental delay concerns the ability to set priorities, a child with attention deficit disorder cannot decide which of the many stimuli bombarding him is the one to get his attention. He is captured by everything he sees and hears. An ordinary classroom with pictures, books, educational equipment, and classmates presents a whirlwind of exciting stimuli. He is compulsively and continuously in motion.

Some children can be helped by a medication known as methylphenidate. (A careful pediatric and psychological examination should be performed prior to the administration of the medicine.) The medication can enable a person to focus on a primary task and not be distracted by stimuli in the environment. Medication often is discontinued for summer vacation when it is less important for the child to concentrate, and usually it is possible to discontinue the medication as a child matures. As the child grows into adolescence, he usually gains the capacity to control his activities and impulses on his own. Possible side effects of the medicine include a rise in blood pressure, a decrease in appetite, and sometimes a decreased rate of growth. Usually these problems go away when the medicine is discontinued, and even the child whose growth has slowed usually catches up with time. It is important for a child who is taking methylphenidate to be under careful medical supervision.

Children who experience difficulty in settling in to a classroom situation with many opportunities for distraction benefit from small classes and opportunity for one-to-one relationships with teachers. In many school systems, it is possible to arrange such a program.

Bed-Wetting, or Enuresis

Although most children achieve control of urination during both day and night by the age of four, a few are unable to master it that quickly. Most have achieved control by the age of seven, but a small group struggle with this problem until early adolescence. And there are occasional adults who still have difficulty overcoming bed-wetting.

Children who experience enuresis are usually considered in two groups: those who suffer from primary enuresis, that is, a child over five years of age who has never achieved dry nights; and those suffering from secondary enuresis, a child who has been dry at night for some time, but suddenly begins to wet the bed as in earlier years.

For youngsters with primary enuresis, the problem usually occurs because they sleep very soundly, and the usual discomfort of a full bladder that awakens most children fails to arouse them. "A bomb could go off, and he wouldn't awaken" or "He never wakes up during a thunderstorm" are comments made frequently about these children. Parents of youngsters with primary enuresis frequently report that they also had this difficulty during their own childhood.

Secondary enuresis comes about for quite different reasons. A child who begins to wet the bed after a period of having dry nights may be suffering an infection in the urinary tract, the onset of a metabolic disease, or may be experiencing some form of stress. A simple examination of the urine can determine whether infection or metabolic disease is the cause. If either of these conditions are present, prompt treatment usually results in disappearance of the bed-wetting.

Psychological stress may come from a variety of causes. A parent may be away, a new sibling may have been born, or a close relative may have died. A move to a new home or starting a new school may also cause stress for a child. (I once conferred with a group of parents of first-graders in which half the children were wetting the bed. The cause? Their new teacher was inexperienced, and her disciplinary approach was quite out of place for children of this age.)

Whatever the cause, remember that it represents a problem over which a child has very little control. It isn't a child's fault that he sleeps so soundly that he fails to awaken with a full bladder, or that he has an infection or diabetes, or that he is experiencing a stressful time in his life. Scolding, spanking, making a child wash sheets, or any other punitive approach has no place in the treatment of enuresis. The child who bed-wets is already upset, and feels inadequate and discouraged about his problem. He wants to stop bed-wetting just as much as his parents want him to.

Avoiding fluids in the evening, and being awakened and taken to the bathroom by parents late at night may help a child to achieve control. Some parents find that making the child an active participant in the search for a remedy is helpful. One recommended method is for you and your child to make a joint shopping trip to purchase a loud alarm clock. Then at night, help your child to set the clock for a time two to three hours after he goes to bed. When it rings, encourage him to get up, go to the bathroom and urinate, and then return to bed, setting the alarm again for a similar period. Although some children sleep so soundly that the alarm fails to awaken them, this method has helped a good number of others to overcome the problem.

Stuttering

Many preschool children experience stuttering; however, it occurs more commonly in boys than in girls. In most instances, this is a perfectly normal phase of development, which occurs because of a child's inability to utilize his tongue and mouth muscles as fast as his mental activity demands. It rarely indicates any psychological disturbance or permanent difficulty. Patience and encouraging your child to speak slowly are the best ways of helping your youngster. Eventually the child will be able to adapt his verbal activities to the speed of his thought processes, and the problem will disappear. Very rarely, particularly if there is a family history of stuttering, a child may benefit from speech therapy. Your local superintendent of schools or the commissioner of education in your state capitol can refer you to the appropriate place to receive help with this problem.

Imaginary Playmate

Many children, particularly those who are highly intelligent, carry on long conversations with imaginary playmates. This activity in no way suggests any mental disorder. It is only a problem when it involves a large proportion of the child's day, thus interfering with other normal activities. If your child has such a playmate, share with her the fact that you know, as she knows, that this is a pretend game, and that you agree that sometimes it is fun to pretend. In this way you can play along with the child, yet at the same time encourage her to understand that it is a game. Usually a child begins to abandon her imaginary playmate when she starts to develop a circle of friends with whom she plays.

10. Common Stresses That Alter a Child's Behavior

Infants, toddlers, and young children are happy and delightful to be with much of their waking hours. However, there are moments when a toddler or young child presents an entirely different kind of behavior. He becomes whiny and demanding; he has little interest in eating, often pushing the food away; or he awakens with frightening dreams. His bowel and urine control may suddenly disappear. He tolerates frustration poorly. Temper tantrums may appear to an increasing degree.

"It's difficult to comfort him," remarked a mother of one of my three-year-old patients. "I don't know what's the matter. He's been such a good child. Now he's impossible. He's acting like a baby."

Children commonly exhibit some behavioral changes prior to a family trip, a long-awaited visit from grandmother, or some other such alteration in family activities. Early mornings and late afternoons are also times when difficult behavior is sometimes the norm. In the morning, a child may be anxious about leaving home to go to a daycare center, nursery school, or elementary school—even one she has attended for quite some time. (This is particularly common following a school vacation or when a child has been home because of illness.) Discomfort and whininess late in the day may be due to exhaustion from a full day at day-care or school. A child often manages to maintain acceptable behavior throughout the school day, but finally, when she returns home, she collapses with exhaustion. "I can't keep it in forever, Daddy," exploded a five-year-old girl when her "letting go" at the supper table exasperated her father. "I have to let it out sometime."

If your child's difficult behavior seems to dominate her day, you should consider the possibility of a physical cause. Sometimes illnesses can occur without overt signs other than behavioral ones. Take your child's temperature. If it is elevated, arrange to take your child to see the doctor. Teething, inflammation of the middle ear, viral and bacterial or parasitic intestinal infections, allergic reactions, or food intolerances may be present and can alter a child's behavior. Another common, but largely unrecognized, cause of abnormal behavior is accumulation of lead in the body due to ingestion or inhalation of this toxic substance. Families who live in old homes where lead-based paint was used in the past should be particularly conscious of this as a possibility.

If there is no sign of illness, you will want to evaluate whether stress may be the cause of your child's difficulty. If you're moving or expecting a new baby, you may already have your answer. Any type of change in a family may cause significant stress for a young child. Common family events that produce changes in behavior include the birth of a baby, changes at school, the illness or death of a close family member or friend, the absence of a parent, an anticipated or actual move to another home, job changes, unemployment, and interpersonal conflicts between adults in the family, including separation and divorce. We will discuss several of these events in more detail, but in general, openness and honesty concerning any stressful events are what will help your child the most. For example, although there is no need to tell her weeks in advance about a lengthy trip you must take, she should know about it as soon as it becomes part of the family discussion. A child's imagined version of what is being hidden from her is almost always far worse than the actual event. The more realistic you can be about any upcoming stresses, the easier it will be for your child.

If a child's reaction to something interferes significantly with eating, sleeping, or the ability to play with friends or enjoy school, consult your pediatrician, a child guidance clinic, or a family service agency for professional assistance in helping your child cope with the stress.

One fact is certain: Slapping, hitting, or spanking a baby, toddler, or child, or inflicting pain in any way is never a solution to a child's disturbing behavior. Parents who lose control themselves and inflict corporal punishment are models for children. When they slap or spank a child at a moment of exasperation, it can only teach a child that when he is angry or dissatisfied, he, too, should slap or hit other people. One cannot convince a child to *stop* hitting by hitting him! It does, however, teach him to incorporate into his own thinking the idea that "When I get bigger, and I'm angry at someone, I will hit. That's what my parents do when they are angry with me!"

Let's consider some common sources of stress for children.

Pregnancy

Consider a mother's pregnancy. Early on, a woman usually feels tired and preoccupied. She responds a bit less promptly than before to her toddler's or child's demands. A child's reaction is to be even more demanding! What can you do to relieve this situation? First, try to remember that a toddler or young child is sensitive to any subtle changes in the way a parent provides care. There will be a reaction to even a minor alteration in your parenting. Paying additional attention to the child during this time may be one solution, but you might also arrange for a relative or babysitter to help out regularly in order to provide a respite for yourself during the pregnancy.

Toward the end of the pregnancy, a young child should,

if practical, be shown the hospital where you will deliver. Some hospitals encourage visiting tours for children, providing an opportunity for the child to develop an image of where you will be while away from home.

If you leave for the hospital in the middle of the night, awaken your child, if possible, to say good-bye rather than have him discover in the morning that you disappeared while he was asleep. If your hospital provides sibling visiting privileges, by all means take advantage of it. If it doesn't provide for family visiting, ask for it! Daily phone calls to your youngster are also important. Some mothers hesitate to have their children visit or phone, thinking that the toddler or young child will be even more upset by the contact. There may be tears, but this is far less upsetting than for a child not to see his mother at all. If he doesn't see her or have contact by telephone, he may assume she has disappeared forever!

When a mother returns home, a child is likely to have mixed feelings about the arrival of a sibling. Although glad to have his mother back, at the same time he is likely to feel somewhat displaced by the baby who is now the center of attention. This is a normal reaction. A young child needs help in coping with these feelings. At the baby's feeding time, many mothers find it helpful to offer an older child a snack to remind the child that she is concerned about meeting his needs as well as the baby's. And in some families, time for nursing also signals a time for the older child to be read a story.

A return to immature behavior is common at this time. A preschool child may resort once again to his bottle, favorite teddy bear, blanket, or thumb for comfort. If he has achieved toilet training and is dry at night, he may experience relapses to soiling and wetting. He may start talking baby talk and acting like an infant or toddler in other ways as well.

If you have not already moved your child into a big bed, this is not the time to do so. Let your toddler remain in his crib and make other arrangements for the baby. Perhaps you can borrow a crib or a bassinet. If you put the baby in what has been the child's crib, your older child is likely to feel more deeply than ever that he is being dispossessed.

At a later date, he can make this transition with greater ease.

Changes at Day-Care Center or School

Changes in a child's day-care center, nursery, or grade school can produce stresses that result in behavioral changes at home. Perhaps a favorite playmate has left the classroom, or no longer rides on the school bus. Or maybe a favorite teacher or aide has been absent. You may want to visit your day-care center or school to determine whether there have been personnel or other changes and whether the program is still suitable for your child. (You may want to consider making an unannounced visit to get a better feeling for what is going on.) You have a right, indeed, an obligation, to learn as much as possible about the program and about the people who care for your child in your absence. Day-care center or nursery school staffs should always be willing to work with you in trying to understand your child's behavior.

Illness in the Family

Illness of a family member or close friend is a common stressful experience for toddlers and children. Whether it is a parent who is ill or a close relative or friend, the preoccupation and concern of the adults alter considerably the way in which a child's needs are met.

When it is a parent who is ill, it is important to be honest and direct with a child even as young as two, explaining that you don't feel well and that's why you're grumpy, or that's why you're not going out. Even a twenty-four-hour flu that keeps a parent in bed for only a day can be alarming to a young child who thinks of her parents as invincible. Reassure your child that she will definitely be taken care of. She also needs to know that the changes in the way she is being nurtured are not because she did anything wrong.

Parental Absence

A young child may react when a parent has been away for a business trip or a much-needed vacation. He may be clingy and demanding upon the parent's return. You must realize that when you leave your child, he can only experience this as a temporary loss of a very important person he loves and depends on for care. No matter how competent a substitute caretaker may be, a child may still react when you return home. However, this does not mean that the trip was a mistake. These experiences of frequent short absences of a parent help to build a child's capacity to tolerate normal anxieties concerning separation from the adults who provide care for him.

Moving

Moving from one house to another is a common stress in the lives of young children. One problem is that it is difficult for a child to conceive of what is going to happen. What does moving mean? Do the walls go? Does the rug? What about the bed? And how will Grandma know where to visit? Books such as the *Berenstain Bears' Moving Day* by Stan and Jan Berenstain (Random House) can help explain the upcoming event. It's also important to talk at length about the fact that *all* her toys will go, too.

As you pack, provide your child with a small box or bag for her to pack the things that she most treasures. That box might best go with you, rather than on the van. (If it goes on the van, label it clearly so that it will be one of the first you find when unpacking.) On moving day itself, be sure your child has the opportunity to visit her room one last time to see that it is totally empty. There's no better way to convince a child that you really have packed all her belongings!

For the first few days after the move, a child may ask repeatedly to return to the old house. It takes days and sometimes weeks to become accustomed to the new surroundings. You can help by telling her that you understand why she liked the old house, that, in fact, you liked it, too, but that "Now we are living in this house, and soon you will like this house as much as the old one." Pointing out the new home's virtues, such as a porch or a downstairs playroom, the larger yard, or the proximity to a park or pool will also help your child adjust more quickly.

Family Problems

Unemployment and job changes or changes in parental working hours are disruptive in any family, and it is important to realize that these are stressful events for a young child. Try to explain any schedule changes, and be tolerant if your youngster takes a while to adjust. For example, it may not seem important to you that because of a scheduling change your child won't see his father at breakfast, but it may be a significant loss to him. Reminding a child that he can be with his father at another time helps with the adjustment.

All families also have moments of interpersonal stress. No matter how hard adults may try, tense moments associated with arguments, angry outbursts, and hurt feelings do alter the way a parent nurtures a toddler or young child. These episodes often cause a child to become upset and develop disturbing behavior. Verbal and physical abuse of adults or children, or bizarre behavior resulting from drug and alcohol abuse on the part of adults in the family can be terrifying to young children. Some children isolate themselves and retreat to a room to be alone; others become frightened and want to be cuddled.

Obviously, it would be preferable if a child did not have to witness extreme tensions between parents. Every child, however, is going to see or overhear family arguments, which are part of every household. Although upsetting at the time, these experiences can be more easily overcome if you let the child know that the unpleasantness is over and that everything is okay. For example, if you think your child has overheard an argument, later, when you've cooled off, you may want to say, "Daddy and I disagreed over something, and we were very angry at each other. But now we've worked it out, and everything is okay." If the child can then participate in a three-way hug, all the better.

Or, if you've been upset by an event outside the family, you might say, "I've been very upset about something at work lately, but it's been straightened out now. I hope I'm not going to be upset when I come home anymore." After all, disturbing experiences are part of life, and your child should know that anger is something everyone experiences, but it is not a permanent state of affairs. Any child will develop stronger problem-solving skills if she has seen difficulties worked out successfully at home.

Separation and Divorce

Often, there are stresses in a relationship between husband and wife that can be resolved only by separation or divorce. It is important to consider how this dissolution of the family is viewed by a young child. Long before parents separate, a child may sense or witness the turmoil, quarrels, prolonged silences, and open or controlled anger that characterizes the relationship between the parents. Whatever form the adults use to manifest their dissatisfactions with each other, a child is aware that all is not well. And just to make it even more difficult for the youngster, parents living under the tensions created by the marital discord have less and less energy to devote to nurturing a child.

Any child who lives in an intact family has the expectation based on past experience that an absent parent will always return. When the absence represents a separation and one parent has moved out of the home, a child still looks forward, with hope for the time when the parent returns. When the parent fails to return, or comes for only a brief visit, a child's trust is shattered. Visitation, either at the home or elsewhere, is important, yet it cannot replace the ongoing presence of both parents. Statements such as "Daddy and Mommy both love you very much, and you still have a mother and father. But we just find that when

Mommy and Daddy are living together, things go very poorly and we are unhappy" are the best one can do to explain the separation to a child.

It takes a long time for a child to understand and adapt to the dissolution of the family. He will vascillate between anger, despair, and being grief stricken, as he deals with feelings of desertion. He may blame himself, wondering what he did to cause his parent to leave him.

A child should be told that nothing he did caused this separation to take place. All too often a child concludes that somehow it is his fault that a parent left. A child often tries to persuade the mother or father who has left to move back, saying, "I'll be good if you come back."

Explanations of why parents separate will not eliminate a child's feelings of loss and abandonment, but sharing the facts truthfully and openly aid a child in his struggle to understand and cope with these stresses.

One can expect a child to react to separation and divorce in many different ways. First, he is likely to cling to the remaining parent. He may burst into tears with little or no provocation. His appetite may decrease. He may have difficulty going to sleep and suffer frightening nightmares. At times, he may openly express anger at the parent who left or the remaining parent for not preventing the other one from leaving. If a child has achieved bowel and urine control, he may regress in this area.

If a child is in school, it is important to share with the teacher the fact that there are problems at home. This enables the school to be understanding and tolerant of the child's restlessness and other changes in his behavior during this stressful time.

It is difficult, of course, for the adult who is dealing with his or her own feelings about the dissolution of a marriage to be sensitive and supportive of a child whose needs are intensified during this time. Caring for a child who is upset and demanding, even though one can understand the reasons for this behavior, is exhausting, particularly in the absence of a supportive partner. You may want to enlist the aid of grandparents, a regular babysitter, or family friends who will help out.

It is often helpful to discuss the situation with your pediatrician or a social worker. They will be able to suggest ways of dealing effectively with your child's needs. Counseling may help to clarify your own reactions and feelings and enable you to focus on what helps the child most as he copes with his anger and sadness over the separation of his parents.

It is unfortunate that during child custody disputes, adults often lose sight of the primary goal, which should be to work out arrangements providing for the best possible way to meet a child's nurturing and psychological needs. All too often a child becomes a pawn in a legal battle, which has little or no relevance to his welfare. Again, a pediatrician, child psychiatrist, social worker, or other neutral person can often be helpful in determining optimum care for a child when a family unit dissolves.

Plans for visitation with the parent who has moved out of the home are important. A child needs constant reminders that he has both a mother and father who love him. Whatever agreements parents reach in terms of custody and visitation, it is important that the child know the schedule and that these plans be implemented as unfailingly as possible. A child's disappointment when a father or mother fails to honor a prearranged appointment intensifies the feelings of being abandoned. Parents must remember that although a divorce may be an event that they can deal with and adapt to with some degree of finality, a child's needs for a father and a mother continue. Frequent visits with the absent parent provide opportunity for the child to receive additional support and attention. A child needs to grow up feeling that even though they are all no longer living in the same house, he has two parents, neither one of whom has deserted him.

11. Sex Education: Laying the Groundwork for a Healthy Attitude

You may wonder when and how to begin sex education with your child. But if you think about it, you'll realize that you began teaching your child about it at birth. When you hold, cuddle, feed, bathe, and diaper your baby in a gentle, loving manner, you initiate satisfactory feelings about your child's *being* and about his or her *body*. This is an important basis for experiencing happy and satisfying sexual relationships in later life.

Basically, sexuality means being at ease with one's role as a male or female, first as a baby, then as a toddler, child, adolescent, and finally, as an adult. A child also develops feelings about his or her sexuality by observing the manner in which a mother and father relate to each other, and how they each share in the child's care. Your child will also derive satisfaction in his or her gender and sexual role in later years by observing the way you as a parent enjoy your role as a man or a woman.

Self-Discovery

A baby explores all parts of the body as the ability to control hands and fingers develops. Just as a baby grabs and pulls at the nose, ears, lips, and toes, he or she will also handle the genital organs—it is as normal as handling any other part of the body. A little boy discovers and handles his penis and scrotum; a little girl probes her vagina. These manipulations are often pleasurable and may cause a baby to laugh or giggle.

Unfortunately, many adults remember that in their own childhood this behavior was considered unusual or damaging to the body. Nothing is further from the truth. Be as matter of fact as possible when your baby handles his or her genital organs; remember that this is normal behavior.

It is also important to name the genitals just as you would any other body part. Just as you would say *nose* when your baby points to his nose, you should also say *penis* when the child touches it during a diaper change. There is no advantage to using substitute words for appropriate anatomical terms; this only necessitates relearning correct words later.

During the second or third year of life, a child notes the anatomical differences between boys and girls. Recognition of and curiosity about these differences are universal. A boy observing a female baby or playmate may ask, "Where is her penis?" or a girl observing a litle boy may ask, "What's that?" pointing to his penis. The little girl may also want to know, "Where's my penis?" Your answers should be simple, stated in a way that makes you feel comfortable. To the little girl, you might say, "You are a girl, and girls have vaginas—not penises. You are like mommy and will grow up to be a woman like her." To a little boy you might say, "You are a boy; boys have penises. You are like daddy and will grow up to be a man like him."

Direct, simple answers will probably satisfy your child's immediate curiosity. However, expect your child to ask further questions. Repeated questioning does not indicate that you have failed in your explanations. Rather, your child needs further discussion about the complexities of body differences as he or she struggles repeatedly to understand the human characteristics of being male or female.

A young child, particularly boys who participate in swimming and other sports activities, often are concerned about the different appearances of circumcised and uncircumcised penises. You will want to explain why one boy's penis appears different than that of other boys. You might simply state that some parents believe that the tip of the foreskin should be removed early in infancy, while others think it isn't necessary. One should realize that questions about circumcision may recur frequently as a child matures.

A little boy observing his father in the nude may also wonder why his father's penis is so much larger than his. The explanation can be very direct, such as "When you grow to be as big and tall as your daddy, your penis will be bigger, too."

Establishing Private Times

A preschool girl often is curious about the nude appearance of boys and girls and adult men and women. Peeking when family members dress or go to the bathroom, and playing "doctor" occurs frequently in these years. At the same time, your child will often prefer not to undress in the presence of adults other than the family. Your child's wish for privacy should be encouraged and respected.

You can also begin to teach your child that certain activities, such as masturbation, are private. When your child's handling of his or her genitals occurs at times that are disturbing to you, such as when you have friends visiting, you can say, "Your body is very private. If you want to feel that part of it, I wish you would go to your room where you can be all alone and have privacy."

You as a parent instill important basic attitudes in your child for respect of one's body and person in these early years. Your own needs for privacy should also be considered. If you are uncomfortable when your child appears in the bathroom or in the bedroom, tell him or her that this is a private time for you. Just as she likes to be alone sometimes in her room, this is a private time for Mommy, or Mommy and Daddy. A child should have his or her own bed, and preferably not sleep in your bedroom.

Of course, one cannot discuss privacy without acknowledging that there may be times when a young child climbs out of bed and bursts into your bedroom during lovemaking. As disconcerting as this interruption may be, you can best handle it by commenting, "This is a private time when grown-ups love each other very much. Sometimes you want to be alone. This is a time when we want to be alone." Of course, it may not be easy to convince your child to return to his or her bedroom. However, firmness is important, both for your sake and also for your child's.

Establishing Body Privacy

There is one subject concerning privacy that needs special emphasis. Although it is normal for a child to explore and handle his or her body and genital areas, it is very important for a child to understand that one's body is private. You may observe that a family member, friend, or other adult seems to have an undue interest in cuddling, handling, and fondling your child's body. This is unhealthy for your child. I suggest that you trust your intuitive feelings and tell this person that such handling of your child's body is inappropriate. Whether you arrange to stop seeing him or her depends on the situation, but you should clearly communicate to your child that his or her body is private and that you will always back him or her in the desire not to be touched or held in a certain way. Teach your child to say "No! No!" to anyone who "touches you and you don't like it."

Whenever your child has been cared for by a babysitter, you should encourage discussion of what took place while you were away. If your child comments that the sitter "hurt," "touched," or "was feeling me," you should not ask this person back. If your child tells you that the sitter removed his or her own clothes or the child's clothes without reason, you should also be concerned. Even if abuse and molestation have not yet occurred, the possibility is that they may take place in the future. Obviously, the handling of a child's body and genitals by an adult or the request that the child handle an adult's body is unhealthy. It initiates fears and anxieties, which negatively affect a child's ability to relate in a sexual manner in adulthood.

If you are the least bit uncomfortable about leaving your child with any adult, trust your instincts and make other arrangements. A child needs your protection from adults of this kind.

Concerns about Masturbation

You may note that your child is spending considerable time handling his genital areas or masturbating. This is in no way harmful to a child; it does not damage a young child's mind or body. However, when a child is preoccupied with masturbation for long periods, you should consider what other interests and activities are available during the day. A bored child who has little opportunity to socialize with other children or with adults tends to spend more time masturbating than does a child who has many opportunities for playing and socializing.

Sex and Pregnancy

A young child observes and comments on the bodily contours occurring in pregnancy by saying, "Mommy, why are you getting so fat?" or "Why is Mrs. Smith's tummy getting so big?" Your answer can be honest and factual: "Mommy's (or Mrs. Smith's) abdomen is big because there is a baby growing inside in a special place called the uterus." (Locating the site of the pregnancy in the uterus is important because a child often believes a baby grows in the stomach and worries about the baby being surrounded by the foods ingested at the last meal.)

Your child will probably ask many questions: "How does the baby eat?", "How does he get out?", "How does he go to the bathroom?" or "Is it a boy or a girl?" You should answer such questions as honestly as possible. You may want to draw a picture indicating the uterus and birth canal, or you may want to use one of the many books available for children that deal with conception, pregnancy, and delivery. (Suggested books include: *The Wonderful Story of How You Were Born* by Sidonie Matsner Gruenberg, Doubleday, 1970; *How New Life Begins* by Esther K. Meeks and Elizabeth Bagwell, Follett, 1969; *What to Tell Your Child about Sex*, Child Study Association of America, 1969; *Becoming* by Eleanora Faison, Eleanora Patterson Press, Putney, Vermont; and *How to Tell Your Child about Sex* by James Hymes, Public Affairs Pamphlet no. 149, Public Affairs Committee, New York).

How a baby receives nourishment through the umbilical cord and placenta is fascinating to young children. You can point out your child's own belly button, where the cord was attached when he or she was inside your body. You will want to tell your child that when the baby is ready to be born, you will go to the hospital where the doctors and nurses will help the baby come out. If you know that you will be having a cesarean delivery, you may want to share this plan with your child, stating that the baby is too big to pass through the birth canal, and the doctor will make a special opening in the abdomen through which the baby can come out.

In most instances, you will not know the gender of your baby, but you can tell your child that as soon as the baby is born, you will learn that it is a boy or a girl. If you have had an amniocentesis and know the sex of the baby, pass this information on to your child. Your doctor may arrange an ultrasound examination during pregnancy to determine the position and size of the baby. Be sure to ask the nurse or technician who does the exam to give you a picture of your baby in the uterus so that you can share with your child how the baby looks inside of your body.

You may wonder about utilizing common fantasies involving a stork bringing a baby or the idea that a mother chooses a baby from a supply at the hospital. These explanations confuse a child. Indeed, a young child observes his mother's enlarged abdomen during pregnancy and her return to normal shape after delivery. He may have felt the baby kicking inside of his mother. A child wonders about the contradictions between what he observes and what he has been told, and he becomes hopelessly confused.

Of course, a child may well ask how the baby gets into your body, and direct honest answers are important. To ignore questions or answer in an offhand way can communicate to your child the idea that it is "not to be discussed." Depending on your child's age, you might want to convey all or part of the following: "There is a very special kind of loving between grown-ups. A man's penis fits into a woman's body in a special place called the vagina. This loving makes a woman and man feel very good about each other. This is called sex, or having intercourse. Sometimes when a man and a woman have sex together, a daddy seed passes from the man's body into the woman's body. When a daddy seed, called a sperm, and a mommy seed, called an egg, meet, a baby begins to grow."

A child may be bewildered by this explanation and may ask, "Does it hurt when Daddy puts his penis in your vagina?" You might answer in your own words, but you probably want to communicate that "it feels very good, so good that a man and woman who love each other do it frequently. A baby doesn't always grow when a man and woman love each other in this way."

Although a young child cannot yet comprehend the complex feelings of adult sexual relationships, your direct and honest answers set the stage for important further discussion in later years. At this phase of development, your comments should be simple but accurate, and as matter of fact as possible.

The goal of sex education in these early years is to help a growing child become comfortable with his or her gender. This offers an important base that will lead to later satisfaction in one's role as an adult man or woman. These early discussions should also help to establish and maintain open communication between parents and a young child.

This will allow continuous opportunities to discuss sexuality and sexual relationships naturally as a child matures into adolescence and adulthood.

12. Keeping Your Child Healthy and Happy When You're Not There

On many occasions you will leave your youngster in the care of others. For his or her well-being and your peace of mind, you will want to do your best to select the right setting for your child.

There are three arrangements in which children are generally left in the absence of a parent: (1) the caregiver (babysitter) who comes into your home to take care of the child; (2) a day-care setting, either family day-care or community day-care, which many parents use when they return to work; and (3) nursery school where many parents send their three- and four-year-olds for a few hours a day, believing it is advantageous for a child to participate in a flexible program in a small setting before entering kindergarten.

In my opinion, the ideal arrangement for the care of an infant or toddler in a parents' absence is to remain at home in familiar surroundings with a relative or other person whom the baby or toddler knows and trusts. When such an arrangement is impossible, the next best plan is for an infant or toddler to be in the home of a relative or friend or in family day-care with a few other children. A community

112

day-care center may be satisfactory for a child of two or
older; however, younger infants and toddlers do better in a
home setting with a small number of children.

The In-Home Caregiver

If you do not have a friend, relative, or neighbor to look
after your child in your absence, word-of-mouth is a good
way to find someone kind and trustworthy. Some families
also do well placing ads, using placement agencies, or
posting the job on bulletin boards at a local college.

If you are looking for someone to do occasional baby-
sitting, try to find a person who is available regularly so
that when you need a sitter you can use a person familiar to
your child.

If you're hiring full-time help, you will want to sound
out the person's feelings about such subjects as playtime,
discipline, safety, and promptness. Give the person the opportunity to talk about other jobs she has had and how she
has handled various situations that arose. Be certain, too,
that she is the type of person who will follow your wishes,
rather than doing as she pleases. Many people also look for
nonsmokers. And make sure that your child has an opportunity to meet the person before he or she is hired. Even an
infant can have a strong reaction, positively or negatively,
and you should have the opportunity to observe how the
caregiver interacts with your child.

You should clarify ahead of time what you expect from
your babysitter and whether you consider housework as
part of the job. Also establish whether the sitter is allowed
to have visitors (many parents feel they are too distracting).

Try to arrange for the person you plan to employ to visit
once or twice while you are at home so that your infant or
child becomes acquainted with this person in your presence. Explain to your sitter the various bathing, feeding,
and bedtime routines; the familiarity of these procedures
provides stability and support for a child in a parent's absence.

Every sitter should be given basic emergency information. (See **Chapter 20, First Aid at Home,** for a list of numbers that should be posted by each phone.) In addition, be sure to leave the number where you can be reached, whether at work, a friend's house, restaurant, bowling alley, the theatre, or anywhere else. All too often, I receive calls from babysitters because a child is sick or injured and the sitter is unable to reach the parents. Also, be sure to leave the name and phone number of a relative or close friend who can be called in an emergency.

In addition, show your sitter where you keep flashlights, the fire extinguisher, and the first aid kit, and how to turn off gas, electricity, and water.

If the child is about to go down for a nap or to bed when the caregiver is due to arrive, I suggest that she be permitted to put the child down. Why? Imagine how it must feel for a baby, toddler, or child to be tucked in by a parent and then upon awakening from a dream, to be greeted by another person? This is a common and unnecessary crisis, which can easily be prevented by having the sitter put the child to bed.

Parents often wonder how an infant or young child is affected by their absence. As a child develops trust and confidence in the sitter, he or she can usually accept short absences with relative ease. However, there is always a joyous relief when a parent returns. Many parents who are out for the evening will awaken a child when they return home, thus reassuring him or her that they have returned. One mother found it helpful to discuss with her children what they would have for breakfast, placing a cereal box and breakfast dishes on the kitchen table so that the children could look forward to the next morning when the family would be together.

And one last but very important point. If you are delayed in your return home, do call and tell your sitter that you will be late. It is difficult for a sitter if parents do not return at the agreed-upon time.

Selecting a Day-Care Program or Nursery School

If you are looking for a day-care program or nursery school, your community probably offers a variety from which to choose. There are an increasing number of home day-care centers in which one or two adults provide for four to six children in the home. Many churches, synagogues, the YMCA or YWCA, Jewish centers, and other community agencies offer child-care programs. Some independent day-care centers or nursery schools also offer programs for the care of infants and young children. Educational institutions, hospitals, and a growing number of companies provide child-care services as well.

How do you find a quality day-care or nursery school in your community? Ask your friends with children for suggestions, or talk to your child's doctor. In addition, some communities have parenting groups that list available programs.

Location, cost, and operating hours are very important, but you should also look carefully at the program you are considering. Call to set up an appointment. When you visit, look for men and women who communicate a feeling of warmth and interest. You should feel welcome and sense from them a genuine interest in you and your child. Staff members of a child-care center or nursery school must love children and place a high priority on helping them find pleasure in their achievements and supporting them in moments of stress. These staff members play important roles in a young child's life. You should feel that they are trusted friends. Look, too, for staff permanence, so that your child can anticipate having a familiar person to provide for his or her needs each day.

The setting itself should be pleasant, with ample space for physical activity, both indoor and out. Young children need opportunity to run, climb, and tumble to work off their excess energy and to gain satisfaction in learning how to control their bodies. At times, a child may need the opportunity to be alone and away from the stimulation of other children and adults, so there should also be nooks and crannies where a child can rest alone on a cot or mat.

Upon first entering a day-care program, your child may cling to you and experience some weepy moments. He is accustomed to having his parents or other close relatives care for him, so this new situation is unsettling. As a result, he may treasure his bottle or a favorite toy or blanket more than previously, or a child who has been toilet trained may soil a few times under the stress. But once having made the adjustment, chances are your child will thrive.

As time progresses and you develop a relationship with the staff, be sure to share with them events that occur at home and that may affect your child's behavior. A recent illness, a birth of a sibling, a move, or the death of a family member may be stressful experiences that decrease a young child's ability to cope with day-to-day activities. A staff member who is aware of these personal events can be supportive and understanding of the child when his or her behavior differs from the usual pattern.

Benefits of a Group Experience

What are the benefits for a young child in a day-care center or nursery school experience? There are many. Learning to tolerate the anxiousness associated with entering a new setting and meeting new people are important growth experiences. Quite frequently, attendance at a day-care center or nursery school represents a child's first opportunity to learn that there are teachers and other adults who love her and have an important role in providing for her care.

A three- or four-year-old child also benefits from the opportunity for spontaneous group play. At first a child may play alone, hugging, feeding, talking to, and scolding his doll while carefully putting it to bed. He may imitate in posture and mannerisms his mother or father. As a child matures, he involves other children in this activity and may say to a friend: "You be the daddy and I'll be the mommy." A few minutes later there may be an exchange of roles; a young child may be the baby or he may ask his friend to be the baby. A few minutes later he pretends he's a policeman or a fireman, a doctor or a truck driver. He drives his tricycle furiously through the yard screaming, "Get out of my way, beep! beep! I'm going to a fire!" This type of spontaneous play among children is very enriching and usually an enormous amount of fun!

Organized games based on the capacities, interests, and maturational levels of children are another important aspect of a nursery school or day-care program. Singing, dancing, playing percussion or other instruments, listening to records or to stories, taking turns on the slide, setting the table for lunch, preparing for a trip to another part of the building, and making decorations for a holiday celebration are common examples of structured play. These group activities, during which children learn to work together for a common cause, to wait, and to take turns or exchange equipment, are maturing experiences. States of tension, anger, and hard feelings are inevitable in a child's life. Learning to cope with these feelings is an important task of this age. A child learns that there must be certain rules that she must accept if she wants to be part of the group. She learns how to cope with the frustrations of waiting and comes to realize that sharing is an important part of peer interaction.

A group program provides opportunities for a child to learn by doing, move about freely, use moments for structured and unstructured play, and develop her own skills and resources to learn to play and mature. Teachers guide a child through the process of adaptation and separation, providing a substitute for the parents as the child develops. They support and enjoy the child's successes and help her grow and mature in all areas. A child, given reasonable support and guidance, will meet these challenges and is then ready to move on to the next series of challenges offered by kindergarten and elementary school.

13. When a Child Loses a Loved One

At what age is a child able to begin to grasp the concept of "alive" and "dead"? Probably earlier than you might think. Even a very young child realizes that a dead goldfish is unable to swim in the tank; the child sees that a bird lying lifeless on the ground cannot fly or sing, and he sadly realizes that a cat or dog lying stiff in the street can no longer play with him in the yard. Three-year-old Bobby, upon discovering that the nursery school's guinea pig had died during the night, placed his hand on the stiff body and said with solemnity: "There is something in him that can't come out anymore." It is quite apparent that Bobby had some grasp of what it means to be dead.

Despite our wish to protect our children from sadness, at some point a child will inevitably experience loss through death of a relative, friend, teacher, or other person whom he loves and who loves him. In order to understand and to cope with the feelings accompanying a death, a child desperately needs your comfort and support at this time.

Death of a Pet

The death of a pet or other animal offers the opportunity to help a child, even one as young as two or three, to begin to comprehend what it means to be alive and to be dead. One can clarify a child's grasp of this difficult concept by saying, "When someone dies, they just lie very still. They don't move, or breathe, or talk, or feel anything. They just rest forever. It's like a tree leaf that falls to the ground. It's the end of life."

It is important to avoid associating the deceased state with being asleep, for such a comparison is likely to create anxiety for a child who begins to wonder if she, too, may die while sleeping.

Flushing a dead goldfish down the toilet or tossing a dead hamster into the rubbish or burying a cat or dog secretly at night is unwise. This robs the child of an opportunity to begin to conceptualize the meaning of being alive or being dead. She should have a means of experiencing the grief associated with the loss of a pet, while still having the comforting presence of family members.

A child may ask to bury an animal in the backyard, with an appropriate marker placed over the site. She may want to say a short prayer, demonstrate sadness, and even shed tears of grief. The planning and carrying out of the ritual are part of an important growth experience for her. They acknowledge the finality of the death and acquaint a child with how human beings use rituals to help to get through a time of sadness.

Death of a Loved Person

The death of a beloved family member or friend is a far different experience than the death of an animal, of course. However, a child who has experienced the death of a pet or other animal has some basis for understanding the concept of being alive and being dead, and is thus more able to grapple with the finality of the tragic loss of an important person in his life. We all wish, of course, that a child could be spared the loss of someone he loves and who loves him. Indeed, adults often wish so strongly to protect a child from suffering with his feelings of loss that they avoid telling the child what has happened to an important person in his life. This is unfair, for it leaves a child bewildered and desolate as he grapples with his intense feelings of sadness.

When a relative or close friend is dying, a child senses that something unusual is taking place within the family. Numerous phone calls, constant coming and going of relatives, hushed conversations, and the frequent appearance of tears on the faces of family members create an overwhelming atmosphere of restlessness and gloom in the family. A child observes that everyone is preoccupied and acting strangely. He may wonder what awful thing he has done to cause his caretakers to be less available to him just at the time he needs them most.

The aura of gloom in the home as a family anticipates a death can be very frightening. You should explain to your child why you are sad and out of sorts at the moment. You can do this by commenting, "I want you to know that Grandma (or whomever) is very sick. I think about her all the time." When the death is imminent, one might say, "Grandma is quite sick. The doctors and nurses are doing everything they can to make her comfortable. She is so very sick that I am afraid she might die."

A child, just like many adults, may fail to grasp totally the possibility that his loved one is about to die and leave him forever. However, telling the child of the expected event ahead of time makes it easier when the death does occur to say, "You remember a few days ago when I told you that Grandma was very sick and I said she might die? Well, I have something very sad to tell you. She did die a few minutes ago."

Be sure to be specific in your choice of words. Euphemisms are often lost on children. Saying "We lost Grandpa" fails to communicate the true facts. Indeed, one five-year-old commented, "Well, if he's lost, why don't you go look for him?"

All losses are difficult for a young child, but there is a particularly difficult adjustment surrounding the death of a parent or other adult who provides the majority of a child's care. It means the loss not only of someone she loves and who loves her, but also the loss of the person who provides for her daily needs. Whenever possible, it is helpful to arrange for one person, a relative or a housekeeper, to assume a major responsibility for the care of the child before the death of the primary caretaker. This assures a child that at least her basic physical needs will be taken care of when her primary person is no longer available.

A child who suffers the loss of an important person in her life may wonder whether this could happen to other people who love and care for her. Reassurance must be realistic, for who knows when any one of us will die? It is best to say, "I don't think it will happen to me for a long, long time." At this point it is wise to add the names of close relatives and friends with whom a child has had a long and trusting relationship, commenting that they, too, will be available to provide for her care.

A discussion of what happens to a human being after death should present honestly the beliefs of the family. The idea of a life hereafter offers comfort to many adults. Yet, it is a difficult concept for a young child to grasp. A child may conceive of Heaven as a place from which one can return, or telephone, or mail a letter.

When family members possess a strong religious belief, it is appropriate to share this with a child in forthright terms. One might say, "The body of a person who dies is placed in a special box in a cemetery. I like to believe that part of the person we love, his or her spirit, the things we love about them, rests in a special place called Heaven, far, far away where there is no pain, hunger, or suffering."

Every child is quick to sense adult insincerity. A disbelieving adult who offers a child a concept of life hereafter, hoping that somehow this will be helpful, only creates confusion for a child. In this instance, it is far better to be honest, saying, "I do not know exactly what I believe happens after a person dies. I do know, however, that Grandma will no longer be with us. We will all miss her very much."

Some families consider sending a child to stay with neighbors or relatives for a few days, hoping to spare him the confusion and tension in the household at this sad time. I believe a child suffering a loss needs his own room, bed, toys, and familiar surroundings, which provide a degree of comfort and support. A child also needs extra cuddling, food he likes, and reassurance that his basic needs will be met.

The Funeral

Is it appropriate for your child to attend a funeral? I believe a child of four or older should decide this for herself. You might explain in simple terms that the family members and friends will gather together as a way of saying good-bye and that the minister, priest, or rabbi will speak about the person who has died. You can describe this service by saying, "There will be prayers and music. The body will rest in a special box called a casket. Everybody there will be very sad. I may cry. Lots of grown-up people will cry."

The gathering of friends and relatives and the ritual of the funeral service can be supportive and comforting to a child, just as it is for adults. When your child does choose to attend a funeral, a close friend or relative should be assigned the specific responsibility of sitting with her if you cannot. Members of the immediate family are likely to be so preoccupied with their own grief that they are unable to provide comfort and support for a child. If a child finds the service overwhelming, she should be allowed to leave with her adult friend.

If a child chooses not to attend, you should arrange for someone whom she knows and trusts to care for her. Hiring a familiar babysitter to come or allowing her to attend nursery school may be a good arrangement. You should tell a child that you will return soon. When you do return, even though you are bound to be grief-stricken, try to spend a few minutes cuddling and talking with your child. She needs to know that you care about her at this critical moment.

Your child may ask to visit the cemetery a few hours or

days after a funeral. The fresh gravesite substantiates the fact that the loved one is buried there. The ritual of the funeral and the visit to the cemetery serve as a focal point for both child and adult to begin the difficult task of adapting to the finality of the loss of a loved one.

Grappling with the Loss

A child demonstrates in many ways how difficult it is to accept the finality of a loss. A six-year-old child I know set the table for many weeks with a place for the deceased grandmother who had lived in the household. Another child, a week after the death of her grandmother, said, "Grandmother called and told me she would be here for dinner on Sunday, just like she always used to come before."

Comforting a child when she wishes with such intensity that her deceased relative would return is not easy. You might try saying something like, "It would be nice if Grandma were able to be here, wouldn't it? I miss her very much, too. Remember we had the funeral service and said good-bye to her? We will have to remember many of the happy times we had when she was able to be with us."

The loss of a sibling or a close friend is an extremely difficult experience for a child. If it is a sibling who has died, the child may find that his parents are so preoccupied with their own grief that they are not readily available to offer the support and comfort needed by the surviving child. As one child told me years after the death of his brother, "My parents were there all the time, yet not there for me." Fortunately, in many families, relatives and close friends can be helpful at this difficult time. Remember, children are going to be desolate and depressed for many weeks, just as adults are. They need support and time as they grieve and mourn in their own way. (For additional information, see *The Bereaved Parent* by Harriet Sarnoff, Crown, 1977.)

As your child deals with the stress of the loss, immature behavior patterns may recur. He may become angry and strike out against other adults and friends. A bottle or treasured doll or blanket, discarded many months before, may suddenly make a reappearance. It may be difficult for him to leave the house, or he may be restless and unable to settle in to normal activities.

Be sure to notify your child's teacher that the family has suffered the death of a close relative. Otherwise, your child's restlessness and periods of crying, poor appetite, and possible soiling will be misunderstood. The teacher will be in a much better position to offer comfort to your child if he or she knows the reason for the child's behavior.

A child who has suffered a recent loss is likely to become anxious when her parents are away from home, fearing that they, too, might fail to return. When you have suffered a recent loss in your family, you should always tell your child where you are going and when you will return, even when you leave home only briefly. (This is a good idea in any case.) If you are delayed, phoning to let your child know you are on your way is always a good idea.

As a result of the death, a child may also dread illness, even a minor one. She may fear she will die. Whenever a bereaved child is sick, no matter how mild the illness, explain that her symptoms are that of a minor illness and that she will get well. If you take her to the doctor, be sure to explain to the pediatrician in advance about the recent death in the family. The doctor may be unaware of it and will be much more understanding and reassuring with your child if briefed on the events that have caused the child's anxiety about her own health.

While helping someone cope with loss is one of life's more painful tasks, you should remember that a child needs to be close to an adult he loves and trusts at this time. There is no harm if adult and child burst into tears and cry in each other's arms. Indeed, this crying together often offers a child permission and support to release the feelings of sadness that are inevitable as a child grapples with the loss of someone he loves.

Remember, too, that you should think in terms of comforting your child—not in terms of preventing him from being sad. He has every reason to be sad (as you do) as he struggles to come to terms with the finality of it all. A child needs time to mourn and grieve, just as adults do.

Traditional ways in which your family deals with loss will be as important to your child as they are to you. Anniversaries of the death, a birthday, family holidays such as Thanksgiving or Christmas or Sunday dinner are bound to be sad times. Some families do special things on the person's birthday or the anniversary of the death. Other families attend church or synagogue or visit the gravesite. Adults can help a child by saying, "Today is the day Grandma died," or, "Today is Grandma's birthday. It is sad that she is no longer able to be with us. I miss her very much. I know you do, too." These conversations support and comfort a child in his sadness.

Ultimately, it is the happy memories of the loved one that you want to preserve. The earlier you can begin to reminisce about happy times and enjoy sharing appropriate pictures with your child, the better able he or she will be to cope with the loss.

14. Special Needs of the Adopted Child

Adoptive parents have all the same joys, satisfactions, and surprises as any other parent. However, there are two particular areas where parents of the adopted child have extra tasks to perform: establishing a health history for the child; and deciding when and how to tell the child he or she is adopted.

Establishing a Health History

A child who is raised by natural parents will probably present few surprises when it comes to general health. If the family has a history of allergies, any reactions to certain foods, to dust-catching items such as stuffed animals, or to pollen will lead the family to suspect an allergy, which can then be treated promptly. By the same token, the family with a history of ear infections will guard their child's hearing closely once they suspect the youngster has inherited this tendency.

Too often, however, the adopted child has no such history to build on. You can make your own life easier and provide a real service to your child by asking for a complete family history when the child is placed with you. Ideally, this history should include information on the parents (including age) and grandparents, details of the pregnancy and delivery, condition of the baby at birth and while in the hospital, and any details of her health and behavior in the period before permanent placement. Many foster mothers write a beautiful description of an infant's progress and the details of her sleeping and feeding, which can be of great help to new parents.

If you are adopting a child with special needs, you will want to discuss her condition with your doctor, the agency pediatrician, or a social worker. Ask about the details of the child's illness or handicap and the specific medical care that will be required in the years ahead. The more you know, the easier parenting will be.

Adoptive parents should also request details about ethnic derivation and educational and vocational characteristics of the biological parents, to provide background data for the adoptee when he or she is old enough to seek this information. In some instances, the biological mother writes a letter and requests that the placement agency give it to the adoptive parents. This serves as a valuable link in later years when the adoptee inquires about his or her family of origin. The need to be connected in some way with one's biological past is important for all human beings.

Telling Your Child about Adoption

Adopted children need to be acquainted early in their childhood with the fact that they were adopted. They should certainly be told before they start school, in order to protect them from learning about their adoption from people outside the family. Some parents postpone indefinitely acquainting a child with this information. This is a poor idea. If not informed by parents, a child usually learns about the adoption by overhearing adult conversation or from playmates who know of her origin, or in later years, a child may rummage through the house and discover adoption documents. To learn the facts of origin from other than the parents can only cause serious confusion, distrust, and bitterness. By telling the child early on, adoptive parents give her the security to be able to say, "I've known I was adopted ever since I can remember."

When the child hears the news, she may have difficulty comprehending the facts of her early existence. "Why didn't my mother want me?" "Why did she have me if she couldn't keep me?" These are common questions. An appropriate answer might be: "Although you did grow in another woman's body, I am the mommy who fed you, bathed you, and took care of you since you were a very little baby. Since your mother and father were unable to care for you, they made arrangements for us to take care of you, and we do love you very much."

A child finds love, trust, and confidence in his adoptive parents, and in turn they find satisfaction, fulfillment, and permanence in having a child. The child who is secure in this relationship is likely to ask repeated questions about his origin. However, too often adoptive parents consider that when a child seeks information about his background, it indicates that they have failed. Absolutely not! It is very natural for an adoptee, particularly in adolescence and adult years, to wonder about his or her natural family. Adoptive parents should share as much information as they have about the birth parents in order to help a child form an image of them. The child may ponder over the information for months and then ask a few more questions, only to remain silent again for a time.

Many adoptees seek to re-establish contact with birth parents. Searching for one's "roots" is common as adoptees try to fit the pieces of their past into the present. Some child placement agencies and psychiatrists suggest that when the adoptee has a compelling desire to re-establish a relationship with the natural parents, it should be implemented if at all possible, providing, or course, that the biological parents are available and agree to the reunion.

Adoptive parents who are open and honest with their

children have proven time and again that when the excitement of locating a natural parent is over, the children still consider that their real home is with the parents they have lived with since early childhood.

III The Healthy Child

15. Obtaining the Most Help from Your Doctor

Your child's pediatrician is your most valuable professional resource when it comes to safeguarding the health of your child. This chapter provides suggestions on how to make the most of this relationship, regardless of the reason for your call or visit.

Phoning the Doctor

Much of your relationship with your child's doctor will be over the telephone. Although at some point you may have to call because your child has experienced a serious accident or seems extremely ill, most of your calls will be for less alarming reasons. You may be concerned because your child has a high fever but no other symptoms, or you may be worried because your youngster has no fever but is quite listless. Other reasons may vary from a rash that has persisted despite medical treatment, to a cough that just won't go away—any type of health problem your child may be experiencing. Or parents may have a developmental concern, bothersome enough that they don't want to wait until the next well-child visit. If you're thinking of calling but are hesitant, most doctors would say to call. They would rather have you err on the side of caution than take a chance with your child's health.

Many pediatricians have established a certain time of the day as a "telephone hour." Except in an emergency, try to call during this time. These special hours are the perfect opportunity for you to discuss your concerns. The doctor will be less busy than during regular office hours, and most phone hours are scheduled at a time of day when it is still possible to bring the child in for an office visit, if necessary.

Before you phone, make a list of your questions. If your child is sick, note down the symptoms so that you'll be able to give the doctor full and complete information. Jot down what symptom came first, whether or not your child has any fever, and how the child's behavior or personality is affected by the illness. A child who demonstrates a high temperature elevation, yet continues to play normally, is less worrisome than a child with a slight fever who is uninterested in his or her toys and surroundings.

Be sure to have pencil and paper with you at the time of the call. In some instances, your doctor may recommend over-the-counter preparations, and you'll want to note down the name of the medication and the appropriate dosage. If medication is advised, be sure you understand exactly how and when it is to be administered.

When Your Child Is Sick

Now let's consider an office visit for a child that has suddenly become ill. You may have already talked with your child's doctor on the phone, and he or she suggested that your child be examined. Once at the office, don't be surprised if your doctor asks you to repeat the history of the illness, even though you did explain these details in the phone conversation. Remember, your doctor may have talked with ten or twenty other parents since the conversation with you earlier in the day. He or she needs to be reminded of the specific details in order to determine a proper diagnosis.

What information should you share with your doctor? First, when did your child's symptoms initially appear? Was there a fever at that time, or has it come on later? If later, how much later? Has the child demonstrated fretfulness, irritability, cough, sniffles, vomiting, or diarrhea? Has he lost interest in his surroundings? Is he eating? These are important clues that will enable the doctor to evaluate the seriousness of your child's illness.

Also tell your physician if anyone in your family, any playmates, or any adults who care for your child are suffering from any illness. (It is important to remember that when an adult suffers a relatively mild viral illness with only moderate malaise and abdominal discomfort, the same viral illness contracted by a child may cause high fever and intense discomfort.)

Be sure to tell the doctor if you have any specific concerns related to your child's illness because of a previous experience with yourself or among friends. You might say, "This worries me because when I was his age, I had these symptoms and ended up in the hospital with pneumonia," or, "This scares me because my neighbor's child had similar symptoms, and now she's being treated for leukemia."

When you share thoughts of this nature with your doctor, she will understand your concerns and will explain in detail what she finds on examination. In most instances, she will be able to reassure you and eliminate the possibility of any serious disease.

A frequent reason that parents bring their child to the doctor is because of a disturbing cough with no fever or any other significant signs of ailment. Usually a child with this complaint is happy and active, yet has been coughing for weeks, often more intensely at night. It will help your doctor considerably if you can remember when the symptoms first began. For example, when a child starts coughing in mid-August and continues through the fall, the doctor will probably consider the possibility of a ragweed or mold sensitivity, since these two substances usually begin to fill the air at that time of year. Or if your toddler begins to suffer respiratory congestion shortly after you discontinue breastfeeding and substitute a milk mixture, milk sensitivity is a possibility. The more specific your observation, the easier it will be for the doctor to arrive at an appropriate diagnosis and treatment.

What will your doctor look for when she examines a child who is sick or has a chronic cough? First, she will consider your child's general demeanor, whether he is feverish or not, the degree of alertness, and whether he is involved with what's happening about him or is listless and uninterested. The doctor will examine the skin, ears, mouth, tongue, eyes, and throat, looking for evidence of infection. She will also check for enlarged lymph glands in the neck, armpits, and groin, will observe the breathing movement, and will carefully note any unusual sounds emanating from the larynx. She will listen to the chest for unusual breath sounds and to the heart to determine pulse rate, quality of sounds, and the possible presence of a murmur. She will palpate the abdomen looking for distension and enlargement of the liver or spleen. She will flex the child's neck to determine whether stiffness is present.

Your doctor may also want to obtain a culture of your child's throat to determine the presence of a specific pathologic bacteria known as Beta Hemolytic Streptococcus, which causes what is known as "strep throat." If your child has been urinating frequently, the doctor may ask you to collect a urine specimen to examine for the presence of infection in the bladder or upper urinary tract. (Urinary tract infections are much more frequent in girls than in boys.)

Often the doctor will conclude that your child is suffering from a viral infection that is prevalent in the community at the time. You will probably be warned that in the next few days your child may suffer nausea, dizziness, headache, cramps, diarrhea, or upper respiratory symptoms. The doctor may suggest administering aspirin or acetaminophen to relieve malaise and fever and will advise that you offer lots of fluids, but not to be concerned about a decrease in appetite for the time being.

If evidence is found of strep throat, a bladder infection,

pneumonia, or inflammation of the throat, ears, or tonsils, the doctor will probably prescribe appropriate antibiotics for a seven- to ten-day period.

Ask your doctor to write down the specific instructions for administering the medication. If the instructions are for ten days, but your child seems better in three days, *be sure to continue to give the medicine for the prescribed length of time*. The full course of antibiotics is necessary to completely rid the body of the infection. And if your doctor asks you to return for a follow-up visit, do so! This is particularly important when a child suffers an ear infection, since a persistent low-grade infection may interfere with hearing even though a child presents no other symptoms. A re-examination of a child's urine after treatment for a urinary tract infection is also important to make certain that the condition is completely cured. Low-grade asymptomatic urinary tract infections may persist and lead to significant problems in adulthood.

You may wonder why your doctor doesn't prescribe antibiotics for all illnesses. The reason is because antibiotics rarely alter the course of viral infections. They are effective only in treatment of bacterial infections. What's more, the indiscriminate use of antibiotics may cause an upset in the normal balance of bacteria in the body and can result in significant distress, particularly in the gastrointestinal tract.

When Your Child Is Injured

Whenever you take your child to a doctor because of an injury from a fall or an auto accident, try to obtain the specific details of the mishap. Of particular importance is whether a child suffered a loss of consciousness initially and how he or she has been acting since the injury. Your doctor will examine your child carefully and may arrange for X rays or a CAT scan to determine whether a significant head injury is present. Repeated exams are very important in checking on your child's well-being.

If there is pain or abnormal positioning of any bone or a limitation of movement in any part of the body, your physician will also arrange for an X-ray examination to determine whether a fracture is present. Consultation with orthopedic colleagues may be necessary.

Whenever your child is referred to another physician for consultation or care, ask your pediatrician to explain to you and to your child what is going to happen to him and why. A child as young as two can understand explanations, and it will help him to adapt to what is taking place. A child's needs must be respected and understood.

If physicians other than the child's primary doctor are going to be involved in the care of your child, ask who will assume the major responsibility for your child. In many instances a child's pediatrician will assume this role, using colleagues with specialized expertise as consultants. This arrangement has many advantages.

Sometimes a child's hospitalization may be at such a distance from the pediatrician's office that continued care by the primary physician is impossible. However, your child's pediatrician should be kept informed of what is happening while a child is under the care of specialists; he will thus be available when you have questions. The more a child's primary physician is involved, the better, since both you and your child have long-standing feelings of trust in the doctor.

Well-Child Visits

Whenever your child has an appointment with the doctor for a well-child checkup or you have asked for a visit because you have specific concerns, you can expect your doctor to devote more time for discussion than when your child is being seen for an acute illness or injury.

Before examining your child, the doctor will probably ask you to describe her daily activities, emphasizing any changes since the previous visit. Important changes occur month by month during the early months and years of life as a child gains increasing skill in the control of her body, how she communicates, and how she relates to people. Although each child develops in his or her own unique way, there is an orderly pattern of development common to all human beings, and making note of your child's development will help the pediatrician assess your child's overall well-being.

Your doctor may inquire about your child's enjoyment of each phase of development; feelings of pleasure and accomplishment are important to enable your child to move on to the next higher level, such as from crawling to walking. Adult caregivers, particularly parents, play an important role in how a young child develops. Your doctor will suggest ways of expressing pleasure as you observe your child's increasing capacity to move about, communicate, play with toys, and interact with people. Your role is as the "cheering section," stimulating your child to want to make continued progress as rapidly as his maturing body will allow. Without this adult interest, a child often fails to develop to his fullest potential. Be sure to ask your doctor for suggestions for ways to provide maximum stimulation at each level of development.

After the age of six months, when your child becomes increasingly mobile, your doctor will emphasize the importance of safety precautions. Household accidents, ingestion of poisons, burns, falls down stairs and out of windows, and automobile accidents are, alas, common events in the infant, toddler, and preschool years. Your doctor will advise you on safety measures you should take (see **Chapter 18, Preventing Accidents**, for additional information). A child needs to have free and protected space for play, but he also needs to recognize that there are "no-no's." A child will be unable to understand these restrictions all at once, but in due time, if parents are consistent and firm, a child learns to control his own activities.

You may be surprised at how much time your pediatrician spends discussing how to prevent accidents. But remember that accidental injuries are by far the most important cause of morbidity and mortality in childhood. And even if your doctor fails to mention safety car seats and seat belts, do use them!

When it comes time for the physical exam, the doctor will record your child's height and weight and, on infants under a year, the head circumference. Your doctor will tell you whether these measurements indicate growth within normal limits. Then he will examine your child's head, eyes, ears (checking hearing with a bell or other noise-maker if the child is under three, and with a tuning fork if three or over), throat, palate, tongue, teeth, heart, abdomen, genitalia, legs, and feet. Depending upon the child's age, the doctor will want to observe your child's ability to sit, crawl, run, climb, and communicate. With children three and over, the doctor will probably check vision and blood pressure.

You may have specific concerns about your child, and by all means bring up your questions. Your doctor cannot help you if he doesn't have any idea what your concerns are. All too frequently parents leave a doctor's office with many concerns unresolved because they never asked the appropriate questions. It helps to make a list of questions before your appointment.

You may be surprised when your doctor states that certain behavior you are concerned about is normal and healthy. For example, the toddler who clings to a blanket or toy and demands it whenever he leaves home or when he is about to go to sleep is actually quite normal. The use of a favorite item, sometimes called a transitional object, represents a phase in development in which a child invests some feelings in this toy or blanket. He is able to consider the item "a little bit of mother" and substitutes it for her presence. You can be proud of the child who, instead of clinging to mother, is able to move ahead to the next phase in which the favorite item serves as a parent substitute when he is anxious or lonely.

Or you may be concerned because your toddler plays in another room only for a short time and then returns back for a hug and a kiss. Your doctor will tell you that this periodic return to the parent is for "recharging," which enables a child to take off again for another independent venture. Gradually, a child will return less often and be able to go farther and farther away for increasingly long periods of time.

Many of the concerns parents have about their infants, toddlers, or young children represent normal, healthy ways in which a child grows up and meets the challenges of each phase of development. As your doctor listens to your concerns, he will probably point out that infants, toddlers, and young children often go through difficult periods during various phases of development. A parent should expect such moments to arise and should realize that they are perfectly normal. In most cases, they will be conquered and resolved, and then another may arise. For example, all of the following children are going through a normal phase of development, even though their behavior may be quite troublesome at the time:

- The nine-month-old is upset when his mother leaves.
- The toddler has yet to learn boundaries and climbs on the kitchen table and into the sink.
- The two-and-a half-year-old cannot yet control his bowel movements and urine flow.
- The four-year-old has not yet learned the meaning of "what's mine" and "what's yours."
- The five-year-old is acting out in response to her first months in a highly structured elementary school.

Some children approach these events with relative ease, but for others, each new challenge represents real difficulties.

Your pediatrician will be able to tell you when he thinks your child is having more than the usual difficulty in mastering some of these challenges. He may offer some specific suggestions as to how you can support your child as she struggles with these developmental hurdles. Or the doctor may decide that your child needs special help and may refer you to a colleague, social worker, child development expert, or a child psychiatrist who has special training in helping young children who are having a difficult time.

Do remember that it is important for you to recognize some of the problems your child may be experiencing and discuss them with your doctor. Your recognition of the fact that your child is having unusual difficulty in meeting certain stresses reflects your sensitivity and understanding of the child's needs. Early intervention and help in the preschool years are important because they may enable a child to grow and mature in a satisfactory manner in order to be able to adjust to elementary school with relative ease.

Your doctor wants to be helpful, but he can only offer his professional skills and knowledge if you share with him your concerns about your child.

16. Immunizations

Routine immunizations of infants and children have greatly reduced the incidence of many diseases that were responsible for widespread illness and death in the United States as recently as half a century ago. Smallpox has been almost totally eliminated throughout the world, so that vaccination for this disease is no longer necessary. Diphtheria, tetanus, whooping cough, poliomyelitis (polio), measles, mumps, and German measles are encountered rarely in the United States and other countries with comparable immunization programs.

You may question whether the rarity of these infectious diseases eliminates the need for continuing the immunization of infants and children. It does not! Smallpox is the only disease of this group for which immunization can safely be discontinued.

Protection against diphtheria, tetanus, whooping cough, poliomyelitis, measles, mumps, and German measles is imperative. It is only by continuing to immunize infants and children that the low incidence of these diseases can be maintained. With increasing travel to and from all parts of

143

the world, there are many opportunities for the nonimmunized individual to contract these diseases from persons who live in areas of the world where immunization programs are less available than in the United States. Many children and adults from such areas may carry disease-producing organisms in their noses, throats, and body secretions, thus offering easy exposure for unimmunized individuals. People who carry these organisms are rarely sick, and they are usually completely unaware that they can spread disease.

By the same token, many children and adults immune to polio may nevertheless carry a disease-producing virus in their saliva, stools, and urine, and thus may be a source of infection for unprotected individuals. The occasional epidemic of polio in recent years among children who have not been immunized illustrates the continuing need for protecting infants and children.

What immunizations will your infant and child receive? Diphtheria and tetanus toxoid and whooping cough (known as pertussis) vaccine are administered in a combination known as a "DTP shot" three times in the first year at one- or two-month intervals. These preparations are usually injected in the thigh or in the back of the upper arm. Poliomyelitis vaccine, composed of attenuated strains of three types of polio virus (hence known as trivalent polio vaccine), are administered orally two or three times in the first year at two-month intervals. At fifteen months, a combination of measles, mumps, and rubella vaccine is administered.

Recently a new vaccine that protects against Hemophilus influenzae type B infections has become available. This bacteria causes epiglottitis, meningitis, pericarditis, septic arthritis, cellulitis, and pneumonia. Infections due to this organism are likely to be quite serious and can be fatal. The American Academy of Pediatrics recommends that this vaccine be administered to all children between the ages of two and five.

Booster DTP shots and oral polio doses are repeated at eighteen months and at four to six years, just before admission to kindergarten. Most physicians eliminate the whooping cough component after the age of six, but continue to administer diphtheria and tetanus toxoids at five-to ten-year intervals during childhood and adolescence.

An infant or child normally develops minor soreness and swelling at the area of the DTP injection. The child may also develop a slight fever and bodily aches lasting a few hours following the injection. Rarely, a child experiences a high fever, crying that lasts for more than three hours, and irritability for several days. When a prolonged period of discomfort follows the initial DTP injection, most physicians eliminate subsequent injections of the pertussis vaccine because the administration of additional amounts may produce severe reactions and even cause significant interference with normal development. Because it is only the pertussis vaccine to which the child is reacting, a special preparation of the diphtheria and tetanus toxoid can be administered at regular intervals, leaving the child at risk only to whooping cough. In the case of a child who has had a strong reaction, the risk of whooping cough is less hazardous than the likely possibility of a subsequent severe reaction to the pertussis vaccine.

Toddlers and children receiving the measles vaccine, either singly or in combination with mumps and rubella vaccine, may develop fever, aches and discomfort, and a faint measles rash five to ten days later. There is rarely any significant reaction to the injection of mumps or rubella vaccine, or the oral administration of trivalent polio vaccine during infancy and childhood.

Do conditions in infancy and childhood dictate that you should postpone or eliminate these immunizations? Yes, there are a few. For one, when an infant or child has a fever or other sign of illness, it is wise to postpone the injections. In addition, live virus vaccines, such as trivalent polio or measles, mumps, or rubella vaccines, should not be administered, either by injection or orally, if a child or close family member suffers a deficiency in immune defense systems, either due to disease or as a result of chemotherapy or radiation treatment for a malignant condition, or is being maintained on steroid medication. Even the attenuated viral form of the poliomyelitis, measles, rubella, and mumps viruses used for immunization may have to be avoided if a child or another family member has any decrease in immune defenses. (The possibility of contagion, although rare, is to be avoided since the result could be fatal illness for the person with decreased defenses.) If you have any questions about whether your child should receive immunizations, discuss them with your physician before the vaccine is administered.

Pertussis vaccine should not be administered to a child with progressive neurologic disease, since people in this group are believed to show an increased incidence of reactions to this vaccine.

Some Special Procedures

There are many special vaccines and other preparations available for exceptional circumstances. Children over two years of age with a deficiency in the ability to defend against infections due to chronic renal disease, surgical removal of the spleen, or decreased resistance associated with sickle cell disease are particularly susceptible to pneumonia and other illnesses caused by the pneumococcus. Pneumococcal vaccine should be administered to these children.

Influenza vaccines providing protection against the prevalent infecting virus should be administered to children with cystic fibrosis, chronic renal disease, severe cardiac disease, and other debilitating illnesses. Meningococcal vaccine may be recommended by your physician when a member of a family experiences illness due to this organism.

Exposure in infancy and childhood to certain strains of hepatitis may require administration of hepatitis vaccine. Also, animal bites in which rabies is suspected call for careful observation of the animal over a two-week period. If this is impossible, administration of rabies vaccine along with passive immune globulin may be indicated. (See the section on Scratches, Cuts, Abrasions, Puncture Wounds, and Animal Bites in **Chapter 20, First Aid at Home**, for more information on possible rabies exposure.) You should discuss the need for injections with your physician, local health officer, or a representative of the Center for Disease Control in Atlanta, Georgia (phone: 1-404-329-3311).

Passive Immunizations

Passive immunization, that is, the injection of gamma globulin, a preparation of human blood with preformed antibodies to specific diseases, is advisable for temporary protection when an infant or child is exposed to a serious disease to which he or she is susceptible. Administration of gamma globulin may be indicated when a young baby is exposed to measles for which he or she has not received immunizations; or in the case of any infant or child exposed to certain types of hepatitis; or if a child is suffering from immune deficiency and reduced capacity to resist viral disease.

Suspected or actual exposure to rabies is another instance where passive immunization, utilizing specially prepared materials in addition to the administration of active vaccine, is advised.

Travel

Special immunization for cholera, yellow fever, and typhoid, and administration of globulin preparations to protect against hepatitis are recommended for travel to certain areas of the world where these diseases are prevalent. Information as to when it is appropriate to obtain these injections can be obtained from your physician, your local or state health department, or in a pamphlet entitled *Health Information for International Travel*, Superintendent of Documents, U.S. Government Printing Office, Washington, DC 20402.

17. Your Child's Teeth

At what age should you begin to be concerned with your child's teeth? The answer is simple: shortly after birth! Even before the teeth have erupted, it is important to provide adequate concentration of fluoride in the diet. Evidence that the ingestion of fluoride from the earliest days of life inhibits cavity formation in later years is impressive. The administration of appropriate amounts of fluoride has no detrimental effect on infants, children, or adults.

Fluoride may be present in adequate concentrations in the natural water supply, or in many communities it is added as the water flows through the filtration plant. Your local water company or health officer can provide information regarding the fluoride concentration in your water supply. If the concentration is less than one part per million, ask your child's doctor or your dentist to recommend an oral fluoride preparation for your infant. This important substance is usually administered with vitamin drops. If you are nursing your infant, you should add fluoride to your baby's diet (even if there is adequate fluoride in your water supply) because the fluoride substances ingested by

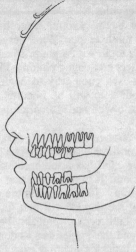

Baby and permanent teeth

nursing mothers are poorly excreted in breast milk.

If your baby is bottle-fed and has difficulty sleeping, you may be tempted to prop the baby's bottle in the early months of life to aid him to go to sleep. As noted earlier, it is unwise to offer a bottle filled with milk or fruit juice or sugar solution as a pacifier while asleep. The sugary substance in the milk mixture is deposited on the teeth and frequently initiates the process of cavity formation, particularly in the upper front teeth. If your infant must have a bottle at night, try using plain water.

Food habits established in the toddler and preschool years initiate a lifelong dietary pattern. Candy, pastries, cookies, marshmallows, chewing gum, cocoa, sweetened flavored juices, and soda should be avoided. What foods can be substituted for these popular items? There are many. Fresh fruits, raw vegetables, sliced cheese, natural fruit juices, yogurt, soups, and finger sandwiches with whole grain breads are popular foods during the preschool period.

Why do some children have a predilection for cavity formation? We do not know the answer. But we do know that dietary measures and fluoride supplements markedly reduce the tendency to form cavities.

At what age should you begin cleaning your baby's teeth? As soon as the first tooth erupts. Wipe or gently brush the front and back of a tooth with a gauze square or soft brush twice a day. Toddlers and young children like to brush their own teeth. This is a good way to begin the tooth-brushing habit, but your help will be important for some time. Utilizing toothpaste with added fluoride is recommended by most dentists.

When is it appropriate to arrange for a child's first visit to a dentist? Two and a half or three years of age is a good time, unless, of course, your child has a toothache or inflamed gums or a chipped tooth. It is important that your dentist "has a way with children." Tell your child the truth about what will happen: that the dentist will first look at the child's teeth with a special mirror, will probably have a toothbrush on a tiny motor, and that sometimes as dentists take care of a person's tooth, it tickles and may even hurt a little. Be as matter of fact as possible. Then let your dentist take over responsibility for telling a child what will happen.

A common accident when a child falls is for a tooth to be fractured or knocked out completely. When this happens, wipe the tooth free of dirt, wrap it in a gauze square moistened with saliva or warm water, and transport your child and the tooth to the dentist as rapidly as possible. Sometimes a tooth can be replanted by your dentist. With a chip or fracture, immediate dental care is important to preserve the nerve and body of the tooth.

Appropriate cleaning of teeth and repair of cavities in the preschool years, even with the primary set of teeth, is important, for neglecting dental care in the early years can lead to serious gum and tooth decay in later life.

18. Preventing Accidents

If you were told of some simple steps you could take that would greatly contribute to your child's chance for continued good health, wouldn't you take them? Of course. Then please read this chapter carefully. Taking a few safety precautions to prevent accidents could make all the difference to your youngster.

Accidents are a leading cause of injury and death during infancy and childhood. Indeed, only in the first year of life do any other causes—birth injuries and congenital malformations—supercede accidents as a cause of death. What can be done about this major health problem? A great deal. Taking a few precautions now can provide you with relative peace of mind about your child's safety.

Car Safety

Auto accidents account for a large proportion of injuries and deaths in the early years of life. In 1975, 10,400 children were killed riding in cars. According to Dr. Leon Robertson of the Department of Epidemiology and Public Health at Yale University School of Medicine, the correct use of specially designed infant and toddler car seats and seat belts for children would reduce by more than one-half the number of vehicle occupant deaths of children one year or older.

For this reason, a baby's first car ride home from the hospital should be in a car seat. Many hospitals have instituted programs of loaning or renting infant-sized carriers to parents at the time of discharge, thus firmly demonstrating The First Ride—a Safe Ride motto of the American Academy of Pediatrics.

Why are infant carriers, car seats, and seat belts so important? It's very simple. These restraints reduce the chance of an individual being thrown forward against the inner body of the car or the windshield at the time of a crash. The common habit of holding a baby, toddler, or child on one's lap is particularly dangerous. The impact occurring at the moment of an accident is likely to propel a baby or child out of the adult's arms, forward against the car frame or windshield. And the myth that restraints are necessary only on long car trips or when riding on main highways is unfounded. The majority of car accidents occur during short trips around the neighborhood.

There are many different types of car seats available. When you shop, be sure that the seat you're considering conforms to federal standards, or better yet, check to see if it is recommended by an advocacy group, such as the Committee on Accident Prevention of the American Academy of Pediatrics, whose standards are even higher than those set by the federal government.

Some car seats are bolted to the frame of the automobile; others are held in place by the car's regular seat belts. Infant carriers are designed to be positioned facing backward so that, in a collision, the baby would take the impact of the crash through his or her back. Seats for older babies (approximately nine months old or about eighteen pounds) and toddlers face forward. In order to avoid buying another seat for your child, shop for one that will do double duty. It can be installed as a backward-facing seat for the new baby and repositioned to face forward for the older baby and child. Once your child has reached about forty pounds, she will be more comfortable in a device featuring a cushioned seat that elevates the child enough to see out and a guard that goes over her and is held in place with the car's regular seat belt. For optimum safety, car seats should always be used in the back seat.

Your pediatrician will be able to recommend suitable carriers and restraints. Or write for information to the American Academy of Pediatrics, Box 927, Elk Grove Village, IL 63007, or to Physicians for Automotive Safety, P.O. Box 430, Armonk, NY 10604.

By consistently using the car seat for your child and a

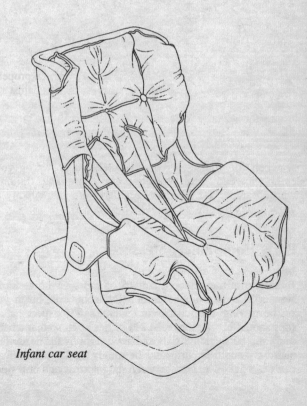

Infant car seat

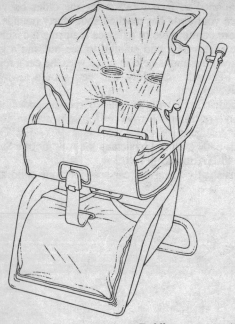

Toddler car seat with shield

seat belt for yourself, you will likely be providing your child with additional protection for a lifetime. Children whose parents use restraints regularly are more likely to grow up continuing the habit themselves.

Early Home Safety Measures

Safety for the newborn begins, of course, with the crib. New cribs must follow federal safety standards, but if you are borrowing one, check for several safety aspects. Crib slats should be no more than 2⅜ inches apart so that a baby can't slip between the slats and get caught by his head. The mattress should be firm and fit snugly at the sides. If an adult can fit two fingers between the mattress and crib side,

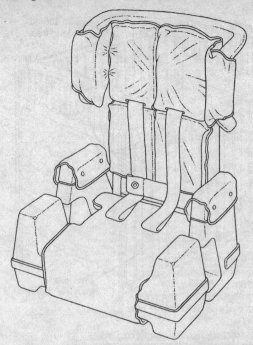

Booster car seat for children over age 3.

the mattress is too small, and a baby's head could get wedged between the side rail and the mattress. The level of the mattress should be twenty-six inches or more below the top of the elevated rails of the crib so that a toddler cannot lean over and fall out. Locking mechanisms must be secure. Paint should be lead-free.

In addition, keep the following in mind: Pillows do not belong in a crib; a baby can suffocate. Before the baby is able to sit up, remove any cords that hold toys strung across the crib; and remember that bumper guards can serve as a step, so as your child becomes more active, you will want to remove them as well.

Parents soon learn that even a young infant can twist

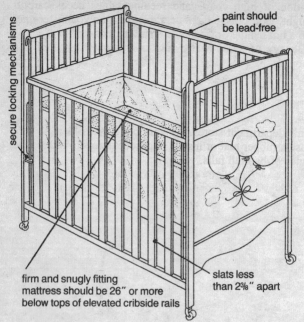

Crib meeting federal specifications

and squirm, and if unattended, is in danger of rolling off a changing table or bed. Arrange equipment and supplies so that when changing, dressing, or bathing the baby, all necessary equipment, including a disposable bag or pail for soiled diapers, is close at hand. This reduces the possibility of an adult's stepping away "for just a second" and providing the baby an opportunity to roll over and fall to the floor.

Holding a baby on one's lap while drinking hot liquids or smoking is dangerous, since even a young infant may surprise you by reaching out and grasping the coffee cup or cigarette, burning child and/or adult in the process.

Coffee pots, toasters, and hot plates should not be placed on a dining table if a baby or toddler is sitting at the table, either on a chair or on the lap of an adult. And the location of high chairs and feeding tables needs careful thought. Don't place them near a stove, or a youngster may grab a hot handle or tip over a steaming pot.

Beware of foods heated in a microwave! Although the container may remain cool to the touch, the liquids or foods inside may be much hotter—so much so that feeding them to a child can cause serious burns.

Bathtime safety for infants can be increased with the use of a molded foam cushion, which is available at most children's department stores. As your child gets older, be sure to use a rubber mat or install skidproof decals to reduce the chance of bathtub falls.

And *never* leave an infant or young child unattended in the bathtub—even for a moment. That leaves just enough time for a child to fall forward and possibly drown. A child who is too young to bathe himself is too young to be left alone in the tub.

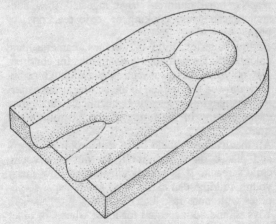

Sponge padding for bathing infants

Babyproofing Your Home

All babies and toddlers require close supervision, but the babyproofed home allows you the freedom to fix a cup of tea or go to your room to change shoes without worrying that your child is in imminent danger of harm. Given enough time, any child can get into some sort of trouble (many children discover how to open childproof latches, for example), but the child whose environment is basically safe can have the freedom to explore on his own without creating constant worry for you.

Potential problems to watch for vary from dangling cords to broken toys. Following is a list of some particular hazards.

- Matches, cosmetics, nail polish, perfume, birth control pills, aspirin, vitamins, tranquilizers, thyroid pills, sleeping pills, pins, needles, screws, paper clips, thumbtacks, jewelry, hairpins, peanuts, and mothballs are but a few of the potentially dangerous items that are too often easily within reach of small children. When ingested, these substances can cause choking or toxic reactions, or both.
- Button batteries, used in watches, cameras, and calculators, are particularly dangerous for children. Not only can these substances cause choking, but if swallowed and lodged in the stomach, the batteries disintegrate, releasing chemicals that may cause erosion of the lining of the gastrointestinal tract.
- All medications should be in childproof containers and placed on a high shelf, far out of a young child's reach. It is remarkable indeed how many young children can easily open safety caps, sometimes with more ease than can adults.
- Toys should be inspected for loose wheels or other parts, and dolls for loosely attached buttons and plastic eyes. Small parts should be removed, and loose button eyes can be snipped off and replaced with a few stitches of black thread.
- Toy boxes with heavy lids present a significant hazard. Fatal strangulations have been reported when the lid has fallen on a child who has leaned in to retrieve a toy. Toy chests with a removable,

unhinged lid, sliding doors, or no lid at all are far preferable.

- Lead-based paint chips are another common hazard, and can cause lead poisoning if a child eats them over a long period of time. Lead-based paint should be thoroughly removed and the area repainted or covered with safer materials.
- Kitchen tools, knives, forks, scissors, guns—even toy guns (which can be poked in the eye)—are potential hazards and should be well out of the reach of an infant or young child.
- Dangling electric cords attached to toasters, irons, or floor lamps are enticing. A crawling infant or mobile toddler can be expected to yank any hanging cord within reach, thus pulling the iron, lamp, or toaster off the table onto his head. It is unsafe to leave a mobile infant or toddler alone in a room with a lighted fire, cooking apparatus, oil lamp, or electric, kerosene, or woodburning heaters. A child's normal curiosity can easily lead her to touch any apparatus, not understanding the dangers of receiving an electrical shock or being burned.
- Electric cords and open electric light sockets can cause severe electric shock and serious burns if

Electrical socket cover

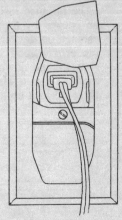

Electrical outlet cover

chewed or fingered. An outlet cap (a simple plug-like cover available at most children's equipment and hardware stores) should be placed in each un-used outlet. An outlet shield is a protective cover that goes over an outlet even where items are plugged in. These shields allow you to continue using the outlet while deterring a child from play-ing with the plugs and outlets. In addition, use cord holders to keep loose wires out of the way of awkward feet and curious hands.

• Storage areas are a common hazard in many homes. The cabinet under the kitchen sink, where polishes, bleaches, soaps, caustic cleansers, paint solvent, and other strong materials are often stored, is a particularly dangerous spot. The infant or toddler, observing that his parents frequently get things out of this area, may make a beeline for it if the door is left open. Soon he is busy pouring pol-ishes or caustic cleaning materials on his skin or drinking the soaps, detergents, or other cleaning substances. Infants, toddlers, and young children are generally undeterred by the pungent odors or tastes. Placing a safety lock on the cupboard doors offers some security, and various types are avail-able. A "keyless lock" is a plastic catch designed to be installed inside cabinets and drawers. It can be opened by tripping the catch from within the cabinet or drawer. However, safety latches, no matter how good, can really only be counted on to slow a child down. Children are extremely inge-nious. There is also no guarantee that you won't forget to lock up a cabinet one day. For these rea-

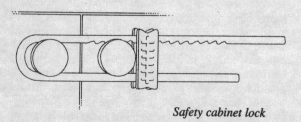

Safety cabinet lock

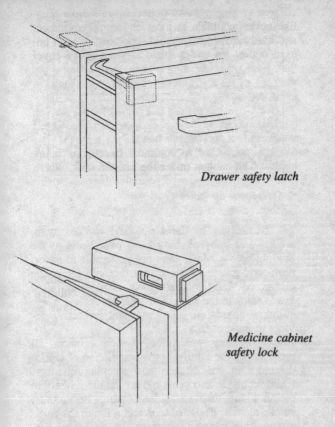

Drawer safety latch

Medicine cabinet safety lock

sons, I suggest that, for additional security, dangerous materials should be stored high out of a child's
reach.

- Stairs offer a particularly intriguing invitation to a
child, whose curiosity stimulates her to go every-
where she can. Be sure to place a gate at both the
top and bottom of all stairways. Your baby will
learn to climb up before learning to go down, so
you don't want her to climb to the top with no safe
way to descend. Infants in walkers are a particularly dangerous combination. They commonly pro-

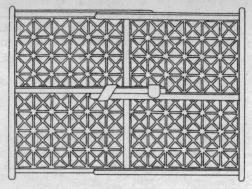

Safety gate for stairs

pel themselves to the stairs and topple down, walker and baby pitching head over heels to the landing below. Mesh gates are preferable to accordion-style gates, which offer a foothold for young climbers. Many toddlers have also gotten their heads stuck in the accordion-style gates.

- Window guards are also important protective devices to prevent falls.
- Another safety precaution, which protects all members of the family, is the installation of smoke detectors in the kitchen and sleeping quarters. Children under four years old are far more likely to die in a fire than are older children and adults; smoke alarms, designed to detect a fire at the earliest possible moment, increase the chance of survival for all family members.

Outdoor Safety

Outdoor areas also need to be checked carefully for potential hazards.

- It is too much to expect an infant, toddler, or preschooler to understand safe limits, so outdoor play areas should be fenced in, preferably excluding the driveway. To a young child, the whole neighborhood, including adjacent yards, driveways, and the street, is considered his or her personal play area unless a fence indicates otherwise.

- Toolsheds, garages, and basement work areas should be carefully locked at all times so that lawn mowers, garden tools, saws, fertilizers, pesticides, and work tools are out of reach.

- Ingestion and contact with leaves and berries from household or garden plants can produce serious toxic reactions in sensitive individuals. Rhododendron, hemlock, yew, philodendron, dieffenbachia, jade plant, holly, pokeweed, poinsettia, Swedish ivy, woody nightshade, black elder, African violets, and poison ivy are a few of the common plants that can cause serious systemic reactions. Ingestion may cause irritation and swelling of tissues of the mouth and tongue. Nausea, vomiting, and respiratory distress may also occur. Ingestion of poisonous mushrooms may produce critical illness within a few minutes. Perhaps the best way to protect your child is to make a list of your indoor and outdoor plants (including trees) and call your local poison control center. They can tell you if any of your greenery poses a potential hazard.

- Another increasingly common accident results from children playing with electrically operated garage doors. A popular but frightening game is "beat the door," in which a child operates the door's closing mechanism and then the child or a friend tries to run in or out of the garage before the door closes. This is extremely dangerous. Even school-age children can be killed if the door comes down on them. Parents who have electronically controlled garage doors should have the switch placed far out of children's reach.

- Backyard pools, Jacuzzis, unprotected swimming areas, brooks, ponds, drainage ditches, and culverts are areas where drowning can occur. If your backyard borders on any of these hazards, be sure to fence off access to that area. Even swimming pools must be fully fenced! And if a child is at a beach supervised by a lifeguard, remember that adults still need to watch their own youngsters. The most efficient lifeguard is unable to observe everyone on a crowded beach. By all means, arrange swimming lessons for your child as soon as she is interested. Certainly by age five, most young children are eager to learn to swim. The American Red Cross provides special classes for young children in most communities. Learning to swim at an early age increases children's confidence in themselves, and it may also save their lives.

19. Establishing Good Health Habits

Instilling good health habits among family members is an important aspect of promoting your child's good health. Parents often fail to realize the important role they play in establishing patterns that have a lasting effect on a child's health in adult life.

Eating

Take the most common health problem in America today—overeating and obesity. Significant obesity exists in approximately ten percent of all children. Once a child becomes obese, he or she is very likely to maintain this status throughout his or her lifetime. Obesity causes children considerable unhappiness during childhood, and it leads to increased incidence of coronary heart disease, high blood pressure, strokes, gall bladder disease, and diabetes in adulthood.

Feeding patterns initiated in infancy and childhood often

firmly establish the habit of overeating. Take, for example, the way in which parents feed their infants. A breast-fed baby who is satiated stops suckling and a mother's milk flow ceases. His judgment tells him to stop eating and he does and that's the end of the meal!

But a bottle-fed baby's feeding experience may be quite different. Adults feeding a baby may find that after ingesting three-quarters of the amount in the bottle, a baby goes off to sleep. However, a mother or father often feels that it is a shame to "waste" the last ounce in the bottle, so the parent may urge, coax, or, indeed, demand that a satiated baby "wake up and finish" the last ounce. The baby responds, probably so he can go back to sleep, by ingesting the last ounce, thus providing an intake of more calories than is necessary. This causes a deposit of fat cells in the body tissues, which remain throughout life. Thus, at an early age, the tendency toward obesity is already determined.

Offering a baby or toddler a bottle of milk or fruit juice at odd hours to relieve fretfulness or loneliness also leads to overeating. This common pattern not only increases the caloric intake beyond what is necessary, but it also establishes the idea that whenever one is tired, unhappy, or out of sorts for any reason, one eats! (Dental decay, as discussed in Chapter 17, results from the practice of offering a bottle of milk or fruit juice at bedtime or during the night, since the food deposited on the teeth remains there all night, providing a fertile field for cavity formation.)

The common admonition to "finish your dinner so you can have dessert" establishes in a child's mind that there is something particularly desirable about sweets. It is better to offer these foods as a routine part of the meal rather than as a reward for having finished the previous course.

Family eating habits are difficult to change. A child growing up in a family where eating is practically an all-day affair and obesity is common is likely to develop similar patterns of food intake in adulthood.

Try to establish healthy eating habits for your child from the very beginning. And if your own habits set a poor example, now is a good time to change.

Smoking

Adult smoking is another example of social behavior with serious long-term health problems for both the adult who smokes as well as the children who are exposed to it. In spite of widespsread reports that demonstrate the clear relationship between cancer of the lung and smoking, vast numbers of adults do smoke. This is not only unhealthy for the parent, but it is irritating to the lungs of young children, particularly those who have allergic tendencies. But worst of all, smoking by a parent or other adult in the home establishes a model that becomes firmly fixed in a child's mind.

Children who grow up in homes where parents smoke are far more likely to smoke than are children who grow up in nonsmoking homes. Parents should realize that the example they present is enormously important in determining whether their children smoke in adolescence and adulthood. Unless parents stop smoking, there is little chance of decreasing the habit of smoking in the next generation.

Drinking

Patterns of drinking alcoholic beverages by adults who nurture children are another important influence on how youngsters conceptualize appropriate behavior as they enter adulthood. It is common for adults to have a cocktail before dinner, a glass of wine with a meal, or a few bottles of beer at the backyard picnic. This represents acceptable adult utilization of such beverages. Offering a child a glass of fruit juice as his drink, with the comment that when he grows up he can have wine, beer, or cocktails, is an appropriate way of including a child in the common pattern of drinking with the family.

It is, however, quite another matter when adults in the family drink to excess as a relief from stress. A young child may not understand the motivation for her parents' drinking, but she does grow up observing that when adults are tired, exhausted, or discouraged, they drink alcoholic beverages, often to excess. This pattern of using alcohol as a solution to some of life's problems becomes firmly established in a child's mind.

In addition, children suffer when nurturing is uneven and inconsistent because of the different manner in which adults function when under the influence of alcohol. This inconsistency in the parent's ability to care for a young child produces uncertainty in the child's mind as to what can be expected from adults. It severely undermines a child's feelings of confidence and trust, which are the basis for psychological stability in childhood and adolescence. Any family in which alcoholism interferes with normal relationships should seek professional help from a counseling agency. Your pediatrician will be able to refer you to an appropriate social agency or counselor.

IV Illness

20. First Aid at Home

In becoming a parent you assume a wide variety of roles, including first aid expert. Should your child or other youngster get hurt, it is vital that you be prepared to clean and bandage the cut or scrape, or with a more serious injury, that you be knowledgeable enough to provide proper care until you can obtain medical help.

This role is such an important one that many parents take first aid courses in order to be better prepared for emergencies. Typically, these courses provide basic advice on accident prevention as well as lifesaving information such as how to perform artificial respiration on a child or how to save a youngster from choking. (Contact the American Red Cross or the local Y to locate courses in your area.)

In the meantime, every parent needs a well-stocked medicine cabinet. To be properly equipped, you should have on hand the following:

- Tweezers
- Band-Aids, sterile gauze squares, cotton, rolls of bandages, and adhesive tape

- Syrup of ipecac to induce vomiting
- Hot water bottle
- Ice bag
- Aspirin or acetaminophen
- Bland ointments, such as petrolatum or zinc oxide ointment
- Nasal aspirator
- Rectal thermometer

In preparation for an emergency, the following information should be posted near all telephones in the house:

- Child's full name
- Pediatrician's telephone number and address
- Parents' telephone numbers at work
- Telephone number of nearest poison control center
- Address and telephone number of nearest hospital emergency room (and brief instructions as to how to get there)
- Telephone number of police
- Telephone number of fire department
- Telephone number of ambulance service
- Address and telephone number of pharmacy
- Name and number of nearest neighbor who would help
- Parents' names
- Address of house

In addition, the following information will help you properly treat minor injuries and know what your participation is in treating a major one.

Scratches, Cuts, Abrasions, Puncture Wounds, and Animal Bites

Scratches, cuts, abrasions, puncture wounds, and animal bites should be washed gently yet profusely with soap and water to remove dirt and foreign material. Applying a cool compress with continuous pressure will usually control the blood flow. If bleeding continues for more than twenty minutes, or if the laceration exposes muscle tissue, or if the skin edges are separated widely, surgical repair may be necessary to promote healing and minimize the scar.

Lacerations of the tongue, gums, and palate are common in young children. Bleeding may be profuse at first, but in most instances, sucking ice chips will reduce the blood flow, and in due time it usually stops. Suturing is rarely necessary within the mouth.

Animal bites should be treated as any other laceration, with *one very important exception*: If the injury is the result of a bite by a skunk, bat, raccoon, fox, unimmunized cat or dog, effort should be made to capture the animal and arrange for a two-week observation by a veterinarian or health officer. Should any signs of illness in the animal develop, appropriate diagnostic studies are imperative to determine whether rabies is present. (Rabies is a potentially fatal disease transmitted by contact with saliva of an infected animal.) If the animal is found to be infected, or if the animal cannot be captured for observation, you should immediately talk to your doctor about the advisability of administering rabies immunizations to your child. Administration of appropriate vaccine is imperative if there is any possibility that the child has been exposed to a rabid animal.

Nosebleeds

Nosebleeds are common in childhood. The bleeding is usually due to an irritation of the skin tissue in the inner part of the nose close to the surface. Quite frequently, a child with frequent nosebleeds has a parent or sibling who also experiences nosebleeds, suggesting an inherited pattern of vessel configuration close to the surface. A blow to the nose, irritation from a cold or allergic reaction, or simply picking at the nose can also cause the nose to bleed.

Squeezing the nostrils with your fingers or applying firm pressure to the nose with ice wrapped in a handkerchief or washcloth usually stops the bleeding within a few minutes. To prevent the blood from running into the stomach and causing nausea and vomiting, have the child sit up so that the blood flows out. If the bleeding continues more than twenty minutes, call your physician. Children with frequent nosebleeds, particularly if associated with the appearance of black-and-blue spots elsewhere on the body, should be examined by their doctor. A systemic disease interfering with the clotting mechanism may be present.

Eye Injuries

Irritation of the eyes from exposure to dust, soaps, bleaches, or disinfectant can be treated by flushing the eye with lots of cool water. If a child complains of continuous pain, covers his eyes because of discomfort from the light,

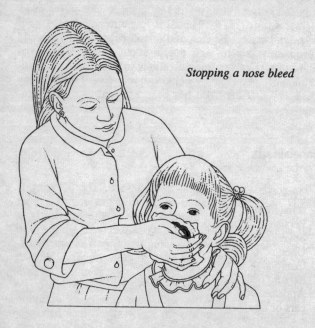

Stopping a nose bleed

or says that his vision is blurred, evaluation by a physician is important to determine appropriate treatment and prevent permanent injury. If the eye appears very red or otherwise distorted, the doctor should also be consulted.

Head Injuries

Blows to the head are common during infancy and the toddler and childhood years. The majority of these injuries are slight and inconsequential, resulting only in an abrasion, scratch, or a swelling of the face or scalp. Cold compresses to reduce swelling are the best treatment. If the child returns to normal behavior and activities after a few moments of appropriate crying, she probably has suffered no significant injury. However, if the child is injured in a fall from a changing table, down a flight of stairs, out a window, or in a bicycle or auto collision, she is at risk for internal damage.

How can you differentiate between the many insignificant blows that children experience almost daily and a serious head injury? If your child loses consciousness for even a moment, he should be examined by a physician, even if the child seems fine. It is important to have a detailed medical examination on record so that if symptoms develop later, a comparison can be made.

In addition to a period of unconsciousness, there are a few other signs that suggest an injury of a critical nature may be present.

1. Excessive sleepiness with decreasing levels of consciousness
2. Persistent vomiting
3. Severe headaches
4. Unequal pupils
5. Complaints of seeing double or of blurred vision
6. Seizure or weakness of one side of the body
7. Appearance of clear fluid (cerebral spinal fluid) in the ears or nose

Whenever any of these symptoms appear shortly after an injury, medical evaluation is imperative. A severe contusion, a fracture of the skull, or internal bleeding may be present.

Choking

Infants and toddlers have an uncanny way of finding small objects, such as buttons, coins, safety pins, deflated balloons, thimbles, pieces of hard candy, dolls' eyes, and other pieces of toys. And once they find them, it is natural for children to place these and similar objects in their mouths. Generally, the item will be spit up, or if swallowed, it usually enters the esophagus, passes into the stomach and intestinal tract with ease, and appears in the bowel movements within 48 to 72 hours, producing no serious consequences. Rarely, a foreign body is stuck in the esophagus, in which case it is necessary to remove it under anesthesia through the use of an esophagoscope.

In some instances, a foreign body will enter the respiratory tract and be lodged in the larynx, trachea, or lower down in the lungs, blocking the upper airway. This presents an immediate threat to life and requires removal. If a child can speak or breathe and is coughing, then the obstruction is incomplete; heroic maneuvers may be postponed for the short time it takes to get your child to the doctor or the emergency room of the nearest hospital.

Action must be taken immediately if a choking child is unable to breathe or make a sound. To aid the victim, stand or sit, and place the baby or toddler in a tilted position lying face down against your thighs, with the head lower than the body. Using the palm of your hand, deliver four quick blows to the child's back with a firm, downward thrust. Repeat if necessary.

This procedure usually causes ejection of the foreign body and restores the air passage. If it fails, hold your child or infant on your lap with his back against your abdomen. Place the index and middle fingers of both hands on the child's abdomen, well below the rib cage and

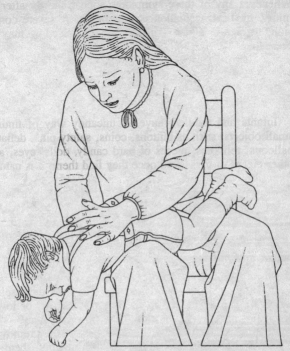

Aiding a choking child (also see page 178)

slightly above the navel. Gently press into the abdomen with a quick upward thrust. Repeat if necessary.

Burns

Sunburn may range from mild redness to severe blistering with exquisite tenderness, pain, fever, headache, and chills. Mild redness begins a few hours after exposure, and the peak intensity of the reaction will occur twenty-four hours later, fading over the next few days. Treatment consists of cool compresses or bathing the child in a tub of cool water with baking soda or cornstarch added. Offer

Another position for choking victim

your child as much fluid as possible. Aspirin or other anti-inflammatory drugs as well as sunburn creams are also helpful.

Prevention is, of course, a preferable treatment. Initial exposure to the sun should be for only a few minutes at a time. Very effective sunscreen lotions are available and should be used on children to prevent burning.

Burns from scalding water, picnic fires or fireplaces, hot pots and pans, spattered grease, and electrical cords can also occur all too easily. Immediate profuse bathing with cold water or ice is currently advised. If the skin is broken, wash carefully with soap and water to decrease the chance of infection. Any child with severe blisters or deep raw lesions below the superficial skin area should be seen promptly by a physician. When burns are severe or widespread, hospitalization for definitive treatment and prevention of infection may be necessary.

Sprains and Fractures

Twisted ankles resulting in minor bruises and sprains are common in toddlers and young children. A sprained joint usually becomes swollen within 15 to 30 minutes after the injury, and may turn black-and-blue within the next twenty-four hours. Cold applications reduce the extent of the swelling. In most instances, a child will limit his or her own activity sufficiently. Occasionally when the pain following an ankle injury is intense, it is wise to arrange for an X ray. Fractures of ankle bones may be present, and a child will need a cast to encourage the healing process.

When a child twists or fractures a wrist or arm, apply cold compresses and prevent movement as much as possible until the child can be seen by a doctor.

Poisonings

Vitamins, aspirin, perfume, nail polish and remover, alcohol, medications, bleach, paint, fertilizer, plant food, kerosene, gasoline, shampoo, mushrooms, deodorants, and plants such as philodendron, dieffenbachia, jade, holly berries, yew, pokeweed, poinsettia, and Swedish ivy are just a few of the poisonous items that young children accidentally ingest.

If you suspect your child has ingested something poisonous, call your doctor or the poison control center in your area at once. (These phone numbers should be posted near your telephones.) They will tell you what to do. In most cases, they will recommend that you induce vomiting. If so, give the child three teaspoons of syrup of ipecac followed by three ounces of water. If vomiting fails to occur within twenty minutes, repeat the dose of syrup of ipecac and water.

However, do not induce vomiting without first consulting your doctor, or a staff member at the poison control center or the hospital emergency room. If your child has ingested a material such as ammonia, bleach, lime, lye, a strong acid, oven cleaner, toxic petroleum, or such products as cleaning fluids, gasoline, furniture polish, and paint thinners, then vomiting is *not* recommended. The doctor or staff member of the poison control center or hospital emergency room will tell you what to do.

Chronic poisoning due to ingestion of paint chips containing lead, inhalation of lead fumes, and playing in areas adjacent to parkways where lead materials settle on the playground is far more common that most of us realize. Recent studies reveal significant damage when lead concentration is only moderately elevated, a hazard that has too long been unappreciated. If your child shows signs of significant behavior changes, and there is no obvious sign of illness, ask your pediatrician about the possibility of lead poisoning (see Lead Poisoning in the **A to Z Guide** for more information).

Injuries to Teeth

When a child falls and bangs her teeth, you should arrange for her to see a dentist as soon as possible. A nerve root may be damaged, and immediate treatment can save the tooth. (Even if the tooth has been knocked out, it can often be replanted. Wrap the tooth in a warm, moist cloth and take it and your child to the dentist immediately.)

When the tooth cannot be replaced it is important to determine whether a piece of it is imbedded in the gum. Frequently, a tooth darkens several weeks after the injury, indicating that serious damage has occurred. Sometimes an abscess occurs above or below the tooth. In either case, examination and treatment of the damaged nerve are important.

Artificial Respiration

As a parent, you do not want to confront the thought that one day you might find your child has had an accident and is not breathing. But if this were to happen, you would need to know how to perform artificial respiration. Although reading the following information may give you a basic idea of what to do, artificial respiration is a procedure that actually should be learned *and practiced* in a first aid course. (Your local American Red Cross will help you find appropriate courses in your community.) Then, should you ever be presented with such an emergency, you will feel more comfortable with what you must do.

However, even if you are able to start artificial respiration, keep in the back of your mind that what you really need is *help*. While beginning the procedure, call out for someone else to help you (if only by phoning the doctor, police, or fire department for you). Or, if you're alone, start thinking of how you can get the child to the phone with you (since you may have to be breathing for him) in order to make the call yourself.

Here is the procedure:

1. Place the child on his back. If necessary, turn the child's head to the side and, using your hand or a cloth, clear his mouth of vomit or any object.
2. Providing that there is no neck or back injury, open the air passage by gently tipping back the head so that the chin is pointing upward. If there is a possibility of injury to the neck or back, open the air passage by gently pulling open the jaw without moving the head. This movement alone may start your child breathing again.
3. If breathing has not resumed, pinch off the nostrils with one hand and place your open mouth over the child's mouth (with an infant your mouth goes over both the mouth and nose), forming an airtight seal. Give four quick, gentle breaths.
4. Remove your mouth and watch and listen for a return of

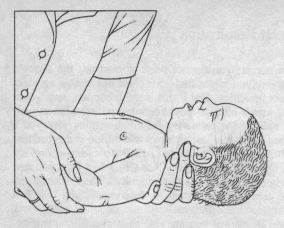

Artificial respiration—Step one: tilting the head back

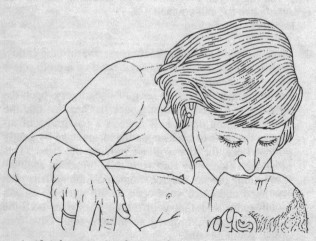

Artificial respiration for an infant

Artificial respiration for a child

air. If there is none, check the child's head and tongue positions to be sure the air can pass easily.

5. Repeat the four quick breaths. If you still don't see or hear that air is leaving the lungs, you may need to try to dislodge whatever is stuck in the airway. Use the procedure for choking earlier in this chapter. Turn the child on his side and slap him between the shoulder blades. Check to see if anything was dislodged; you may need to use your finger to explore the back of the mouth.

6. Place the child on his back again. Tilt the head back and start again with four quick breaths.

7. Once you see that air is passing, give an infant or small child a new breath every three to four seconds, or sixteen to twenty per minute, using gentle puffs of air. Continue until the child breathes on his own or until medical help arrives. (Even if the child starts breathing, watch him closely as you may need to begin artificial respiration again at any time.)

21. Allergies

Exactly what is an allergic reaction? It is the tendency for an individual to experience discomfort and significant symptoms in response to repeated exposure to certain substances, such as foods, medications, plants, pollen, mold, dust, or animal dander. This response does not occur in individuals who do not possess this capacity to react.

If you or your spouse has allergies, chances are your child will, too, since allergic individuals tend to inherit the physiologic ability to react adversely to offending substances.

Whether your child's allergic reaction takes the form of a stomachache or respiratory symptoms, your most important task is to pay close attention to his or her food intake and to exposure to pollen, dust, mold, and other airborne substances in order to determine the cause of the allergy. Identification of the offending substances is the first step in helping a child with allergies.

One word of caution in your search for a cause: Just because your child had no reaction to Grandma's new puppy the first time the two of them romped does not mean that Fido is not the culprit if your son now returns from every visit to Grandma's with a runny nose and red eyes. In order to develop some allergies, a person usually must encounter the offending substance more than once and become sensitized to having an allergic reaction. (That's why food allergies do not always show up the first time a child tastes the food.) So don't be too hasty in ruling out certain items just because a first exposure did not cause a problem. A child *inherits* the tendency to have allergies, but usually sensitivity to an offending substance takes time to *develop*.

Early Allergies: Milk and Various Foods

Allergic reactions may appear as early as the first few weeks of life. Cramps, vomiting, and diarrhea in an infant ingesting formula with a cow's milk base suggest an allergic reaction. Because the allergy may not show up for a week or so, parents are often surprised when the problem turns out to be the milk mixture.

The usual pattern is for a baby to tolerate the milk mixture for the first few weeks and then begin to experience increasingly severe abdominal discomfort after eating. In some instances, the sensitivity to cow's milk produces bleeding in the gastrointestinal tract with subsequent anemia and failure to gain weight. Sniffles and congestion in the throat and trachea are also manifestations of milk allergy in infants. Substitution of a soybean milk mixture may offer dramatic relief, although many infants sensitive to cow's milk are also unable to tolerate soybean mixtures. If so, feeding a synthetic milk mixture usually solves the difficulty.

Although human milk is the ideal nutrient for infants, cow's milk in a mother's diet may produce cramps, gassiness, abdominal distention, and diarrhea in a breast-fed infant who is allergic to cow's milk. Elimination of cow's milk in the nursing mother's diet will often relieve the baby's abdominal discomfort. Peanuts, wheat, chocolate, fish, and eggs are other foods the nursing mother may eat that can cause an allergic infant to experience cramps and diarrhea. These symptoms represent a reaction primarily in the baby's gastrointestinal tract.

Gastrointestinal sensitivity to milk proteins usually diminishes in the second half year of life. If your pediatrician suggests that a baby with a milk allergy may be able to tolerate milk now, offer an initial trial of a few ounces of evaporated milk, commercially prepared formula, or a powdered milk preparation. Frequently an infant with milk sensitivity can ingest cooked milk with little difficulty because the heating process in preparing these products alters the milk's protein, making it less likely to cause allergic reactions. Feeding unboiled milk from the carton or bottle may result in the reappearance of the gastrointestinal symptoms.

Also be aware that the nature of an allergic reaction may change during early childhood, so don't be fooled by the subsiding of one set of symptoms. If you have an allergic child, those symptoms may well be replaced by others. For example, the ingestion of cow's milk may no longer cause gastrointestinal discomfort as a baby reaches her first birthday, but it may result in the appearance of congestion in the nose, throat, and trachea. The young child who seems to "have a cold all the time" is often suffering from sensitivity to cow's milk. Eliminating milk from the diet often produces dramatic relief.

Careful attention to the moment of onset or worsening of allergic symptoms will often reveal the cause. When a baby who is weaned from the breast to a milk mixture, or a formula-fed infant who is offered whole milk develops gastrointestinal or respiratory symptoms a week or so later, it suggests that he is suffering an allergic response to the cow's milk.

Sometimes it is difficult to be certain when these symptoms represent a stomach or upper respiratory illness, or when they are allergic in origin. If your child has no fever and the symptoms continue for several weeks, you should begin to suspect an allergic basis and substitute one of the various preparations of cooked milk.

When the ingestion of milk in toddler or preschool years results in abdominal discomfort with gaseous distention and loose bowel movements, the possibility of lactose intolerance, another common disease, should be considered. This condition due to a deficiency in the intestinal enzyme lactase, reduces the child's ability to digest lactose, the sugar in breast or cow's milk. However, whether abdominal discomfort in early childhood is due to an allergy to milk or an enzymatic deficiency, the elimination of milk in the diet often results in dramatic improvement.

Of course, a baby may suffer reactions to foods other than milk. Eggs, wheat, peanut butter, corn, and chocolate are common offenders.

If several individuals in your family are allergy-prone, you would be wise to postpone offering your baby solid foods, particularly eggs and wheat, until he or she is six months or older. There is less chance of an allergic reaction in an older baby. Any addition to a baby's diet should be offered in small quantities, one at a time, at five- to seven-day intervals. Intestinal discomfort or the appearance of a generalized rash following the addition of new foods suggests food sensitivity.

Food Sensitivities and Behavior

Many parents report significant changes in their child's behavior following the ingestion of certain foods, particularly substances containing naturally occurring salicylates (see below for a list of foods containing salicylate). Other children are sensitive to foods containing mold. Food additives, colorings, and preservatives, particularly yellow dye, often are added to liquid medications and are also common offenders.

Children with the tendency to react to certain foods become restless, agitated, and quarrelsome shortly after ingesting the offending substances. The changes are often dramatic. The conflict and frustration of normal life experiences become overwhelming. Frequent episodes of anger and temper tantrums occur. A child with this sensitivity may find it impossible to concentrate in school and instead, jumps up and down in his seat and wanders around the classroom.

Whether the symptoms are due to an unusual allergic response or represent a direct toxic effect on the body—particularly the brain—is unclear. Whatever the cause, parents whose children possess this tendency can—and should—become quite expert at recognizing which foods need to be eliminated from the child's diet.

There are three main groups of foods that frequently cause a sensitive child to respond in this unusual way.

- Salicylate-containing foods include almonds, apricots, blackberries, boysenberries, raspberries, peaches, prunes, grapes, cucumbers, tomatoes, cloves, apples, apple cider, currants, gooseberries, strawberries, plums, oranges, and pickles. Aspirin also contains salicylate.
- Mold-containing foods include mushrooms, milk, cottage cheese, cheese, sour cream, buttermilk, vinegar, wine, beer, cider, pickled meats, smoked meats, and bread containing yeast.
- Artificial coloring and additives are present in bologna, salami, frankfurters, prepared meat loaf, ham, frozen fish, ice cream, diet drinks, colored margarine, colored butter, mustard, soy sauce, and toothpaste.

In addition, children with hay fever, asthma, or eczema may experience behavioral disturbances after ingesting milk, chocolate, corn, cane sugar, wheat, citrus fruits, eggs, and soybeans.

You may find it worthwhile to eliminate these possible offending substances from your child's diet. If his behavior improves, you might begin to add some of the foods very gradually, keeping a careful record. Soon you will be able to discover which foods or groups of foods produce this type of behavior. Children as young as five often recognize which foods evoke discomfort and will reject those foods spontaneously, realizing the relationship between the food and their bodily feelings. (Further information about the relationships of diet and behavior is available in Benjamin Feingold's *Why Your Child is Hyperactive*, Random House, 1974, Claude Frazier's *Coping with Food Allergy*,

Quadrangle Books, 1974, or Richard F. Grabers' *Parents Book of Childhood Allergies*, Ballantine, 1983).

In some individuals, these sensitivities disappear by adolescence; in others, the reaction continues throughout life.

Allergic Rhinitis—Affecting Nose and Eyes

Itching and sneezing as well as inflammation of the nasal tissue and eyes, accompanied by congestion that obstructs the airways, constitute a common allergic condition in young children known as allergic rhinitis. These symptoms often represent a sensitivity to airborne mold, pollens, weeds, grasses, dust, feathers, or animal dander. (As noted earlier, ingestion of milk, particularly in a child with a history of gastrointestinal irritation from milk in early infancy, may also cause these respiratory symptoms.)

You may find it difficult to distinguish whether your child's symptoms are due to an infectious or allergic process. A young child experiencing one cold after another and who "sniffles all the time" may be suffering an allergic reacton with superimposed, recurrent upper respiratory infections. When the nasal congestion and itchiness of the nose continues for weeks on end, or if your child frequently rubs her nose with her hand in what has come to be known as the "allergic salute," you can safely conclude that allergy is responsible for at least some of her symptoms.

Thinking back to when the child's symptoms began is important in helping to determine the cause. If they started in mid-August, the increase in airborne ragweed pollens in the eastern United States might be the cause. Or if symptoms appear following the addition of a new family pet, sensitivity to animal dander may be the problem.

To verify a suspicion, you may need to remove the substance when possible. Dusting carefully, eliminating feather pillows, covering mattresses, and removing rugs and curtains may be important. In some instances, a favorite pet may have to be sent to the neighbors for a vacation. If a child's symptoms disappear while the animal is out of the house and reappear upon the animal's return, you may have to conclude that the animal dander is an important factor in your child's symptoms.

The best treatment for this type of allergy involves removal of the offending substance from the diet or the environment, whenever possible. Although it may be impossible to prevent a child who inherits allergic tendencies from developing symptoms at some time in his life, avoiding exposure to common substances that are known to cause difficulties will often relieve the symptoms.

Oral administration of antihistamine preparations relieves much of the discomfort, although some preparations cause children to be sleepy.

Atopic and Contact Dermatitis

Atopic dermatitis, or eczema, is a common skin eruption occurring in infants and toddlers. Characteristically, red inflammatory lesions appear initially on the face, neck, and inner part of the elbows and backs of the knees, and then spread over the body. The lesions often become crusty and weeping. Intense itching is common. A child's tendency to scratch increases the inflammation. Secondary superimposed bacterial and fungus infections commonly intensify the inflammatory process.

The cause of atopic dermatitis is not totally understood. Children experiencing this skin condition often develop respiratory forms of allergy in later years.

Sensitivity to specific foods is an important contributing factor in many instances. Common foods that may intensify this skin condition are milk, eggs, wheat, chocolate, peanuts, fish, and corn. Elimination of these foods often produces dramatic improvement. You can then begin adding the foods one by one at five-day intervals to determine which of them is likely to be one of the causes of the skin inflammation.

Eczematoid skin lesions often flare up when there are significant changes in the environment, such as when the heat is turned on in the fall, particularly in a home with hot-air heating. Seasonal atmospheric changes, such as the mid-August appearance of ragweed pollens in the air, also can exacerbate symptoms. The addition of a gerbil, guinea pig, hamster, dog, cat, or rabbits to the household may be a factor responsible for intensification of the rash.

Oral administration of antibiotics and topical treatment usually control the infection. Antihistamine preparations administered orally reduce the discomfort of the itching. Oatmeal baths are also soothing. Creams containing lanolin derived from wool fat should be avoided since the wool fat often irritates the skin and intensifies the inflammation in many infants.

In allergic individuals, contact dermatitis, which usually develops a few hours after a sensitive individual has had contact with an offending substance, may occur from contact with wool, strong soaps, nylon, bubble bath, plastic belts, wristbands, dyes, nail polish, leather, and shoe polish. Eliminating these offending substances is usually curative. Soothing lotions (except for lanolin-containing preparations, since the wool fat they contain may be irritating), oatmeal baths, and oral antihistamine preparations often relieve the discomfort. However, avoiding the offending substance is, of course, the best treatment.

Many children who may or may not suffer other allergic conditions may develop an allergy following contact with poison ivy, oak, or sumac. Contact dermatitis develops a few hours after a sensitive individual has had contact with leaves of the offending substance. This contact may occur directly or it may be the result of being exposed to smoke and soot-containing particles of toxic leaf and oils. In the latter instance, the individual experiences a typical reaction and may be quite unaware of the exposure.

Hives

Hives, also called urticaria, are red, itchy lumps with clearly defined edges that appear on the skin. They often show up in allergy-prone children. These skin lesions, or wheals, may occur anywhere, and usually spread over the body within an hour of the initial lesion. They then may disappear in a few hours, only to reappear later. Hives are often brought about by ingestion of specific foods, particularly nuts, peanuts, fish, shellfish, eggs, mushrooms, and peas; and by drugs such as aspirin, penicillin, and any preparation containing yellow dye, known as tartrizine. Artificial food dyes and flavors are also common offenders. Rarely, a child develops these lesions following contact with a cat or dog or other pet. Handling plants or being bitten by an insect can also cause this reaction. Oral administration of antihistamines and cool baths are soothing until the lesions disappear. In severe cases, steroid medication and adrenalin injections may be necessary.

Scabies

Scabies is a highly contagious skin condition caused by a tiny invisible parasite, which burrows into the skin. It appears commonly on the exposed areas of the body, particularly around the wrists and ankles, as well as over the chest and abdomen. The intense itching associated with the presence of this parasite is an allergic reaction to the protein in the body of the organism. Because the body is reacting to this substance, the rash and discomfort may continue for several weeks after appropriate treatment has killed the parasites.

Conjunctivitis

Toddlers and preschool children with a predisposition to experience allergic reactions frequently suffer inflammation of the outer covering of the eye, known as conjunctivitis. The eyes appear red and puffy; itchiness is a prominent feature; and nasal irritation and discharge are often present.

This condition may be a reaction to a sudden increase in dust, pollens, or molds in the air or to direct contamination of the eye tissues with animal dander on the hands after a child has been in contact with a pet. Washing the eyes with a solution made by dissolving one-half teaspoon of salt in a cup of warm water is soothing and relieves the inflammation. Oral administration of antihistamic preparations is also helpful.

Asthma

Asthma is a chronic allergic reaction that takes the form of an episodic respiratory condition caused by the obstruction of the bronchial tubes (the small tubular structures of the lungs serving as passageway for inspired and expired air). Coughing, difficulty in breathing (particularly during expiration), and wheezing occurs due to a swelling of the lining of the passageways, the overproduction of mucous, and spasms of the muscles encircling the narrow tubular passages. Asthma is one of the leading chronic health problems in childhood.

An asthmatic attack may be brought about by a viral or bacterial infection or exposure to cigarette smoke, perfumes, dust, animal dander, chemicals, weeds, pollen, mold, or the ingestion of specific foods. Sudden atmospheric and temperature changes, as well as participation in exercise, can also bring on an asthmatic attack.

Usually a child begins with continuous coughing, followed by an increase in the rate of respiration. Audible wheezing, particularly on expiration, is apparent. The expiratory phase of breathing, which normally is shorter than the inspiratory phase, becomes prolonged. Parents and children can learn to recognize the early phase of asthma in which the expiration begins to be prolonged, often even before there is any coughing. Administration of appropriate medication at the outset frequently eliminates a severe episode and enables a child to continue normal activities in school and on the playing field.

There are a variety of medications for treating asthma: bronchial dilators such as theophylline, beta adrenergic drugs such as metaproterenol, steroids such as prednisone, and inhalants such as metaprotenol and Cromolyn. It is important to remember that whichever medication your doctor prescribes, the preparation should be administered at the first sign of a respiratory difficulty and continued for several days. In severe attacks, the repeated injection of epinephrin (adrenalin) may be necessary to relieve the discomfort.

Preventing the onset of an attack is advisable, so it is worth spending the time to determine what initiates your child's symptoms. You can then take steps to reduce the likelihood of an attack.

Exercise commonly precipitates an attack in some children. A few minutes of activity in a gymnasium or in a sports activity is followed by a tight feeling in the chest, and shortly, wheezing ensues. The oral administration of bronchial dilators or other medications prior to participating in the exercise program enables the child to engage in the activity without experiencing respiratory symptoms. For the child whose attacks are caused by exercise, it is wise to give the medication before he or she embarks on any marked exercise program.

Environmental controls are also important in treating an asthmatic child. Pollutants and other substances in the air commonly provoke an attack, and house dust, often containing a tiny insect known as the house dust mite, is a common factor. For this reason, removing curtains, rugs, rug pads, feather pillows, and easy chairs, if possible, can be helpful. Washing and cleaning drawers and closets with a damp cloth will also help reduce the amount of dust in a child's bedroom. Upholstered furniture, kapok-filled pillows, feather pillows, horse hair mattresses, and stuffed toys should be eliminated. Pets should not be permitted in the bedroom of a child who suffers wheezing.

For the family with an asthmatic child, radiant heat is the best kind, and the next best is steam or hot water. If hot air is the main method of heat in your house, the filters should be changed annually and the pipes cleaned. In some instances it is wise to shut off the heat and use a portable electric radiator when a child's sniffles, coughing, or skin rash is seriously discomforting. It can make a dramatic difference.

Plants, particularly those of the chrysanthemum variety,

and insect repellents containing pyrethium, commonly irritate the child's respiratory tract and initiate an asthmatic episode. A sudden increase in the mold concentration, hot, humid weather, particularly in homes with damp basements, is often a precipitating factor. An electric dehumidifier in the basement may be helpful. Electronic air filters, devices that reduce airborne dust and molds in a forced heating system, also offer relief.

Cigarette, cigar, and pipe smoke are irritating factors that should be eliminated completely from the home. Hairspray and face powder may also cause a problem, so the mother may want to use nonallergenic makeup and soaps.

The emergence of tree and grass pollens in the spring, of ragweed and mold in late summer, may often be responsible for the onset of watery eyes, sniffly nose, a cough, and at times, wheezing. Another common cause is the introduction of new rugs, particularly when mats of fiber animal hair are placed under the carpet. A new pet such as a cat, dog, guinea pig, or gerbil may also be causative factors.

There has been an increasing trend in recent years to insulate homes with a variety of substances blown into the walls. Although this may reduce the household heating bill, at times it seals the house so completely that it elevates the concentration of molds and other pollutants, thus providing additional substances that can cause discomfort.

An excellent book dealing with asthma is *Children with Asthma—A Manual for Parents* by Thomas F. Plaut, M.D., from Pedi Press, 125 Redgate Lane, Amherst, MA 01002.

22. What You Should Know about Fever

A parent frequently phones the doctor with the following complaint: "I don't know what's wrong with my two-year-old. She seemed hot, so I took her temperature and it is 102. She's a bit fretful, but otherwise, she seems fine. What should I do about this high temperature?"

You may be surprised to find that in all probability, your physician will have minimal interest in the child's temperature but may ask questions such as: "Is she playful or listless? Is she sneezing, coughing, or vomiting? Is she having any unusual bowel movements? Is she urinating more frequently than usual? Does she have a rash anywhere on her body?"

The answers to these questions provide important information enabling a doctor to focus on the child's basic illness. Fever in itself is not a disease! It is, however, one of the body's most powerful defenses against the invasion of disease-bearing viruses or bacteria. Fever comes about because pyrogens, fever-producing substances, appear in the blood and affect the temperature control center in the brain. Actually these substances raise "the set point" in a way that

196

is quite comparable to the way in which the house temperature is elevated if the thermostat is adjusted.

How To Take Your Child's Temperature

The method used for taking a child's temperature depends on the age of the youngster. Generally, a child must be four or five before he or she is capable of keeping a thermometer under the tongue for the appropriate length of time. For a younger child, taking it rectally produces a more accurate reading more quickly than taking the temperature under the arm.

Whichever method is used, be sure to shake down the thermometer with a few quick snaps of the wrist prior to beginning.

Rectal method: Dip the tip of a rectal thermometer in petroleum jelly for easier insertion. Place the baby across your lap or in the crib, backside up, and gently insert the thermometer about an inch into the rectum. Hold the thermometer between your fingers with the palm of your hand against the buttocks. The temperature will register within about a minute.

Under arm method: Using either an oral or rectal thermometer, place it under the child's arm and hold it there for a full four minutes. (If you use this method, be sure to tell the doctor when you report the degree of temperature. An under arm reading will register lower than a temperature taken orally or rectally.)

Oral method: Using an oral thermometer, slip it under the tongue and ask the child to keep his or her mouth tightly closed, with the thermometer in place, for two minutes.

Although your doctor will probably want to know the temperature reading, the important factor is the cause of the rise in temperature, not the fever itself. Some children with minimal illness will present a high temperature, while a very sick child will have only a degree or less of fever. Therefore, the degree of fever does not always indicate the seriousness of a child's illness. A youngster who has a high

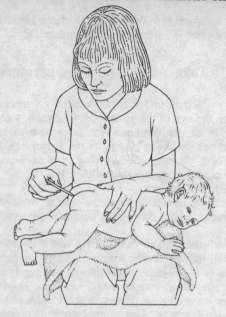

Taking temperature rectally

fever and is alert and playful is likely to be only mildly ill. On the other hand, a child with a moderate elevation of temperature who is listless and uninterested in the surroundings or in playing with other children may be seriously ill. And any child, particularly in the infancy and toddler years, who doesn't "look well" is a cause for concern regardless of body temperature.

It is the symptoms, not the degree of temperature elevation, that help a doctor decide whether your child needs to be examined immediately. If a child is happy and playful or just a bit fretful, the illness is probably mild and your doctor may be willing to wait a few days before seeing him or her. Some symptoms indicate a very specific problem; if so, the doctor will probably recommend an immediate visit. Sneezing, coughing, nasal discharge, and noisy

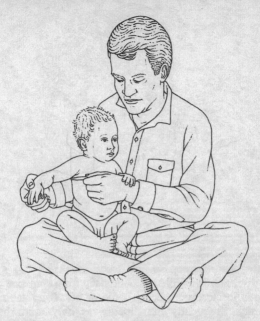

Taking temperature under the arm

breathing suggest the presence of an upper respiratory infection; persistent crying and rubbing an ear suggests an ear infection; vomiting, abdominal cramps, and diarrhea suggest gastroenteritis; increased frequency in urination with discomfort when voiding suggests that a child may be suffering from a bladder or kidney infection. Severe irritability, particularly in infancy and toddler years, unrelieved by cuddling, rocking, or feeding, should always be taken seriously. These symptoms suggest that a child may have a severe headache and may, indeed, be in the early phases of meningitis or encephalitis.

Do share with your doctor information concerning illness in other members of the immediate family or among your child's playmates or teachers at school. Fever elevation in a young child is usually an early sign of a viral or

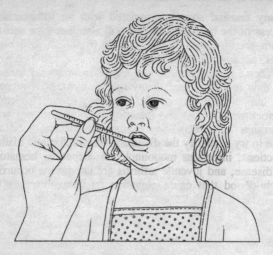

Taking the temperature orally

other disease that a child has contracted from someone who has been in close contact with him or her. If an adult has been sick, frequently the illness was only mild, but a young child who contracts the same infection is likely to be much sicker than the person from whom he or she caught the disease. In addition, infants, toddlers, and young children tend to run high temperatures more quickly with minor illnesses than do adolescents and adults.

Sometimes an elevation of body temperature is the only sign of illness for several days. Often, by the time the definitive signs of an upper respiratory infection, gastroenteritis, or other viral infection appear, the elevation of body temperature has begun to subside.

What does a doctor look for when examining a child with a fever? First, a doctor considers a child's general behavior. As discussed, irritability and inconsolability always suggest the need for close examination. During the exam, the doctor will look at the child's mouth, throat, and ears for inflammation in the respiratory tract or in the ears; he will look for enlarged lymph glands in the neck and elsewhere in the body, common signs of viral or bacterial infection. He will listen to the heart to rule out the presence of any unusual sounds associated with an inflammatory process of the heart muscle. He will also listen for unusual breath sounds in the chest, which would suggest bronchitis, pneumonia, or asthma.

When a child's temperature elevation continues for several days in the absence of any specific symptoms suggesting an upper respiratory infection, ear infection, gastroenteritis, or bladder infection, your doctor may want to arrange for a laboratory examination of the blood and urine to try to clarify the diagnosis. Asymptomatic bladder infections, infectious mononucleosis, hepatitis, hematologic disease, and juvenile arthritis are conditions occurring in childhood that cause elevation of temperature in the early phases with little or no other signs of illness.

Treating the Illness

The majority of infections in childhood are caused by viruses, and administration of antibiotics is useless. However, if a bacterial infection is present in the throat, ears, or lungs, antibiotics are indicated. When a child who suffers from what appears to be a viral illness suddenly experiences a temperature elevation, a complication such as ear infection or pneumonia may be present. In these instances the administration of antibiotics may be necessary.

Upper respiratory and gastrointestinal diseases predictably tend to last five to ten days and usually must be left to run their course. Aspirin and acetaminophen reduce an elevated temperature for the moment, but neither one shortens the disease process. These medications may provide relief from discomfort however, and they are effective for about four hours. After this length of time, a child's temperature can be expected to recur. This reappearance does not mean that a child is any sicker than he was before when the medication effectively began to lower the temperature. It is just that he is still sick and the aspirin or acetaminophen is no longer in the body and is not controlling the temperature.

You have probably heard of possible side effects from the use of aspirin and would like to know exactly what they are. Continued ingestion of aspirin may cause a child to experience irritation and bleeding of the lining of the gastrointestinal tract. Aspirin has also been associated with serious complications when given to a child with chickenpox or influenza. (see Reye's Syndrome in the **A to Z Guide** for more information). For this reason, many pediatricians recommend the administration of acetaminophen rather than aspirin for relieving the discomfort and controlling the temperature.

Parents sometimes ask if their child can have a bath while down with a fever. As a matter of fact, a lukewarm bath is one of the best things you can do. It relaxes aching muscles, is refreshing, and often lowers the temperature. Your doctor will probably suggest a bath as a very good way to reduce fever.

Must the child be kept in bed? There are no studies suggesting that bed rest reduces a child's temperature, shortens the length of an illness, or prevents complications. In most instances a child who is sick prefers to play quietly on her bed or on the sofa, doze, or watch television.

A child should rest at home until her temperature returns to normal and she is feeling up to playing with other children. However, this does not mean that a quick trip to the grocery store—even in cold weather—will do any harm. The best way to judge the proper activity level for your child is to put yourself in your child's shoes. If her sneezing is so annoying that dressing to go out is going to cause additional irritation, then try to stay home. However, if she has been home for a few days and is suffering from boredom, then heading out on a few errands—and for a change of scene—will probably be good for you both.

Seizures Associated with Fever

Occasionally an infant, toddler, or young child who suffers a sudden onset of fever from any cause may experience a convulsion, consisting of jerky movements of the extremities, stiffening of the body, and a one- or two-minute period of unconsciousness. The seizure, known as a febrile convulsion, is the result of the rapid elevation of body temperature. However, in some instances a seizure, particularly if it is prolonged, may mark the onset of a viral or bacterial infection of the central nervous system, or it may be a sign of underlying neurologic disease.

Febrile seizures usually occur under the age of three. There is often a family history of a father, mother, or sibling experiencing similar convulsions associated with fever in their own early years of life.

How does one differentiate between seizures due to a sudden onset of a high fever and the more serious convulsions associated with widespread infection or a neurologic disease? In general, if a child returns to normal activities a few minutes after a seizure, it suggests that there is no acute infection in the central nervous system. It is important, however, to discuss your child's condition and the seizure with your doctor—particularly if it is a first episode. The doctor will probably want to examine your child; she may also arrange for appropriate blood and other laboratory studies. A child who experiences seizures in the absence of fever, particularly if there is any suggestion of developmental delay, should have a careful medical examination and an electroencephalographic study. The administration of anticonvulsant medication may be necessary in this instance.

About one-third of the children who have one febrile seizure will have a subsequent one. Parents also worry that febrile seizures may lead to chronic, nonfebrile seizures, epilepsy, or abnormal neurologic or psychological development. This may happen in a small percentage of children who have febrile seizures. However, when this occurs it is not the febrile seizure that causes these long-term problems. The abnormality of a child's nervous system associated with delay or recurrent seizures in the absence of fever was present before the febrile convulsion occurred.

Some pediatricians recommend daily administration of phenobarbital or other anticonvulsants after a child suffers one febrile seizure, in the hopes of avoiding repeated convulsions. However, in recent years, pediatricians have noted significant toxic reactions, such as abnormal behaviors, sleep disturbances, slow development, and learning difficulties occurring with the prolonged administration of phenobarbital.

Most pediatricians suggest lukewarm baths and the prompt administration of aspirin or acetaminophen at the earliest signs of an illness for a child who has experienced febrile seizures in the past. They reserve the daily administration of anticonvulsant medication for those children with a strong family history of epilepsy, or evidence of neurologic deficit, or who suffer seizures in the absence of fever

23. How to Tell If Your Child Is Sick or Very Sick

Whenever your child is out of sorts—feverish, irritable, and showing a decreased interest in usual activities—you will probably call your doctor, hoping for some definitive diagnosis and suggestions for treatment.

What your doctor will need is an accurate report on the symptoms of the illness (cough? nasal congestion? vomiting? diarrhea? abdominal pain?) as well as information on your child's general behavior. Is she playing normally despite the fever, or is she irritable and uninterested in her surroundings? This information will help your doctor decide whether your child is suffering a mild upper respiratory or gastrointestinal illness with a predictable course, or whether the symptoms and temperature elevation represent the initial phase of a serious illness.

Most parents express great alarm if their child is running a significant fever, but, as discussed in Chapter 22, fever is not a disease. It is one of the body's important defenses against the invasion of disease-bearing organisms. It is the *reason* for the fever that is important, not the fever itself.

The majority of illnesses in infancy and childhood are

viral infections. (Many viral illnesses causing serious illness in times past, such as polio, mumps, measles, and German measles, are now rarely experienced in the United States because of widespread immunizations.) The distinction between whether a disease is caused by a virus or other organism is important, because antibiotics have no effect on the course of viral infections, but frequently do alter the course of infections due to bacteria.

One concern with any illness accompanied by vomiting and diarrhea is that it can cause dehydration in the infant or child due to lack of fluid intake. If fluid is markedly reduced or the vomiting or diarrhea is excessive, you may observe that the urinary output is reduced. (The child is rarely urinating or needs less than the usual number of diaper changes. The need for less than four or five diapers a day indicates dehydration in a small infant.) This is an important observation to report to your doctor. Offering ice chips, or small amounts of breast milk, diluted formula mixtures, or fruit juices may resolve the difficulty, but your doctor will tell you exactly how to proceed.

The following information on a wide range of illnesses should be helpful. The material is organized according to the predominant symptoms to help you more quickly identify an illness, whether or not you are familiar with it. This is by no means a definitive listing of all possible illnesses, but these are some of the more common ones that people worry about. Of course, your doctor should be consulted for an accurate diagnosis and appropriate treatment.

Respiratory and Viral Illnesses

Slight Fever, Sniffles, Cough, Watery Eyes

Respiratory infections due to many different viruses commonly occur in infancy and childhood. Usually, an initial rise in body temperature is followed a day or two later by the appearance of sniffles, cough, watery eyes, and irritability. This phase usually lasts a few days, followed by a convalescent period of a week or so, during which a child continues to cough but manifests little disturbance of normal activities.

These same symptoms may, however, also represent the beginning of a more serious illness, such as ear infection, bronchitis and similar inflammations, pneumonia, croup, or epiglottitis (all discussed later). A baby or child who incurs moderate elevation of temperature and minimal signs of illness for several days and then suddenly demonstrates a marked elevation of fever, ranging up to 103 to 104 degrees Farenheit, is likely to be suffering more than a mild upper respiratory infection.

Moderate Respiratory Illness with Marked Temperature Elevation, Ear Rubbing, or Persistent Pain

Frequent cries of pain or rubbing of the ear with a fist suggests *otitis media*, an infection of the middle ear. (A child who suffers an ear infection during the first year of life is likely to have repeated ear infections with subsequent upper respiratory illnesses.) A toddler or older child often indicates that he has an inner ear infection by pointing to his ear or saying "ear hurt." An ear infection deserves prompt medical attention.

Infections in the middle ear may cause perforation of the eardrum with the result that material drains into the external ear canal. The release of this accumulated fluid relieves a child's discomfort. He may appear quite well at this time; however, a child with a draining ear should receive a course of antibiotic therapy to preclude developing a chronic infection, which can lead to permanent hearing loss or other serious problems. When your child suffers an ear infection of this nature, your doctor will prescribe appropriate antibiotic therapy. He will also ask to examine your child in a few weeks to ensure that the eardrum has healed. Ear infections, if untreated, may lead to a reduction of a child's auditory capacities, which can interfere seriously with the development of language and other psychological skills. (Also see Ear Infections in the **A to Z Guide.**)

Moderate Respiratory Illness with Marked Temperature Elevation, Persistent Hoarseness, Cough

Often, an upper respiratory infection extends from the nose and throat into the lower areas of the respiratory system. *Tracheitis* (inflammation of the windpipe) and *bronchitis* (inflammation in the passageways to the inner aspect of the lungs) are common. The inflammation may be mild and manifest itself only by hoarseness and cough, or it may present a serious obstruction to the passage of air through the respiratory passages. Your child's temperature will likely continue for several days, and coughing may be severe. With both of these symptoms, your doctor will want to examine your child to look at the throat and listen to the chest. (Also see Bronchitis in the **A to Z Guide**.)

Moderate Respiratory Illness with Temperature Elevation, Increased Respiratory Rate, Labored Breathing

Bronchiolitis (an inflammation in the tiny air-carrying tubules deep in the interior of the lungs) is a common illness in infancy and the toddler years. The respiratory rate increases from a normal of 40 a minute to 60–90 per minute, sometimes even higher. Breath sounds are audible across the room; the expiratory phase of respiration is prolonged. The entire chest may heave and the nostrils dilate with each breath. Accumulation of mucoid material in the inner passages becomes thick and tenacious, thus further obstructing the passage of air. A vaporizer in the child's bedroom is very helpful in relieving congestion. Interference with the air exchange can be so extensive that hospitalization for administration of mist therapy and oxygen and intravenous medication may be necessary.

Moderate Respiratory Illness with Fever, Listlessness, Intense Cough, Increased Respiratory Rate

An infection in the nose and throat may spread to one or more lobes of the lung and cause *pneumonia*. When an infant or young child has had the sniffles and a cough for days and then suddenly becomes feverish and listless, with a more intense cough and an increase in respiratory rate, you should discuss with your doctor the possibility that your child may be developing pneumonia. Grunting respirations accompanied by dilation of the nostrils with each breath are also common signs of pneumonia in infancy.

High Fever, Bodily Discomfort, Sore Throat Caused by Lesions

Several other illnesses that begin with fever, discomfort, and sore throat are more debilitating than the usual viral upper respiratory infection. A common viral infection occurring in young children is *herpetic stomatitis*, characterized by a high fever initially, followed in a few days by the appearance of multiple blistery lesions on the throat, tongue, and gums. A child is often miserable due to pain in the mouth and throat. The breath is often foul smelling. Fever elevation and general discomfort continue for several days. The mouth lesions interfere with the intake of fluid, and dehydration, due to the reduced intake, is common. Pieces of chipped ice, ice cream, jello, fruit juices, and carbonated beverages, which are fluids that children will usually take, will help combat the dehydration.

High Fever, Headache, Irritability, Sore Throat

Another common viral infection, *herpetic pharyngitis* (a type of sore throat), produces small red areas, particularly in the back of the pharynx and in the tonsil area. Initially the disease presents with general discomfort, high fever, and headache. Nausea, cramps, and diarrhea often follow. The disease lasts three or four days and then clears spontaneously.

Very Sore Throat, Swollen Glands, Vomiting

Tonsillitis or *pharyngitis* due to the streptococcus (*strep throat*) is common in toddler and preschool years. The throat is quite inflamed and painful; the lymph glands in the neck and elsewhere in the body may be enlarged. Young children may, at the onset, suffer vomiting and abdominal discomfort. A scarlet rash with a fine sandpaperlike appearance may be present. This combination of symptoms is known as *scarlet fever*. Bacteriologic studies of material obtained by swabbing the throat reveal the presence of the Beta hemolytic streptococcus. Whenever your child suffers a sore throat due to a streptococcus, your doctor will prescribe appropriate antibiotic treatment for a tenday period. (Also see Streptococcal Sore Throat in the **A to Z Guide.**)

Barking Cough, Hoarseness, Crowing Sound

Croup, which manifests itself by a barking cough, hoarseness, and a crowing sound with intake of breath, is due to swelling or inflammation of the laryngeal tissues. It is common in infants and toddlers and usually occurs in the fall. The mild form, known as *spasmodic croup*, is due to swelling of the vocal cords in response to a viral infection. Dramatic improvement usually occurs when a croupy child is placed in a room with steam or cool mist. One way to achieve this is to sit with a child in the bathroom with a hot shower running; another way is to boil pots of water on the stove in the kitchen; or place several vaporizers or cool steam humidifiers in your child's bedroom.

A child suffering spasmodic croup should improve after thirty minutes of exposure to steam or mist. If your child fails to improve after sitting in a steam-filled bathroom or near a vaporizer, he may be experiencing a more serious condition, either acute laryngo tracheobronchitis (see below) or an acute bacterial infection. (If that is the case, call your doctor. If your physician is unavailable, take your child to the nearest hospital emergency room immediately.)

If the barking cough, hoarseness, and crowing sound when breathing do not clear up after thirty minutes exposure to mist, your child may have laryngo tracheobronchitis, a viral infection that attacks the larynx, trachea, and deeper areas of the lung. As the disease spreads, thick mucous clogs the air passages, causing respiratory difficulty, hoarseness, and cough. Steam or cool mist and an increase in fluid intake are important ways of treating this condition. But if the inflammation continues and mucous obstructs the air exchange in the lungs, hospitalization may be necessary. (Also see Croup in the **A to Z Guide**.)

Sore Throat, Difficulty Breathing, Drooling, Fever

Epiglottitis, occurring between the ages of three months and three years, also produces respiratory obstruction due to inflammation of the epiglottis, the cartilage located at the base of the tongue. Hemophilus influenzae, type B is the usual cause of this condition; thus, the disease is often known as "flu B-croup."

An infection caused by this organism can have an explosive rate of development. A baby or child may awaken with a sore throat and moderate difficulty breathing. In only a few hours, he may be critically ill. He drools constantly because of the pain experienced when swallowing even minute amounts of saliva. There is usually an elevation of temperature. A common sign of epiglottitis is a plaintive facial expression. A baby frequently sits leaning forward with his hands to the side, extending the neck slightly to allow as much space for the passage of air as possible. Early treatment is imperative. Again, whenever your child's croup is unrelieved within a half hour of being exposed to steam, you should contact your physician immediately. If you cannot reach your doctor, you should take your child to the nearest hospital emergency room as soon as possible. Appropriate antibiotics administered intravenously can be life-saving.

Sore Throat, General Weakness, Fever

Infectious mononucleosis, a viral infection, also causes sore throat and fever. This condition, commonly seen in adolescents, may also occur in young children. Headache and sleepiness, general weakness, and tender enlargement of the lymph nodes in the neck are the most common symptoms. The spleen is usually enlarged sufficiently to be palpable in the left upper abdomen. An elevation of the number of white blood cells occurs in the blood, with an increase in a specific type of lymphocyte; a specific blood test substantiates the diagnosis. This disease lasts a few weeks and is usually mild in young children. No specific treatment exists for mononucleosis. The period of convalescence may be prolonged for several weeks. (Also see Infectious Mononucleosis in the **A to Z Guide.**)

Breathing Obstruction, Wheezing, Difficulty Swallowing

Episodic or recurrent bronchial obstruction, wheezing, and difficulty in swallowing associated with respiratory symptoms may represent an allergic reaction such as *asthma*. It is difficult in the toddler and preschool years to distinguish whether a child's coughing and wheezing are due to an allergic reaction or an infection. Both factors are often important. Oral administration of bronchial dilators reduces the congestion and wheezing to a tolerable level. When the respiratory symptoms continue in the absence of an infection and interfere with normal play activity, careful history and examination usually suggest that sensitivities to pollens, mold, dust, pets, or specific foods are the cause of the symptoms. (Also see Asthma in **Chapter 21, Allergies.**)

Runny Nose, Choking Cough, Body Aches, Headache

Sinusitis (an inflammatory process in the small air spaces adjacent to and below the eyes) may occur, particularly in older children. It is difficult to distinguish between a severe infection of the nose and throat and one that extends into the sinuses. When there is swelling of the nasal tissues, due either to allergy or infection, drainage from the sinuses is impeded and a low-grade inflammatory infection may be under way. Symptoms of sinusitis are a choking cough, purulent (containing pus) nasal discharge, achiness, and headache. Antibiotics and decongestants usually im-

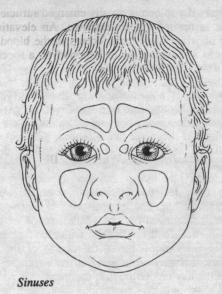

Sinuses

prove the condition markedly. (Also see Sinusitis in the **A to Z Guide.**)

Tenderness of Area under the Eye

A critical infection in the ethmoid sinus, located under the eye, sometimes occurs due to invasion of the Hemophilus influenzae, type B. You should contact your physician immediately if your child presents tenderness or discoloration of the skin in that area.

Tenderness in the Cheek Area

Cellulitis, or inflammation in the cheek, is another serious infection in toddlers and preschool children produced by the Hemophilus influenzae, type B organism. It can quickly become a critical illness, so contact your physician immediately if you note the appearance of a tender mass in the cheek associated with achiness and fever.

Slight Fever, Headache, Skin Rash

Chickenpox is a common viral disease in childhood, usually mild, characterized by slight fever, headache, and a generalized skin rash consisting of inflamed elevated lesions, which at first look like mosquito bites but soon develop blisters and contain small amounts of fluid. The lesions usually start around the neck at the hairline, behind the ears, and on the thorax, but soon appear over the entire body. At times, lesions in the mouth or genital area can be very uncomfortable. The main discomfort is due to itching, which can be relieved by oral administration of antihistamines and starch baths. Children with chickenpox tend to experience nightmares during the course of the disease. Commonly, this may occur early in the infection, in many instances the day before the rash appears.

The disease is highly contagious from the first signs of illness and for approximately one week. A child who has not had chickenpox may be expected to contract it within fourteen to sixteen days after exposure to an individual with the disease. One episode conveys lifelong immunity to this form of the disease. However, the virus often lies latent in the spinal cord, and many years later becomes activated, producing a condition known as shingles, which is characterized by painful red inflammation and blisters in a bandlike lesion extending from the back to the side and midline. These lesions may contain the virus and cause individuals who have not had the disease to contract it.

There is no reason why a child with chickenpox should remain in bed or limit her activity. However, she is contagious during the active form of the disease.

Rarely, a child who is experiencing chickenpox may develop dizziness and become cumbersome and awkward due to the involvement of the central nervous system. This condition, encephalitis, usually resolves within a few weeks with no residual effects, although in rare instances it can be a serious disease.

Many children are extremely sensitive about the appearance of their skin. If your child reacts in this way, you might suggest that he or she wear long sleeves until the lesions go away. Some children even prefer to wear gloves.

High Temperature with Pink Rash Several Days Later

Roseola is a common mild viral infection occurring in children under three. Characteristically, a child experiences a high temperature, often 104 or 105 degrees, for several days with no other signs of illness. Examination is completely normal other than the elevation of body temperature. Suddenly the temperature returns to normal, and a few hours later a faint, slightly elevated pink rash appears on the chest and abdomen and may spread over the entire body. The rash disappears within twenty-four hours.

The sudden onset of the elevation of body temperature associated with this disease is a common cause of seizures in a child who has a tendency to convulse when experiencing sudden temperature elevation.

Vomiting and Lethargy on Fourth or Fifth Day of Viral Illness

Reye's Syndrome is a rare complication of chickenpox and other viral infections. It manifests itself by intense vomiting, irritability, and lethargy. Seizures may occur. A child may be difficult to arouse. The cause of this condition is unknown. If your child is suffering from chickenpox or any other viral infection and on the fourth or fifth day suddenly demonstrates any of these symptoms, contact your doctor immediately. Early treatment is important. If you cannot reach your physician, take your child to the nearest hospital emergency room.

Some doctors believe that the administration of aspirin increases the likelihood of a child with chickenpox or influenzae to experience this complication. Pediatricians, therefore, now recommend the use of acetaminophen instead of aspirin for symptomatic relief during a viral infection.

Gastrointestinal Illnesses

Vomiting and Diarrhea

Vomiting is often the initial sign of any illness in babies, toddlers, or young children. The vomiting may represent the onset of an upper respiratory infection or gastroenteritis due to a virus or bacteria. A child feels nauseated and dizzy, as if she were seasick or airsick. Cramps and diarrhea usually follow this initial phase in a day or two. There may be a passage of five to ten watery bowel movements a day for four or five days.

Treatment of *diarrhea* consists of reducing the intake of solids and making certain that fluid intake is maintained. Breast milk, diluted formula, gelatin desserts, and diluted fruit juices are fluids usually tolerated by infants and toddlers. After twenty-four to forty-eight hours, the number of bowel movements usually diminishes, and you may then gradually reinstitute a regular diet. If the diarrhea persists, it is important to discuss this with your physician. Weight loss, decrease in skin elasticity, reduction in urinary output, disinterest in the environment, or blood in the stool suggests that a baby may be critically ill. Hospitalization for intravenous administration of fluids may be necessary.

When diarrhea is prolonged, your baby may be suffering from a condition other than an infection. Allergy to milk, sensitivity to wheat products, and difficulty in digesting lactose (the sugar in milk) are the common conditions in infants and children that produce diarrhea. Quite frequently an acute viral infection can bring out symptoms of metabolic or digestive problems that were asymptomatic before the illness.

Irritation of the skin in the diaper area is common when a baby has persistent diarrhea. Exposing the baby's body to the air and applying generous amounts of soothing cream help to minimize the skin inflammation.

Continuous Abdominal Pain with Nausea and Vomiting

Appendicitis, an inflammatory process in the small appendage of the large intestine, is rare but does occur in childhood. Continuous abdominal pain and tenderness, particularly if it starts in the middle and moves to the right lower area of the abdomen and is associated with nausea and vomiting, may signal the onset of this disease. Characteristically, a child who experiences appendicitis is unwilling to move about. If you suspect appendicitis, you should contact your physician immediately. (Also see Appendicitis in the **A to Z Guide**.)

Severe Vomiting, Intestinal Cramps

Intussusception is a gastrointestinal condition that occurs in infancy and childhood. In this illness, the intestine telescopes on itself, causing severe episodic pain due to bowel obstruction. Severe vomiting and intestinal cramps are present. A child with this condition experiences intense spasms for a few minutes and then may have five to eight minutes of relief, only to have the spasms start over again. Pallor, sweating, and passage of bloody stools looking like currant jelly are common. Careful examination and an X ray of the lower intestinal tract are important. Frequently, the injection of barium into the colon through the rectum while taking the X ray reduces the intussusception. If this does not happen, surgical intervention is necessary.

Vomiting, Irritability, Lethargy, Stiff Neck

Meningitis is an infection due to a disease-producing bacteria or virus in the tissues entering the brain area. Bacteria such as pneumococci, Hemophilus influenzae, type B, and meningicoccus can produce this condition. Irritability, lethargy, and vomiting are the cardinal signs of meningitis. In infancy, the bulging of the soft spot at the top of the head may be noted. This reflects an increase in the intracranial pressure due to the inflammatory process inside of the head. A stiff neck, in which the infant or child resists flexing, is common. Meningicoccal infection is frequently accompanied by a generalized patchy or blotchy rash.

If you suspect meningitis, contact your doctor immediately, or take your child to the nearest hospital emergency room. Immediate hospitalization is indicated. Diagnosis is confirmed by examination of a few drops of cerebral spinal fluid obtained by inserting a tiny needle into the spinal canal. The presence of abnormal cells, alterations in the protein and sugar content in the cerebral spinal fluid, and bacteriological studies provide information that helps to determine the exact cause of the illness. Intravenous administration of antibiotics is the appropriate treatment for bacterial meningitis. The earlier the treatment is administered, the less chance of residual damage.

A virus infection such as one caused by chickenpox or mumps or a number of other viruses may also produce meningeal irritation and meningitis.

Other Childhood Problems

Short Period of Unconsciousness with Body Stiffness

Many infants and young children suffer a *febrile seizure* (a seizure associated with fever), that is, a short period of unconsciousness associated with stiffness of the body and jerking movements of one or more extremities. This occurs in many infants and children as the result of sudden elevation of body temperature. The eyes usually roll upward, the jaw becomes clenched, the extremities may jerk rhythmically, and the breathing is unusually heavy. The episode lasts for three to five minutes. Quite frequently, a parent of a child suffering a febrile seizure remembers being told that he or she, too, had seizures in childhood with sudden elevations of temperature.

Sponging a child with cool water reduces the fever, and the seizure usually ceases. Within a short period, a child who has suffered a febrile seizure becomes alert and resumes normal activities, as if nothing had taken place. A child who suffers a seizure in association with a sudden elevation of body temperature in the absence of widespread infection may experience similar episodes with subsequent illnesses.

Although the episodes are frightening and disturbing to witness, it is rare for a child to suffer any residual problems. The risk of repeated seizures with the onset of fever can be minimized by the continual oral administration of phenobarbital. Many pediatricians, however, hesitate to recommend the continuous use of this drug because of side effects that may interfere with normal development and activity. Instead, the oral administration of aspirin or acetaminophen to control the elevation of fever during an illness may be recommended.

How can one distinguish between a seizure due to fever caused by a mild illness, and a seizure that might indicate a serious infection or a chronic neurologic condition?

First of all, if a child recuperates within a few minutes and returns to normal play as if nothing happened, it suggests that the convulsion is a reaction to the sudden elevation of body temperature. However, consultation with your child's doctor is important.

When a seizure lasts ten to fifteen minutes or longer, prompt examination is important. The seizure may be part of a response to a critical, generalized infection due to a widespread invasion of a virus or bacteria. The examination of spinal fluid obtained by a lumbar puncture of the spinal canal helps the doctor to decide whether there is a viral or bacterial infection. When examination of the spinal fluid indicates the presence of bacteria, hospitalization for further studies and intravenous administration of antibiotics are necessary.

When a child who has a history of febrile seizures demonstrates learning difficulties, cerebral palsy, or other neurologic deficits or handicaps at a later time, these deficits are generally assumed to have been present before the seizures occurred. There is no evidence to suggest that the seizures themselves cause any of these problems.

Unexplained Fever

During toddler and preschool years, unexplained fever often occurs with few or no observable symptoms. In girls this is frequently the result of an infection in the bladder or other parts of the kidney system. Although urinary tract infections do occur in boys, they are far more common in girls. Sometimes a child with a urinary tract infection will void more often than usual and will complain of pain during urination. A child who has been dry at night may suddenly experience accidents.

Examination of a urine specimen or culture provides laboratory confirmation of an infection in the urinary tract. It is important that such infections be treated with appropriate medications, and a repeat urine examination be done following a course of treatment. If infections occur repeatedly, your physician may order X ray studies to rule out any anatomical abnormality that might interfere with the flow of urine and cause repeated infections.

Protrusion in Groin Area, Severe Pain

An inguinal hernia (a protrusion of tissue from inside the body through the abdominal wall into the inguinal canal in the groin) commonly occurs in infants and young children. Normally, this passageway, extending from the intra-abdominal space, is obliterated in fetal life or early in infancy. If it is not, a hernia sac, a space extending from the abdominal cavity into the muscular layers of the abdominal wall, remains. This space may exist for years with no discomfort. But if a loop of intestine, or in the case of girls a loop of intestine and/or an ovary, slides into this space, swelling and intense pain occur. Nausea and vomiting are common.

The discomfort disappears when the loop or intestine or ovary is manipulated back into normal position in the abdominal cavity. Nevertheless, once herniation has occurred, repeated episodes can be expected. Elective surgical repair is wise. (Also see Hernia, Inguinal, and Hernia, Umbilical, in the **A to Z Guide**.)

Convalescence

Whenever your physician suggests that you administer medication for a prescribed number of days, it is important to continue as he or she suggests, even though your child may seem markedly improved after a few days of treatment. If the full course of medicine is not given, the infection may recur.

Parents often wonder about the need for bed rest. Most infants, toddlers, and children will naturally decrease their activities when they are sick. There is no evidence to suggest that bed rest speeds up recovery. However, when a child is recuperating, it is wise to reduce his opportunity for very active play until he regains his strength.

Do remember that when adults are sick, we tend to reduce our food intake and often ingest unusual amounts of fluids, such as tea, fruit juice, and soup. Unfortunately, when babies, toddlers, and children limit their intake to milk and juices, adults seem to forget that this is a reasonable decision and they want to force children to eat more substantial food. Rest assured that although it may take several days or even a week following the acute phase of an illness before a child regains his usual appetite, in due time he will do so.

During convalescence, a short period of walking or playing out-of-doors, particularly in the warmer parts of the day, is certainly beneficial.

24. If Your Child Needs Hospitalization

No one likes to think about it, but there is a good possibility that at some time your child may need to be hospitalized for treatment of an illness, or an injury, or even for surgery. Although this experience is unsettling, there are many ways you can support your child during this time.

First, it's important to consider the situation from a child's point of view. Hospitals are big and overwhelming institutions. Sleeping arrangements are far different from a child's usual surroundings. He's not in his own bed with his sister in the next room and Mommy and Daddy just down the hall; in fact, none of the surroundings are familiar. What's more, medical treatment inevitably involves some pain and discomfort. If surgery is necessary, a child is wheeled to an unknown distant part of the hospital and put to sleep. He awakens in a strange recovery room, often tied down and experiencing pain. He is taken care of by individuals who are strange to him and who more often than not are dressed in what appear to be odd costumes.

No matter how kind and dedicated the nurses, physicians, and other hospital personnel may be, a child often considers the experience to be punishment for an unknown indiscretion. Indeed, a hospitalized child will often say to a parent, "Take me home. I'll be good."

Advance Preparations

Assuming that your child has not been admitted under emergency circumstances, there are several things you can do in advance to make the hospital experience less traumatic. To begin, try to find a hospital where you can "live in" with your child. A parent's presence offers a baby, toddler, or young child ongoing support and comfort during the inevitable stresses that will take place. Often, the absence of the parent is far more devastating than anything else happening during this period. A child can only think that he has been deserted and left in a strange place where people do all types of mean things to her. As one child said to a parent who visited the day after admission, "I thought you didn't want me anymore."

Since 1971, the American Academy of Pediatrics Committee on Hospital Care has been recommending that hospitals provide living-in arrangements for parents of infants and preschoolers who must be hospitalized. These arrangements not only ease the stress of the stay itself, but can significantly reduce the time it takes for a child to put the hospital stay behind her. If your hospital does not provide for living in, ask your physician to try to arrange makeshift plans for you to stay. It is helpful, of course, when hospitals provide a rollaway bed or couch for a parent to sleep on, but if they don't, it is perfectly possible to work out alternatives, such as bringing in your own folding lounge chair to sleep on.

Whenever possible, a child, even as young as two and a half, should be prepared for the experience. The better prepared she is, the easier it will be to cope with the inevitable stresses of being in the hospital. Explain to your child in simple terms the reason for the hospitalization. You might say, "Your tonsils, the little tissues on either side of your throat, cause you to have lots of sore throats. Your doctor wants to have one of his doctor friends, a surgeon, remove your tonsils so you won't be sick so often." Or, "That painful swelling you have is a hernia. It needs to be fixed." Or, "The muscle that moves your eye needs fixing so that you will be able to see better. You will have to be in the hospital a few days." If surgery is to be performed, you should explain that she will be given some medicine to smell that will help her go to sleep, and she will feel no pain. You should also tell her that you will see her soon after she wakes up from the operation.

At the next appointment, your child's pediatrician should go over the same information. If the child has known the doctor since birth, she will have developed considerable trust and confidence in this person, and it will give the child an additional opportunity to absorb what is going to happen to her.

Some parents decide to "protect" a child by not sharing with him the plans for surgery and hospitalization. This is not a good idea. A child inevitably overhears conversations between the doctor and parent or among adults in his family. He surmises something is being planned for him. If this information is not shared with him completely, his imagination runs wild. He may think that whatever is going to happen to him is so awful that even his own doctor and his parents are unable to tell him about it!

Reading books about hospital stays can provide helpful facts and information. It should also stimulate a child to ask questions, which will allow you to better address his concerns. Four well-known books that might be helpful are: *Curious George Goes to the Hospital* by Margaret and H.A. Rey (Houghton Mifflin, 1966); *Madeline* by Ludwig Bemelmans (Viking Press, 1939); *What Happens When You Go to the Hospital* by Arthur Shea (Riley and Lee, 1969); and *A Hospital Story* by Sara Bonnett Stein (Walker, 1974).

Some parents have difficulty with conversations concerning the hospital because of poor experiences they had as children. However, it is important to prepare a child. She needs to be able to talk freely and know that you, the person she trusts most in the world, understand her fears and are trying to help her cope with these stressful events.

As you prepare your child for a trip to the hospital,

provide him with a small suitcase and encourage him to pack a few personal items he wishes to take with him. A favorite doll, a teddy bear, a few other toys, and paper and crayons for drawing serve as "bridges from home." In addition, young children should take their own bathrobes and slippers, which are far more comfortable than hospital garb!

Many children's units provide an opportunity for a child to have a preliminary tour of the children's ward in order to become familiar with the setting. A nurse, secretary, or another child often serves as guide. As you tour the children's ward with your youngster, be sure to show him the playroom and the beds in the rooms where a parent can sleep (if living-in arrangements are provided). Talk to your child about what you see and encourage him to share with you any questions he might have.

The Hospital Stay

At the time of admission to the hospital, be sure to acquaint the nurses with the important facts about your child, such as the name she prefers, particularly if it is different from her name on the hospital record, foods she likes, habits, and special interests, and the terms she uses for urination and bowel movements. Many hospitals have a special form on a child's chart to record this information so that any nurse on any shift can be familiar with a child's personal preferences before she even enters the room.

Make an effort to learn as much as you can about what will happen to your child. Ask the nurses or doctors about specific details of procedures and then explain to your child what will take place. Knowing what to expect helps the child tolerate painful or complicated procedures. Don't say "it won't hurt" when it will! Rather, you can say, "It's going to hurt some. The doctor will be finished in just a few minutes."

Painful procedures arouse fears in a child that he will suffer attacks on other parts of his body. These common fears, stemming from relatively minor experiences, may be more disruptive to your child than the actual illness.

But despite all you do, your child is bound to be upset. He may be frightened, scared, or just plain angry. This is to be expected and is perfectly normal. The most helpful thing you can do is to be there to support him during his anxious, frightened, and angry moments. No doubt about it—hospitalization is an unsettling experience!

Whenever possible, feed, bathe, and care for your child yourself during this time. Just as an adult would, a child resents it when a stranger dresses, undresses, cleans, washes, and helps him with urination and defecation and administers to him in other personal ways. It is a mistake to assume, as many do, that "he's only a child and doesn't know the difference." These indignities are just as upsetting to a child as to an adult.

Not only does it make your child feel much more secure and comfortable when you care for him, but it will also offer you satisfaction, because you are providing for his basic needs. And don't feel that if your child demands extra attention he is being spoiled. Not at all! Hospitalization, particularly when surgery is involved, is indeed a stressful experience for a young child. Remember that a child who undergoes surgery, whether minimal or major, is bound to feel that his body has been attacked and mutilated. He needs every bit of loving support a parent can provide at this difficult time.

Must you remain at the hospital continuously throughout the stay? No, not necessarily so. Once a baby or young child is settled in and feeling better, a parent will be better able to come and go. However, try always to be there overnight. Nights are difficult and lonely for a young child in a large institution where a nurse may be caring for many children simultaneously.

Remember, too, that a child has little sense of time. When you do leave, tell your child that you will be back for lunch or for supper or at bedtime, rather than "in a few hours." Leave your scarf, a pocketbook, a sweater, or some other familiar item in your child's room, which will serve as a reminder that you will be returning.

The Recovery Period

When your child comes home, you may be surprised at how long it takes her to return to her previous level of behavior. The illness itself is likely to produce discomforting symptoms that frighten a child and interfere with her ability to move about and participate in play. Weakness as a result of the disease or a stay in bed limits her physical activity. Being away from home and the normal routine, and perhaps missing a sibling or the family pet add additional strain during this time.

These various stressful events are exhausting and may cause a child to revert to many infantile and immature levels of functioning. When she returns home she may be irritable, clinging to her parents whenever they are in sight. She may suffer crying spells, temper tantrums, have difficulty in falling asleep, and experience nightmares during the night. A three-year-old may begin to suck her thumb and carry around a favorite blanket or toy as she did when she was two. A child who has achieved bowel and bladder training may suffer a relapse and return to soiling habits previously abandoned. (Although these symptoms almost always occur to some degree, they are far less intense in children whose parents have been able to remain with them in the hospital.)

This period of convalescence is quite normal. It may take a child several weeks or longer to be able to return to normal behavior after being hospitalized. Do have patience!

Helping your child discharge some of his feelings about the experience can be extremely helpful in speeding the recovery. Encourage a preschool child to talk about his experiences, draw pictures or play with dolls, and portray his hospital experience. A child will usually play for hours, acting out repeatedly what happened in the hospital. This will gradually reduce the intensity of a child's reaction to what took place.

And do remember, if a child is belligerent or mischievous or seems to be impossible to please, it is not a question of being bad. He is working off some of his feelings.

Reading books, possibly the same books you read before the child was hospitalized, usually stimulates a child to discuss in greater detail his memory and feelings of what happened. This is another way of helping to reduce the psychological and physical tensions that are inevitable reactions to the stresses of hospitalization.

When a youngster must be hospitalized, it's a difficult time for the entire family. However, the more attention you can give to his fears and concerns, the more rapidly he'll recover from the experience.

25. Chronic Illness

All parents anticipate that their child will grow up to be a healthy adult. Unfortunately, this dream may be altered when a child suffers a handicapping condition or a long-term illness. Common conditions that limit a child's activities include Down's Syndrome, cerebral palsy, hemophilia, congenital heart disease, cystic fibrosis, malignant conditions, deafness, blindness, rheumatoid arthritis, autism, spina bifida, and the difficulties of limited intellectual capacity.

It is always a shock when a doctor confirms a parent's suspicion that a child is suffering from a chronic and serious condition. The first response is likely to be, "It must be a mistake. It can't be. Are you certain?" You will need time to think about what your doctor has told you, and you will want to arrange repeated conferences to discuss in detail your child's needs.

A conference with a social worker who has experience with childhood illnesses is often helpful. Many parents who have a child suffering from a handicapping illness find it helpful to join a support group consisting of parents of children with a similar illness. (Ask your pediatrician about any such groups, or contact the local hospital.) These groups provide opportunity for parents to share mutual successes, failures, and frustrations in caring for a sick child. You will also find that by banding together you can become a member of an effective pressure group working for the improvement of education and health services for handicapped children.

Although specific information concerning what to expect of the particular illness that afflicts your child will best be obtained from your doctor or support group or by reading books and articles on that specific topic, there are two subjects to be touched on here. The first concerns the right of every handicapped child to an education; and the second concerns the importance of helping other children in the family cope with the existence of the illness.

Educational Programs for the Handicapped

The Education for All Handicapped Children's Act (Public Law 94–142), passed by Congress on November 29, 1975, requires each state "to have in effect a policy that assures all handicapped children the right to a free and appropriate public education" in the "least restrictive alternative possible." It is a great boon for handicapped children. As a result, opportunities now exist in all communities in the United States for disabled youngsters to attend a regular school program, or if not, to be enrolled in a special educational program until the age of twenty-one. Many children who in the past received only an hour or less of homebound teaching each day are now attending school. The passage of this law represents a tremendous step forward and reflects the growing acceptance since the 1970s of the idea that government should have some responsibility for citizens who are dependent or handicapped.

When a child participates in an educational program for the handicapped, the parents will usually find a dedicated staff of administrators, teachers, nurses, consulting physicians, social workers, hearing and speech therapists, and occupational and physical therapists who believe that many handicapped children can achieve higher levels of performance than is often realized.

These programs bring together the parents and the school personnel in the daily program and in evaluation and planning sessions. The opportunity to participate in these discussions can eliminate, to a great degree, the sense of loneliness and despair that the parent of a handicapped child often feels. Information about special educational programs for handicapped children can be obtained from your local school superintendent or the state commissioner of education at your state capitol, or from the United States Office of Education, Box 1492, Washington, DC 20003.

Helping Your Other Children Cope

A child living in a family with a sick or handicapped child knows that her sibling is sick and unable to play as intensely as do healthy children. Parents' facial expressions, tones of voice, and phone conversations as well as visits to the doctor communicate in a very substantial way that the sibling is ill. When parents fail to share openly the nature and details of the illness or handicap with their healthy offspring, the other child or children may think that things are far worse than they really are. A healthy sibling should not be forced to bear her worries and fears about her brother or sister's illness by herself. If a well child in your family fails to inquire as to why her brother or sister is irritable and uninterested in playing, or why he's having seizures or unable to walk, you can initiate the discussion by saying, "You must wonder why Bobby is so fretful and cranky and unable to play like other children his age."

You may fear that as you share the fact of the illness with your healthy children that you may burst into tears. This may happen, but it is not necessarily harmful. When a child is sick and unable to participate fully in normal activities, it is indeed sad. Healthy children can be helped to bear this sadness when they have the opportunity to talk openly with their parents about the health of their sick brother or sister. As sad and difficult as these moments may be, it is better to have discussions than for a child to keep feelings pent up inside with no opportunity for relief.

Brothers and sisters often jump to the conclusion that a child's illness is their fault. Healthy children need to be reassured that nothing they did caused their sibling's illness. In addition, children who experience the severe illness or death of a beloved family member or friend sometimes worry that they also might develop a serious illness or die. It is important to recognize that this is a normal reaction. If your child does share these concerns with you, it might be wise to arrange for his own physician to see him and reassure him as to his state of health. It is also wise to explain the reason for your visit to the doctor ahead of time so that he can take time to explain his findings and why he thinks your child is healthy.

Healthy siblings can grow to be extraordinarily compassionate and understanding. You must remember, however, that it is important to provide specific moments of recreation for your healthy children, too. This will give them the special moments they need with you, and they'll return home feeling better prepared to share you with the handicapped child, who may require a great deal of additional attention.

Depending on the nature and seriousness of your child's illness, you may worry that a sibling will ask whether a handicapped child is going to die. You need to be honest and answer as truthfully as you can. For example, you might say, "Right now he seems to be doing all right. If he becomes sicker, I will tell you." Or, "The doctors are doing all they can to help Bobby." If death does seem imminent, adults should share this fact by saying, "It is quite possible that as Bobby gets sicker, he may die."

Although it is difficult for parents and children to realize that a child's life is ending, it is important to discuss this when it is obvious that death is about to occur. Avoiding the conversation means that a healthy child copes alone with her sadness. It is important to be comforting to your child in her despair rather than leaving her alone to bear the burden.

V A to Z Guide to Your Child's Health

Abdominal Pain, Recurrent

Preschool and school-age children frequently complain of recurrent abdominal pain. A child with this complaint usually suffers no weight loss, has no elevation of temperature, or any other sign of illness. Physical examination and laboratory studies of the blood and stools are usually within normal limits. Nevertheless, a child does suffer real pain. The discomfort may last for a few minutes and then disappear, only to recur a few hours or days later.

In a limited number of instances, milk sensitivity, parasitic infections, or anatomical abnormality of the intestinal tract may be the cause. When no specific cause is found, the complaint usually disappears as a child matures. Rest and hot water bottles offer relief. Oral medication is rarely indicated.

Acne, Baby

Pustular lesions on the cheeks, forehead, and chin, commonly appearing in the early months of life. Because of the immaturity of the sweat ducts of a newborn, the ducts can become clogged and cause this condition. These lesions subside spontaneously within a few months.

Adenoids

Lymphoid tissue lying in the back of the nose and extending downward into the nasopharynx. Normally large in infancy and childhood, these tissues diminish in size beginning at about age eight. During infancy and toddler years, recurrent infections sometimes result in marked enlargement of the tissues to the extent that there is interference with breathing through the nose and drainage through the eustachian tubes, which connect the middle ear with the nasopharynx. Surgical removal of the adenoids may be indicated when obstruction is extreme, ear infections continuous, or hearing loss present due to dysfunction of the eustachian tubes. Whenever possible this procedure should

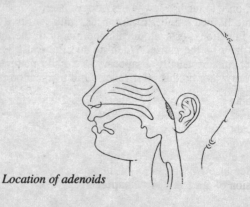

Location of adenoids

be postponed until the age of five when a child is better able to cope with it psychologically.

Albuminuria

An often temporary condition where albumin (a normal protein constituent in the body) is present in the urine, occurring during the acute phase of a minor illness. However, continued presence of albumin in the urine merits further evaluation; it may suggest asymptomatic, abnormal kidney function.

Albuminuria is usually detected during a routine urinalysis ordered by the doctor.

Allergy

The unique capacity of many individuals to experience discomforting or clinically significant symptoms when exposed to specific foods, medications, plants, pollens, molds, dust, or animal danders. This condition tends to be common in certain families. Ten percent of the population will experience significant allergic reactions during their lifetimes.

In infancy, the gastrointestinal tract is the most common site of allergic symptoms. Vomiting, cramps, and diarrhea result when an offending substance is ingested. In toddler years, the reaction usually occurs on the skin; inflammation and itching occur. After the age of four, symptoms such as sniffles, cough, congestion, and wheezing predominate, although contact with toxic plants may produce significant skin reactions.

Avoidance of the offending substances whenever possible is always the best treatment.

See also Milk Allergy in this guide, and for a full discussion of allergies, see **Chapter 21.**

Amblyopia

A diminished visual acuity of one eye, often resulting from an inability to utilize both eyes in a coordinated manner. This condition frequently occurs when one eye tends to swing in or swing out. A child unconsciously suppresses one eye in order to prevent blurring of vision.

If you suspect your child has an eye problem, be sure to discuss it with your pediatrician or take your child to an ophthalmologist or optometrist with specialized training in visual problems of children. Early detection of this condition is important, since patching of the good eye will often stimulate improvement of the visual acuity in the deficient eye. Also see Eye entries later in this guide, and **Chapter 9, Developmental Concerns** for additional information.

Anemia

A deficit in the oxygen-carrying components of the blood. The most common basis of anemia in infancy and childhood is low hemoglobin due to a deficient amount of iron in the body. Administration of iron preparations by mouth usually resolves the problem. Other causes include blood loss, chronic infection, hereditary abnormalities of red blood cells, lead poisoning, gastrointestinal diseases interfering with iron absorption, and other systemic illnesses.

Lethargy, pallor, decreased resistance to disease, irritability, and discomfort are common symptoms that accompany this condition.

If you suspect that your child is anemic, your doctor will arrange for blood tests for a definite diagnosis and treatment.

Animal Bites, *see* Bites, Animal

Antibiotics

A group of drugs effective in inhibiting the growth of many types of disease-producing bacteria and some types of fungi. Antibiotics are used widely in the treatment and prevention of infections caused by organisms that are susceptible to specific preparations of these potent medications. However, antibiotics are not effective against most types of viral illnesses, such as colds, flu, or the chickenpox.

Antibiotics should be taken exactly as directed. If the medication is prescribed for a ten-day period, be sure to give your child the full course. If you stop after three or four days (at which point your child will probably be feeling much better), the antibiotics will not be fully effective, and the infection will likely recur.

Antibiotics are extremely useful when there is a definite indication for them, but indiscriminate use can upset the body's bacterial balance, and the overgrowth of bacteria resistant to these medications may cause significant illness.

Antibodies

Protein substances in the blood that provide resistance to and combat viruses, bacteria, or other foreign organisms. While most antibodies are extremely helpful to the body, antibodies are also what cause allergic reactions to specific foods and/or inhalants such as pollens and dust in individuals who have the unique capacity to react in this way.

Antihistamines

A group of drugs, usually administered orally, that relieve sniffles, cough, watery eyes, and itching due to allergic reactions. In addition, many of the drugs in this class reduce the nausea and dizziness associated with viral infections and car or seasickness. Possible side effects are drowsiness, blurred vision, and dry mouth.

Before using some type of antihistamine for your child, consult with the pediatrician about your child's symptoms and the exact type of medication to use.

Appendicitis

An acute inflammation of the appendix, a small pouch attached to the large intestine. Early signs of appendicitis are nausea, loss of appetite, and moderate pain in the central area of the abdomen. Pain gradually shifts to the lower right abdominal quadrant. Temperature elevation is minimal or slight initially, but rises as the inflammation of the appendix continues. White blood count is low or slightly elevated at the beginning and then begins to rise significantly within a few hours. Rectal examination by means of inserting a gloved finger into the rectum reveals tenderness and the presence of a mass on the right.

If you have reason to suspect appendicitis, contact your doctor immediately. Once a diagnosis is confirmed, immediate surgical intervention is imperative. Delay may lead to a rupture of the inflamed appendix, releasing purulent material into the abdominal cavity and causing a generalized infection known as peritonitis.

Arthritis, Viral

A child suffering any viral infection may experience a complication that involves pain and limitation of motion of one or more joints. This condition, known as viral arthritis, causes discomfort and may last seven to ten days. It can also occur as a complication of viral immunization for such diseases as mumps, measles, or rubella. Rest and administration of aspirin relieve the symptoms. The condition is not serious, although it is often confused with other more significant types of joint disease. See also Juvenile Rheumatoid Arthritis.

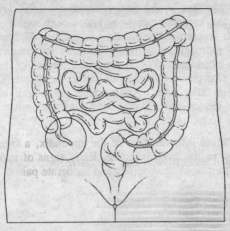

Location of the appendix

Asthma

A respiratory condition associated with pulmonary infections and allergic reactions manifested by labored breathing, difficulty in expiring air, and severe coughing. Oral administration of aminophyllin usually relieves the symptoms. Adrenalin injections may be necessary when an asthmatic attack is severe and prolonged. Occasionally hospitalization for intravenous administration of medications and aerosol suspensions is necessary. See **Chapter 21, Allergies** for a complete discussion of asthma.

Astigmatism, *see under* Eyes, Vision Problems

Athlete's Foot

A low-grade fungus infection (also known as tinea pedis), which produces redness and irritation. It commonly affects the foot in the area between the toes. It is often contracted in public showers and locker rooms, and because it is commonly passed via the bathtub or shower, several members of a family may suffer simultaneously with this condition. Within the home, spread of the fungus can be slowed by washing out the tub or shower stall with ammonia after use. Appropriate antifungal ointments usually reduce the inflammation and discomfort. Recurrence is common.

Atopic Dermatitis, *see* Dermatitis, Atopic

Attention Deficit Disorder

A condition occurring in childhood, also known as hyperactivity or hyperkinesis. It is characterized by difficulty in maintaining consistent attention to the specific task at hand, a tendency to shift from one activity to another, an impulsive restlessness, and difficulty in working toward a specific goal. This condition is four times more common in boys than girls. For more information, see the section on Hyperactivity in **Chapter 9, Developmental Concerns.**

Frequently these symptoms are associated with neurologic deficits, which also interfere with the ability to learn and progress in schoolwork. Careful neurologic and psychologic evaluations are important to understand completely the basis for a child's symptoms and difficulties.

Autism

A poorly understood condition that limits a toddler's or child's ability to develop relationships with other human beings. The autistic child presents, even in infancy, a strong preference for being alone. There is a tendency to treat human beings in the same way in which the child treats toys and furniture. There is little evidence of anxiousness when an adult leaves the room, nor is there joy when the person returns. Autism usually involves a deficit in the development of language.

The cause of the condition is unknown, but in most instances, it is believed that there is a basic deficit from birth. A child with autistic features should be thoroughly studied. Deafness or other neurologic problems may be present. Special educational programs often markedly improve the autistic child's capacity to learn and to relate to other human beings.

Baby Acne, *see* Acne, Baby

Baby Talk

A toddler or preschool child who is capable of using correct words and expressions may sometimes resort to immature language, such as "up me" for "pick me up," particularly when awakening in the morning or when tired after a day in day-care or nursery school. These regressions are common when a child of this age is under stress or exhausted.

Talking like a baby is one way of communicating that a child is finding life at the more advanced level difficult to adapt to for long periods of time. These lapses into abandoned speaking habits are short-lived and disappear spontaneously as a child experiences security and enjoyment at the more advanced level of functioning consistent with his or her chronologic age.

Bacteria

Tiny, single-cell organisms. Some are quite harmless and even beneficial; others produce diseases in susceptible individuals. Bacterial infections can usually be controlled by the administration of appropriate antibiotics.

Bacterial Infections

Acute illnesses in childhood are frequently due to invasion into the body of disease-producing bacteria. Illnesses caused by bacteria tend to be prolonged. The course is shortened by the administration of appropriate antibiotics.

A culture of throat secretions obtained by swabbing the area with a cotton-tipped applicator, or a blood sample offers opportunity to determine the bacterial origin of a disease. If disease-producing bacteria are found in these materials, the administration of specific antibiotics is the appropriate treatment.

Baker's Cyst

A collection of fluid in the tendons located in the posterior aspects of the knee joint. The encapsulated fluid is painless. The lesion may appear and disappear spontaneously. If the condition persists, surgical treatment may be necessary.

Bilirubin

All newborn infants experience a mild elevation of bilirubin (a normal substance found in the body in small amounts) and a minimal jaundice during the second to fifth day of life, due to normal breakdown of red blood cells shortly after birth. Excessive destruction of red blood cells may occur when an incompatibility exists between the blood cells of the mother and of the baby, causing the release of large amounts of bilirubin and producing visible and prolonged jaundice. When the jaundice is intense, phototherapy with ultraviolet light (a process where the baby is placed under special lights) is indicated. In severe cases, an exchange transfusion may be necessary.

Jaundice can also be caused by a generalized viral infection, which produces hepatitis, an inflammatory condition of the liver. Laboratory studies are often necessary to determine the basis for jaundice and what treatment, if any, is in order.

Bites, Animal

Bites by animals of all sorts should be treated as any other laceration; that is, they should be washed with sterile water and dressed with a sterile dressing. If the laceration is deep and extensive, surgical treatment may be necessary. If a child is up-to-date on his or her immunizations, there is little danger of tetanus infection.

Rabies is rarely a danger if the child was bitten by a family pet who has been regularly immunized. However, wild animals, as well as unimmunized dogs and cats, do present a definite hazard. See Rabies later in this guide; also see Scratches, Cuts, Abrasions, Puncture Wounds, and Animal Bites in **Chapter 20, First Aid at Home.**

Bites, Insect

In all probability, your child will be stung by a bee, yellow jacket, hornet, or wasp sometime in her life. Your immediate concern will be how to comfort her and whether or not a serious reaction will occur. The vast majority of insect stings result in painful wounds, but fortunately not serious or life-threatening situations.

The usual or "normal" reaction to an insect bite is a small, red, slightly raised area, painful at first, and then becoming itchy. In most instances, this reaction lasts a few hours and then disappears. Occasionally the swelling may last for a few days and may involve a large area adjacent to the site of the sting. Cold applications and oral administration of antihistamines and aspirin usually relieve these symptoms.

A generalized reaction occurs in less than one percent of the general population. Symptoms may appear immediately after the sting, or there may be a delay of several hours. Mild, systemic symptoms include generalized itching, puffiness of the eyelids, lips, or ears, with itching and redness. Urticaria (hives) in various parts of the body may occur. A generalized swelling of the joints with fever and a generalized rash may appear as long as ten days after the sting.

Symptoms of a more serious nature are swelling in the larynx, manifest by a tickle in the throat, gagging, difficulty in swallowing, or voice change; spasm of the bronchial muscles, causing lightness in the chest or wheezing; and low blood pressure, with dizziness or fainting.

A subcutaneous injection of adrenalin is the immediate treatment for serious reactions. If your child has systemic reactions when stung, it is important to arrange with your physician to have injectable adrenalin available at all times. The doctor may recommend that you purchase an AHA Kit, which is a preloaded syringe with two doses of adrenalin, or an Epe-Pen device, which delivers one dose of adrenalin with relative ease.

If your child has a systemic reaction following an insect sting, you should discuss with your physician the advisability of desensitization, that is, the frequent injection of increasing amounts of insect venom over a period of time. This is particularly important to consider when an individual suffers respiratory, laryngeal, or cardiovascular symptoms following an insect sting. See also Insect Sensitivity in this guide.

Blepharitis

Recurrent inflammation of the eyelids. Usually there is redness of the area just below the origin of the eyelashes. Blepharitis is associated with itching and swelling of the eyelids, which may cause temporary narrowing of the aperture of the eye. Often tiny white scales are present at the base of the lashes.

There is often an associated scaly condition of the scalp. This material spills over to the eyelids, producing irritation and inflammation. When this is the cause, it is important to treat the scalp condition as well. In other instances, blepharitis arises when a child is exposed to pollens, dust, or animal dander to which she is sensitive. Occasionally it occurs as a result of contact with a mother's nail polish or facial powder. In some cases, blepharitis is infectious, so until its cause has been diagnosed, take care to prevent its spread by having family members use different pillows, towels, and washcloths.

Your doctor should be consulted promptly in order to get the problem cleared up. Treatment involves the administration of mild antiseptic solutions or antibiotic preparations to the eye and the removal of as many antigenic and irritating substances as possible.

Blocked Tear Duct

Frequently the tear duct leading from the eye into the nose through which fluid flows is blocked at birth. The result is an accumulation of mucous and fluid in the eye, which normally should drain into the nose through this duct. This obstruction is generally temporary and the duct usually opens in time. In rare instances, the obstruction remains and surgical probing under anesthesia is necessary. This is usually performed at the end of the baby's first year if the condition has not cleared spontaneously by this time.

Blood Pressure, Elevated

As the heart pumps blood through the arteries to all parts of the body, the force of the moving blood exerts pressure on the arteries. Systolic blood pressure is the extent of the force present in the vessels during a heart contraction, and diastolic pressure represents the force existing during relaxation of the heart between contractions.

Blood pressure should be recorded from age three in order to establish a base line for detecting when the blood pressure is elevated. Elevated blood pressure tends to be more common in certain families. If your child's blood pressure is higher than average or there is a history of hypertension among adult family members, it is wise to reduce your child's intake of salt and cholesterol-containing foods and to control food intake to prevent obesity. This dietary approach is a preventive measure that may reduce the extent of high blood pressure in adult life.

Breast Enlargement in Newborns

Breast tissue in both male and female newborns is normally swollen at the time of birth and may increase during the first week or two of life. The enlargement of the breasts is due to an increased concentration of maternal hormones transmitted to the baby before birth.

The swelling of the breast tissue disappears gradually in the early weeks of life. Occasionally a baby's breasts secrete colostrum, known as witch's milk. This also disappears within a few weeks. Manipulating the breast to express the colostrum is unnecessary and may lead to inflammation and infection of the breast tissues.

Breath Holding Spells

Episodic holding of breath following a minor injury or moment of anger or frustration. After a short period of crying, the child gasps, holds his breath, and becomes pale and limp, often losing consciousness. These episodes are most common in the latter part of the first year and during the second year of life. The tendency has usually all but disappeared by the time the child is three.

It is often difficult to distinguish a breath holding spell from a seizure. An electroencephalographic recording of brain waves can usually clarify the diagnosis. The absence of any unusual wave patterns suggests that these episodes represent immature ways of dealing with frustration, rather than seizures. For more information, see the section on Febrile Seizures in **Chapter 22, What You Should Know About Fever.**

Bronchiolitis

An acute respiratory illness in susceptible infants and toddlers, usually associated with a viral infection. The symptoms are due to an inflammation of the lining of the tiny air passage tubes in the lungs, known as bronchioles.

The illness begins initially with irritability, running nose, and slight cough. There is often no elevation of temperature. After three to five days of these minor symptoms, a significant rise in respiratory rate occurs with a noticeable difficulty in expiratory phase. There may be dramatic heaving motions of the abdominal and chest muscles associated with movements of the nostrils. In spite of the respiratory difficulties, an infant or toddler with bronchiolitis may be active and relatively happy.

Occasionally when a child's fluid intake is reduced, supplemental intravenous fluid therapy is necessary. Mist, or, if the condition is severe, supplemental oxygen, is the appropriate therapy.

Cough medicines, antihistamines, and antibiotics generally offer little help with this condition, which usually subsides in three to five days. Also see **Chapter 23, How to Tell If Your Child Is Sick or Very Sick.**

Bronchitis

An inflammatory process of the trachea and bronchi due to the invasion of disease-producing viruses, bacteria, or other organisms. The acute form of this condition is usually preceded by a few days of what seems like an ordinary upper respiratory infection with nasal discharge, slight cough, general aches and pains, and lethargy. Appetite is likely to be markedly reduced. Within a few days a child develops a distressing, dry, hacking, unproductive cough with a tendency to produce gagging and vomiting. Sleeping may be interrupted repeatedly because of the severity of the coughing. Wheezing due to obstruction of the air passage with mucous may be present.

A vaporizer is a must when a child is suffering with bronchial infections, since the accumulation of dried-out mucous in the air passages intensifies the coughing. Most cough medications offer only minimal relief.

When a bacterial infection is present, administration of antibiotics may help to shorten the course of the illness. However, since the most common cause is a viral infection, which is unresponsive to antibiotics, one can expect the disease to take seven to ten days to run the usual course. Also see **Chapter 23, How to Tell If Your Child Is Sick or Very Sick.**

Cafe Au Lait Spots

Discrete, flat, light brown spots about one to fifteen centimeters in diameter. A few such spots are found in many normal individuals, but if there are many lesions, it is wise to have a child examined to rule out any systemic disease. There is no specific treatment to remove the spots themselves.

Caput Succedaneum

Commonly observed in newborn infants, a temporary molding of the skull with lengthening in the long axis. It is the result of pressure on the head during the passage of the baby through the birth canal. There is often accompanying edema, or collection of fluid, in the area between the scalp and the skull bones. The head regains its normal round appearance during the first forty-eight hours of life.

Car Sickness, *see* Motion Sickness

Cardiac Catheterization

A diagnostic procedure involving passage of a tiny catheter through a blood vessel into the heart in order to study pressure, blood flow, and oxygen saturation in the various heart chambers. It is used when there are unusual heart murmurs or evidence of cardiac abnormality.

Cardiac Murmur

Murmurs are sounds detected between the heart beats. A *functional* murmur is due to the movement of blood through the heart and large vessels. This type has a very distinct quality and no pathologic significance; it does not imply cardiac disease. It may be heard at one visit and not at another. Whenever the heart rate is increased, as with an elevation of temperature or after exercise, functional murmurs are more audible than in the resting state.

An *organic* murmur is due to an abnormality in the heart structure or the vessels leading to and from the heart, perhaps a congenital defect or the result of valvular disease (such as rheumatic fever). In order to determine the meaning of this type of murmur, electrocardiogram chest X rays and other studies of cardiac function may be necessary. The sounds of cardiac murmurs usually have a distinct quality, which enables the doctor to differentiate between a functional benign murmur and an organic murmur, which might indicate the possibility of cardiac abnormality.

Carotenemia

A benign condition occurring in the latter half of the first year of life in which the carotene pigment in yellow vegetables such as carrots, sweet potatoes, and yams is absorbed into the body and poorly excreted. The result is that certain skin areas, particularly the nose, ears, palms of the hand and soles of the feet, take on a yellow tinge. The condition is harmless and disappears with time as the body's digestive system matures.

CAT Scan (Computerized Axial Tomography)

An X ray technique that provides cross-sectional images and produces a composite picture that reveals size, shape, and contours of structures within the body. It is very commonly used to determine information relating to structural changes within the brain. A doctor may request it when there is possible neurologic abnormality such as cerebral palsy or spasticity, or when a child is suffering seizures or severe headaches, or if there is evidence of neurologic disorder. Occasionally it is used after a child has suffered a severe fall.

Cat Scratch Fever

A common condition in which a large and tender lymph node appears in the armpits or in the groin following a cat scratch on the arm or leg. The node enlarges two to four weeks following the scratch, which may have been quite minor. The disease is believed to be caused by a virus that resides on plants and is transferred by the cat's claw to the person's arm or leg. The disease itself is usually self-limiting. Rarely, the enlarged gland becomes purulent and surgical drainage is necessary.

Celiac Disease

A term used to describe a combination of symptoms, the most severe of which are chronic diarrhea with foul-smelling stools, weight loss, general discomfort, and weakness. It occurs in infants between nine months and two years of age. Your doctor should be consulted if you suspect your child has celiac disease.

The cause of this condition is deficiency in the ability to digest gluten, the basic protein substance occurring in wheat and rye. Strict elimination of these items from the diet should produce dramatic remission.

Cellulitis

An inflammatory process in the subcutaneous tissues (area just under the skin). Many different bacteria can cause cellulitis, but if it is due to infection with Hemophilus influenzae, type B, it is quite serious. The infection often begins as a reddish, tender, inflamed area of the skin around one eye or in a cheek. The child is flushed and feverish and does not look well. Prompt treatment with appropriate antibiotics is imperative.

Cephalohematoma

A collection of blood and fluid on top of one of the skull bones in a newborn, resulting from prolonged labor. The fluid is absorbed gradually. Frequently a little ring of calcification appears at the edge of the site of fluid collection. It is palpable for several months but disappears in time.

Cerebral Palsy

A chronic disorder of the nervous system due to incomplete development of the brain. This condition is characterized by difficulty in controlling gross and fine muscular movements.

Common signs of cerebral palsy in a baby are difficulties in sucking, unusual stiffness in the extremities, and awkwardness in crawling or walking. As a child with cerebral palsy matures, tremors and twisting movements of the extremities may occur.

A child with cerebral palsy often experiences significant hearing loss, visual deficits, and difficulties in expressive language. It is imperative to have the child completely evaluated physically and psychologically. Gross and fine motor deficits, hearing deficiencies, and language difficulties may suggest that a child is severely handicapped in intellectual function. However, careful psychometric examination often reveals normal intelligence, which has gone unrecognized because of the other problems interfering with a child's capacity to function.

Chickenpox

A common viral disease, usually mild, characterized by slight fever, headache, and a generalized skin rash consisting of inflamed elevated lesions, which at first look like mosquito bites, but within twenty-four hours develop into elevated lesions filled with fluid. The lesions appear all over the body and in the mucous membranes of the mouth and genital areas. After a few days the lesions begin to fade. Many children experience disturbed sleep and frightening dreams in the initial phase of the disease. The main discomfort is the intense itching, which can be relieved by oral administration of antihistamines.

The disease is highly contagious from the day of onset and for approximately one week. A child who has not had chickenpox may be expected to contract the disease within fourteen to sixteen days after exposure to a person who has the disease. One episode conveys a lifelong immunity to that form of the disease.

Rarely, a child who is experiencing chickenpox may develop dizziness and may become cumbersome and awkward due to the effect of the chickenpox virus on the central nervous system. This condition, known as encephalitis, usually resolves itself within a week or two.

Once an individual experiences chickenpox, the virus causing this disease lies dormant for many years in the spinal cord. Suddenly, it may become activated, producing painful redness and blisters in a bandlike unilateral lesion in the back, side, and thorax. This condition, known as shingles, is due to the effect of the chickenpox virus in the adult individual. The lesions contain the chickenpox virus, and the disease can be spread to a person who has not had the disease.

There is no reason to limit the activities of a child who has chickenpox, other than to avoid contact with those who are not immune. Persons receiving chemotherapy treatments are usually susceptible to the chickenpox virus.

Cholesterol

A chemical substance normally present in the body. A high blood level of this substance is associated with cardiovascular disease, heart attacks, and strokes. Cholesterol is present in high concentrations in animal fats, eggs, and dairy products. The American Heart Association recommends reducing the intake of these substances in our diet in order to reduce blood cholesterol levels and perhaps to postpone the onset of significant cardiovascular disease in adults.

Chromosomes

The bearers of the genes that provide the potential for each baby to develop a wide variety of characteristics inherited from the parents. Recent advances in the technique of studying chromosomes obtained from the blood of individuals provide a means of diagnosing and understanding many inheritable conditions. This information is of vital importance to parents who have a child with a genetically determined condition and wonder about the possibility of a similar condition occurring in subsequent babies they may conceive.

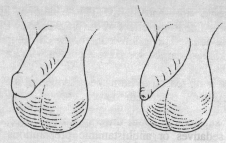

Circumcised and uncircumcised penis

Circumcision

An optional minor surgical procedure in which the tip of the foreskin of the penis is removed, usually during the first week of life. It is often performed for religious reasons or in the belief that it is appropriate. Although there are few medical indications for this procedure, most male infants born in the United States are circumcised. See also **Chapter 2, The Newborn.**

Club Foot

A congenital malposition of the foot due to faulty intra-uterine position. The foot is turned down and inward. In mild instances, the foot can be returned to a normal position by daily manipulation. In more serious cases, a series of plaster casts must be applied. Rarely, surgical intervention is necessary.

Colic

A poorly understood condition occurring in newborns and manifest by paroxysms of abdominal pain, irritability, and fussing or crying, which often lasts for more than three hours. This condition often occurs at the same time each day, usually in the late afternoon or evening. Most infants experiencing colic are highly perceptive. External and internal stimuli that do not disturb most infants evoke distress and pain in these children.

Various remedies such as rocking, application of a hot water bottle to the abdomen, or offering a pacifier help some infants with colic some of the time. The condition usually subsides at about three months of age. In severe cases, sedatives or antihistaminic preparations administered orally are helpful. For more information see Fussiness and the Highly Perceptive (Colicky) Infant in **Chapter 3, The Early Months: From Birth to Four Months.**

Colostrum

A yellowish, transparent fluid secreted by the mother's breasts a few days after delivery. This substance is high in protein and contains antibodies. When ingested by an infant, it offers protection against many infections occurring in the early months of life.

Concussion

An injury to the brain following a fall or a blow to the head, which results in a period of unconsciousness usually lasting a few minutes. Frequently there is an associated memory lapse as to what happened just before the injury. For more information and symptoms that might suggest serious injury, see Head Injuries in **Chapter 20, First Aid at Home.**

Conduction Hearing Loss, *see* Hearing Loss, Conduction

Congenital Heart Disease

A general term referring to an abnormality of the heart developed during fetal life. Newer diagnostic techniques and rapid advances in cardiac surgery provide means of surgically treating many of the congenital cardiac conditions that formerly were fatal.

Congenital Infections

A group of diseases acquired by an infant before birth due to exposure to viral, bacterial, or protozoan disease in the mother. Common diseases that occur during pregnancy and may affect an infant are syphilis (a contagious venereal disease), toxoplasmosis (lesions of the central nervous system), Rubella (German measles), herpes (inflammatory diseases of the skin), and cytomegalic inclusion disease. These diseases may or may not affect the infant's development, depending on the point during fetal life in which exposure occurs.

Congenital Laryngeal Stridor (Relaxation of the Larynx)

A common condition in infancy in which the cartilaginous structure of the larynx is more flexible than usual. Noisy breathing appears in the early weeks of life due to a collapse of the air passage in the larynx during inspiration. Although the sound is disturbing, infants rarely suffer any ill consequences. Many infants with this condition breathe more easily lying on their stomachs. The condition usually disappears spontaneously toward the end of the first year of life.

Conjunctivitis, *see under* Eyes, Irritation and/or Inflammation

Constipation

Difficulty in passing bowel movements is common in infants and young children. When the problem becomes severe, the term constipation is used. Weaning from the breast to a prepared milk mixture, or changing to whole milk frequently produces this problem. The addition of prunes, prune juice, apricots, dates, or figs to the diet usually resolves the difficulty.

Cracks in the membranes at the junction of the anus and skin commonly occur in infancy and may create enough pain upon defecation that a baby retains bowel movements. Gentle application of petroleum jelly or other softening material to the anal tissues is helpful. On rare occasions, specific foods produce an inflammatory reaction of the skin in the anal area, causing significant pain, which restricts the passage of fecal material. Elimination of these foods from the diet often results in noticeable improvement.

Some babies tend to be constipated with the eruption of each tooth.

Contact Dermatitis, *see* Dermatitis, Contact

Convulsion

A short period of loss of consciousness associated with stiffening or jerking movements of the extremities. Febrile seizures (those associated with fever) are of minimal significance (see Febrile Convulsion later in this guide, and Chapter 22). However, a child who suffers seizures should be carefully evaluated to determine that there is no viral or bacterial infection or basic underlying convulsive seizure disorder due to neurologic or metabolic deficit. An electroencephalographic study of brain waves may be used in making this evaluation. If a basic seizure condition is present, prolonged administration of medication is in order.

Corneal Abrasion

A scratch or abrasion on the transparent covering of the eyeball caused by a flying piece of metal, a tiny stone, broken contact lens, fingernails, or other types of foreign bodies. Injury to the cornea is extremely painful. Treatment consists of removal of the foreign body, if present, and careful ophthalmological examination. Anesthetic drops and an eye patch can relieve some of the discomfort, and healing is usually quite prompt once the foreign body is removed.

Corticosteroids, *see* Steroids

Cradle Cap

A scalp condition manifest by adherent greasy white and yellow scaly lesions. The scalp is itchy; secondary excoriation and infection are common. The condition often spreads to the eyebrow area, the skin behind the ears, and the neck, armpit, and groin areas. Although this is not considered to be an allergic condition, the problem occurs more frequently in infants who later develop significant allergies.

Treatment consists of frequent washing with bland shampoos recommended by your doctor and the application of soothing, anti-inflammatory lotions. Careful removal of the scales is advised in order to decrease additional irritation. To remove scales, rub the scalp with mineral oil or petroleum jelly, and use a brush or fine-toothed comb.

Crib Death, *see* Sudden Infant Death Syndrome

Cromolyn

A pharmacologic preparation that often prevents the onset of an asthmatic attack. It is especially helpful when taken prior to participation in a sports event or other physical activity that may precipitate this respiratory problem. The preparation is administered by means of a special inhaler.

Croup

A common condition in infancy and toddler years characterized by hoarseness, a barking cough, tightness in breathing, and a crowing noise upon inspiration. Croup usually begins without warning in the middle of the night. Mild croup, often called spasmodic croup, results from swelling of the vocal cords. It is usually caused by a viral infection. Relief is often obtained by placing the child in steam or mist, either in the bathroom with the hot shower running, in a kitchen with a teakettle boiling, or in a small room with a vaporizer. If a child suffering from croup fails to improve after spending one-half hour in steam, or if he really looks unwell, he is probably suffering from more serious forms of croup, either acute laryngotracheobronchitis of viral origin, or an acute bacterial infection caused by Hemophilus influenzae, type B.

Laryngotracheobronchitis is a moderately severe viral respiratory disease affecting the larynx, trachea, and lungs. It starts like an ordinary cold and spreads through the entire respiratory system, causing difficulty in breathing, hoarseness, and a croupy cough. A child who is severely ill needs hospitalization for mist and oxygen therapy.

The most serious form of croup is due to *epiglottitis*, an

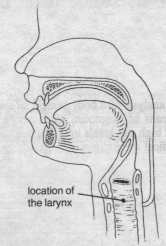

Location of the larynx

inflammation of the cartilage located at the base of the tongue. The infection, usually due to the bacteria Hemophilus influenzae, type B, can be fatal. A child may awaken with a sore throat, have difficulty in breathing, and be critically ill and moribund a few hours later. A child suffering from this disease usually drools constantly, shows difficulty swallowing, has an elevated temperature, and presents a toxic, glassy-eyed, plaintive facial expression. He may lean forward, resting on his hands in front of and a bit to the side of the body in an effort to make it a little easier to breathe.

Early treatment of this infection is crucial. If your child has croup with fever and drooling and shows no improvement after thirty minutes in steam, contact your physician immediately, or take your child to the nearest hospital. Appropriate antibiotics administered intravenously in the initial phase can usually cure the infection. Also see **Chapter 23, How to Tell If Your Child Is Sick or Very Sick.**

Cystic Fibrosis

An inherited chronic disease associated with pancreatic dysfunction, which interferes with the capacity to digest and absorb food. Chronic malnutrition and below-average growth are common. In addition, those suffering from cystic fibrosis are especially susceptible to bronchial and lung infections. An analysis of a body sample of sweat provides an accurate means of diagnosis, since people with cystic fibrosis present high salt levels in their perspiration.

Careful medical supervision, the administration of pancreatic enzymes, and judicious use of antibiotics often result in remarkable improvement in the capacity of these children to participate in normal activities.

Cystitis

An infection and inflammation of the bladder, much more common in girls than in boys. The major symptom is frequent voiding with burning or irritation as urine is passed. Drinking large quantities of water and oral administration of appropriate antibiotics are the usual treatments, and normally cure this condition promptly.

Dehydration

Loss of body fluids due to vomiting or diarrhea. It can be quite serious. If your child is vomiting, suffering excessive diarrhea, and has reduced his fluid intake, offer ice chips, small amounts of breast milk, diluted formula mixture, or fruit juices (as appropriate), to try to avoid dehydration. Also report the condition to your doctor who can tell you exactly how to proceed.

The loss of fluids and essential salts in children can lead to extreme lethargy and critical illness. Absence of tears, sunken eyes, wrinkled skin, dry mouth, a weak cry, and diminished urination are symptoms indicating a serious degree of dehydration.

When it is impossible to replace fluid loss by oral administration of diluted milk mixtures or specially prepared solutions, hospitalization for intravenous administration of fluids may be necessary.

Delayed Language Development, *see* Language Development, Delayed

Dermatitis, Atopic

A common skin eruption in infants and toddlers. Red inflammatory lesions usually appear initially on the face and scalp, later extending over the chest, abdomen, arms, and legs, particularly the inner parts of the elbows and backs of the knees. A child is usually uncomfortable and irritable. Rubbing the affected areas increases the severity.

In some instances, this condition arises shortly after a baby ingests new foods, in which case the new food should be discontinued. In other instances, it is exacerbated by an environmental factor, such as a particular soap or a new pet in the home. Children experiencing this skin condition often develop respiratory forms of allergy in later years.

Oral administration of antibiotics and topical treatment usually control the infection. Antihistamine preparations administered orally reduce the discomfort of the itching. Oatmeal baths are also soothing. Also see **Chapter 21, Allergies.**

Dermatitis, Contact

An irritating inflammation of the skin resulting from contact with materials such as plants, wool, plastic, harsh soaps and detergents, and various topical creams and lotions. In older children, poison ivy is the most common example of contact dermatitis.

Elimination of the offending substance and application of soothing creams usually result in resolution of the problem. If the irritated skin seems infected, consult your doctor. Judicious use of antibiotics may be necessary. Also see other entries under Dermatitis in this guide; and Atopic and Contact Dermatitis in **Chapter 21, Allergies.**

Dermatitis, Fiberglass

A patchy inflammatory dermatitis due to penetration of the skin by fiberglass particles, the source of which may be insulation panels, drapes, or clothes washed in a machine previously used for washing fiberglass materials. Children experiencing this condition respond to removal of the offending material. Topical lotions and oral administration of antihistamines relieve the discomfort.

Dermatitis, House Plant

A contact dermatitis reaction in certain children caused by house plants. Common offenders are the philodendron, geranium, poinsettia, dieffenbachia, daffodil, buttercup, foxglove, lilac, lady's slipper, tulip and narcissus bulbs, magnolia, chrysanthemum, aster, and daisy. Avoidance of the offending plants is the best treatment. Soothing lotions and oral administration of antihistamines relieve an acute episode. Also see Dermatitis, Contact earlier in this guide.

Dermatitis, Monilia

An intensely inflamed, well-demarcated rash, appearing in the diaper area in susceptible individuals due to the presence of a fungus known as monilia or candida. This organism is normally present in the gastrointestinal tract and is eliminated in stools. However, some infants have low resistance to this organism, and the wet moist skin of the diaper area is the site of overgrowth of the fungus, resulting in the appearance of an inflammatory, irritating rash.

Treatment with antifungal creams and soothing lotions usually clears the infection, although it may take several weeks. Occasionally when the infection is prolonged, oral administration of antifungal preparations is necessary.

Dermatitis, Seborrheic

A commonly occurring scaly or crusting eruption of the scalp in early infancy. It usually begins with thin, scaly lesions known as cradle cap. The lesions often progress to sharply defined round or oval patches covered by thick, greasy yellowish crusts. Flakes of this crusty lesion spill over and cause inflammation elsewhere in the body, particularly behind the ears, in the neck folds, on the shoulders, and in the umbilical and diaper area.

Frequently, superimposed fungus or bacterial infections occur. These must be treated appropriately with antibiotic or antifungal agents before the basic lesion will improve. Also see Cradle Cap earlier in this guide.

Dermatitis, Shoe

A common form of contact dermatitis affecting the top surface of the feet and toes. This condition is often mistaken for a fungus infection. A valuable diagnostic feature is that shoe dermatitis rarely affects the areas between the toes, whereas this is the first area affected in fungus infections. Rubber, adhesive material, cement, tanning agents, and dyes are common causes of this dermatitis.

Children suffering with this problem should avoid wearing leather shoes as much as possible. Open sandals and canvas-topped tennis sneakers are beneficial substitutions. Open wet compresses and topical lotions offer relief in the acute phase. Also see Dermatitis, Contact earlier in this guide.

Desensitization

A series of injections that reduces a child's sensitivity to specific pollens, molds, or dust that can cause significant respiratory symptoms, such as hay fever or asthma.

Diabetes

A metabolic disorder resulting from a deficiency of insulin. This problem reduces the ability of the body to utilize and store glucose. Diabetes may become manifest at any age. Two percent of all diabetics have the onset during childhood, and the rate of occurrence in children is highest in two age groups: children of five and six, and those who are between eleven and thirteen years old.

The earliest signs of this disease are hunger, general discomfort, weight loss, urinary frequency, presence of sugar in the urine, and an elevated blood glucose level.

Appropriate administration of insulin and a controlled diet enable a child with diabetes to maintain health and to continue to participate in all normal activities.

Diaper Rash

Most common skin disorder of infancy. The problem arises when an infant's skin becomes irritated by contact with urine, feces, strong soaps, and other abrasive materials in the diaper area. The use of airtight plastic pants over diapers sometimes contributes to this problem because they produce a high concentration of urine next to the skin, causing irritation and a fertile field for the growth of bacteria and fungi. Frequent diaper changes, the use of mild soap, and exposure to the air are the most effective ways of treating this condition. Dusting with medicated powders at each diaper change is often helpful. If the rash persists or seems severe, your doctor should be consulted. When there is a superficial superimposed infection due to bacteria or fungi, specific antibacterial and antifungal therapy may help to eliminate the problem.

Diphtheria

A serious disease that rarely appears in the United States today because of widespread immunization in infancy and early childhood. The symptoms include fever, severe sore throat, rapid pulse, enlarged lymph glands in the neck, and a white, grayish membrane on the throat and tonsils. The disease is serious and life-threatening. Immediate treatment with intravenous antibiotics and injections of antitoxin is imperative. For information on immunizations against diphtheria, see **Chapter 16, Immunizations.**

Dislocation of the Hip

A congenital abnormality of the hip joint in which the head of the femur slides out of the normal position because of a defect in the structure of the pelvis. Early diagnosis is important. Treatment with a special diaper that holds the hip in position while the growth of pelvic bones takes place is often successful in restoring the normal space for the head of the femur. In a few instances, casting or surgical intervention may be necessary.

Down's Syndrome

A congenital condition that results in a child who characteristically has sloping eyes, small facial features, a large tongue, unusual flexibility of the joints, and limited intellectual endowment. Definitive diagnosis is established by chromosomal studies. Many children with Down's Syndrome also have a congenital heart defect. Delayed development usually occurs in all areas.

Special educational programs for children with Down's

Syndrome, as for all handicapped children, are mandated by Public Law 94-142 and available in all school systems in the United States. See the listing for Public Law 94-142 for more information; also refer to **Chapter 25, Chronic Illness.**

Dyslexia

A fairly common disorder in which the individual sees words and letters reversed. "Was" is visualized as "saw"; "b" is seen as "d." This is a common phase in the pre-school years, but when this pattern of visual function continues into later childhood and adulthood, it causes considerable difficulty in reading. There is a strong family history of this condition. Special educational programs can often help a child overcome this functional deficit. For more information, see Dyslexia in **Chapter 9, Developmental Concerns.**

Dysuria

Painful and more frequent urination. This condition is usually due to an infection either in the urethra, bladder, or kidneys. Rarely, these symptoms can be the result of external irritation due to a sensitivity to bubble bath, nylon panties, or other material in contact with the genital area. Examination of the urine helps to determine the cause of the symptoms.

Close attention is imperative when a child has irritation in the genital area or unexplained irritation and swelling of the tissues. Child abuse is often the cause of such symptoms.

Ear Infections

There are two types of ear infections from which your child is most likely to suffer.

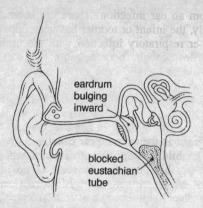

Otitis media in the middle ear

Otitis media: An acute inflammatory process in the middle ear accompanied by pain and the presence of a bulging inflamed eardrum. Diminished hearing is common. An upper respiratory infection usually precedes an ear infection. The swelling of the tissues in the nasopharynx impedes the drainage through the eustachian tube, which connects the middle ear with the back of the throat, thus trapping secretions and disease-producing bacteria in the middle ear, leading to inflammation.

Oral administration of antibiotics is appropriate therapy. Some toddlers and children have a predilection for ear infections, while others seem to avoid them. There is no explanation for this variation in susceptibility. Quite frequently parents of children who suffer recurrent ear infections report that they, too, suffered ear infections in childhood.

Serous otitis: A collection of sterile fluid in the middle ear, which interferes with movement of the tympanic membrane and may cause hearing deficit. This condition may be the result of recurrent ear infections, or it may be caused by allergic swelling of the inner tissues of the ear and eustachian tubes, preventing adequate draining in the ear.

You may wonder how to tell if your preverbal child is

suffering from an ear infection. There are several indications. Usually, the infant or toddler has what appears to be a minor upper respiratory infection with the usual symptoms of sniffles, cough, poor appetite, and discomfort. During the first or second week of the infection, he suddenly becomes more irritable and, at times, is inconsolable. His temperature, which has probably been minimal, suddenly rises several degrees. Another common indication is if the youngster is rubbing or banging his ear, or trying to stick his finger in the external ear canal.

When your child is suffering with an earache, he should be examined by his physician as soon as possible. Untreated ear infections are very painful and may lead to permanent damage and long-lasting hearing deficits.

There are several methods of comforting an infant, toddler, or child who is suffering with a painful ear infection until you can get to the doctor. The oral administration of aspirin, acetaminophen, or cough mixtures with pain-relieving ingredients will temporarily ease much of the discomfort. These medications provide relief for about four hours, so that repeated administration is necessary. Having a child lie down with the affected ear on a warm hot water bottle or heating pad is also soothing. The administration of ear drops can also offer temporary relief.

One word of caution! Often an eardrum will rupture and purulent fluid will be observed in the external canal. When this happens, a child's irritability decreases because of the relief of pain caused by pressure in the middle ear. It is imperative that your physician examine your child when this happens even though the child may feel much better. Chronic ear infections associated with a ruptured eardrum can also lead to permanent damage and a decrease in hearing.

A child who suffers repeated ear infections may develop a collection of sterile fluid in the middle ear (serous otitis), which interferes with normal hearing mechanisms. When this condition is unrelieved by administration of antibiotics and antihistamines or other medications that shrink the lining of the eustachian tube, the surgical implantation under general anesthesia of *plastic ventilation tubes in the eardrums* provides a pathway for the drainage of this fluid.

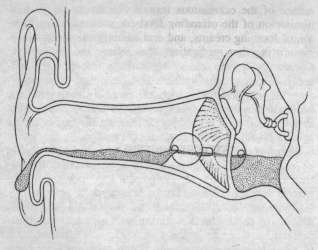

Ventilation tube in the eardrum

The implantation of these tubes may result in a remarkable improvement of hearing. Unfortunately, the tubes are often extruded within a few months, and if the condition persists, reinsertion of the plastic tubes may be necessary.

Also see in this guide, External Otitis (Swimmer's Ear); Hearing Impairment; Hearing Loss, Conduction; Hearing Loss, Sensory; and **Chapter 23, How to Tell If Your Child Is Sick or Very Sick.**

Eardrum, *see* Perforated Eardrum

Eczema

A nonspecific term used to describe a chronic inflammatory condition of the skin, which in many instances is intensified by the ingestion of certain foods or being in contact with dust, pollens, and household irritants. Itching may be intense. Superficial infections often occur on the surface of the eczematous lesions. Treatment consists of elimination of the offending foods or substances, application of soothing creams, and oral administration of antihistamines or other medications that relieve the discomfort. Also see the listings under Dermatitis.

EEG, *see* Electroencephalogram

EKG, *see* Electrocardiogram

Electrocardiogram (EKG)

A graphic recording of electrical impulses reflecting various activities of the heart. Data revealing heart size and rhythm activities aid in evaluating cardiac function. The EKG is among the studies done if a doctor has reason to suspect a heart problem.

Electroencephalogram (EEG)

A recording of electrical waves present in the brain, obtained from electrodes applied to the scalp. Specific patterns of brain waves indicate the presence of a seizure state, which usually can be treated with appropriate medications. Among its uses is helping to determine the cause of a seizure.

Electrolyte Levels

A determination of the blood concentration of various salts in the body to help diagnose the extent of an illness that features vomiting and diarrhea and where dehydration is a concern. When laboratory studies reveal distinctly abnormal electrolyte levels, hospitalization for intravenous fluid replacement may be necessary, particularly in infancy and toddler years.

Encephalitis

An inflammatory condition of the brain due to the presence of a virus or other disease-producing organisms. Encephalitis often represents a complication of a systemic illness, such as mumps, chickenpox, German measles, or other viruses that are rampant from time to time in any community. Symptoms consist of fever, headache, nausea, vomiting, stiff neck, and drowsiness. In most instances, the illness lasts from a few days to a week, and improvement occurs spontaneously. There are, however, types of encephalitis, particularly those transmitted by mosquitos, which cause protracted illness of a severe, and sometimes critical, nature.

Diagnosis of encephalitis is determined by a doctor's examination and laboratory studies of cerebral spinal fluid obtained by a lumbar puncture, or as it is often called, a spinal tap. Also see Lumbar Puncture later in this guide.

Epiglottitis, *see under* Croup

Epilepsy

A condition involving a recurring problem with brief disturbances of the brain in which a child experiences a short abnormal phase of behavior, such as a seizure or convulsion. In a mild seizure, known as a petit mal, a child stops whatever activity she is doing and stares blankly for a few seconds. She is unaware that anything has occurred. Sometimes a child with unrecognized seizures of this nature is accused of daydreaming. Grand mal seizures are more dramatic. The entire body stiffens and there may be twitches or jerking movements that last for several minutes.

A person suffering seizures should have an electroencephalogram to determine brain wave patterns. Appropriate medication can usually control the seizures. Occasionally, however, seizures are associated with serious neurologic disease and can be difficult to cure.

ERB's Palsy

A deficit due to nerve dysfunction in which an infant suffers an inability to move the arm away from the shoulder, to rotate the arm in an outward direction, and to turn the lower part of the arm outward. Occasionally there is a lessening of sensation on the outer part of the arm. In many instances, the condition clears spontaneously; in other cases, some of the problem continues. Physical therapy early in infancy is important to minimize the extent of permanent deficit.

Eustachian Tube

A narrow tube connecting the middle ear with the nasopharynx. See Ear Infections earlier in this guide.

External Otitis (Swimmer's Ear)

A painful inflammation in the external canal of the ear, commonly occurring in swimmers due to the frequency with which moisture collects in this area. The warm moist setting is easily invaded by many different types of bacteria and fungi, initiating an inflammatory process. Excess perspiration, failure to clear the canal of moisture after swimming or showering, and a humid atmosphere are conducive to the development of external otitis. The pain often extends to the pinna, the projecting portion of the external ear, and to the cheek area surrounding the entrance to the ear canal.

Ear drops containing acid solution, antibiotics, and other anti-inflammatory preparations usually cure this condition. Repeated episodes are common. Also see Ear Infections earlier in this guide.

Eyes, Inflammation and/or Irritation

Inflammation of the conjunctiva, the transparent covering of one or both eyes, is common in infancy and childhood. This condition, called conjunctivitis, is characterized by redness, an increase in mucoid secretion, and excessive tearing. It has many causes.

In the first few days of life, it occurs usually as a reaction to the silver nitrate or antibiotic drops instilled at birth to reduce the possibility of an infection contracted during the birth process. In rare instances a baby can contract an infection which is resistant to these drops and other treatment may be necessary.

Inflammation due to irritation from the drops usually clears up in a few days. Occasionally the nasolacrimal duct, which allows passage of tears from the outer eye to the nose, is partially obstructed at birth, causing a temporary accumulation of mucous on the surface of the eye.

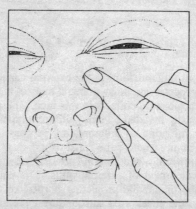

Massaging the tear duct

This can be irritating to the eye and cause inflammation, but it usually clears in a few days. Gentle massage in an upward direction several times a day with a clean finger along the duct located adjacent to the nostril frequently extrudes a mucous plug, establishing the normal passageway for drainage.

In toddlers and older children, conjunctivitis is most frequently due to irritation from dust, pollens, animal dander, or air pollution.

Redness of the eyes may indicate the early phase of many upper respiratory infections as well as other viral diseases. If redness persists beyond a few days, check with your doctor.

Specific isolated infections of the conjunctiva, causing redness, itching, burning, and often pain, is quite rare.

Prolonged inflammation of the conjunctivae, continuous tearing, photophobia (light sensitivity), a hazy appearance or a prominence of the eye in early infancy may be due to abnormal amounts of fluid within the eyeball. This condition is known as glaucoma. Congenital glaucoma is caused by an abnormal obstruction in the pathways that usually provide drainage of the fluid from within the eyeball. Prompt ophthalmologic treatment is important to reduce the possibility of permanent damage to the eye tissues.

Eyes, Positional Abnormalities

Inadequate alignment and poor coordination of movements of the eyes are normal during the early months of life. Prominence of the epicanthal fold of skin, at the side of the nose at the junction of the eyelid, and flattening of the nasal ridge often suggest a deficient alignment of the eyes. Observing that the reflection of a light held before the baby falls on the same spot on both pupils indicates that the eyes are in appropriate alignment. The appearance of abnormality in the alignment is due to the anatomical configuration of the face around the eye, which decreases the amount of visible white portion of the eyeball and narrows the palpebral tissue. As a baby's facial contour matures, the poor alignment disappears.

When is poor alignment and uncoordinated movement of the eyes significant? If inward or outward positioning of either eye is present at six months of age, you should be concerned. The deviation may be due to dysfunction of the muscles that control ocular positioning and coordinated movements. Inability to align the eyes can lead to diminished visual acuity in one eye because of disuse. This condition, often termed "lazy eye" (see Chapter 9), may be prevented by intermittent patching of the good eye, which stimulates the use of the weaker eye. Difficulty in aligning the eyes may also be the result of a variation in focusing power in the two eyes. One eye may be more nearsighted or farsighted than the other, so that it is difficult for the infant or child to focus both eyes together on any object.

An infant of one year with symptoms of this nature should certainly be evaluated and treated by an ophthalmologist or optometrist with special training and interest in eye problems in infants and young children, so as to reduce the chance of permanent deficits occurring in visual acuity and function.

Eyes, Vision Problems

Chronic inflammation of the conjunctivae, excessive tearing, and frequent sties occur commonly in children with visual deficits. Other symptoms suggesting defective visual function or acuity are excessive blinking, rubbing or pressing the eyes, frequent headaches, bumping into furniture, tripping, holding the head in a tilted position, squinting or covering one eye with the hand, or tiring after a few minutes of concentrated drawing or other activity requiring close vision.

Astigmatism in young children, in which the focusing is uneven, is often unrecognized. In this condition a child may have trouble recognizing letters in a book or on the blackboard because he or she cannot see horizontal and vertical components equally.

Many young children who are neither nearsighted nor farsighted cannot consistently converge and hold their eyes

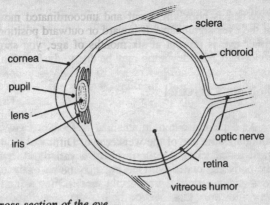

Cross-section of the eye

on a specific point on a printed page. The word they are looking at blurs in and out or seems to jump. One moment they see the printed word; the next minute it has disappeared. These children have difficulty in synchronizing their eye movements along a line. They tire easily and begin to make mistakes inconsistent with their knowledge and intelligence. They may be called lazy; however, the real problem is that the deficiency in visual function is tiring and exhausting, even for a highly motivated child.

A child presenting any of these symptoms should be examined by an ophthalmologist or optometrist with an interest and training in the visual problems of young children. Early recognition and treatment of visual dysfunction are important. Poor vision interferes greatly with a child's growth, maturation, and educational process. In addition, delay in appropriate treatment can result in permanent visual deficits, which could have been prevented. Also see **Chapter 9, Developmental Concerns.**

Failure to Thrive

A diagnosis applied to an infant who demonstrates a lack of normal gain in height and weight. The term describes a symptom that may reflect a metabolic, cardiac, gastrointestinal disorder, dwarfism, or inadequate nurturing. Careful studies are necessary to determine the exact cause of this condition.

Febrile Convulsion

An acute episode in infants and toddlers brought on by a sudden elevation of body temperature, usually due to a viral or bacterial infection. There is usually stiffening of the body associated with jerking movements of the extremities and a period of unconsciousness. Often a family history indicates that one or both parents suffered similar convulsions in childhood. The tendency to experience febrile convulsions is rare after the age of three. A sponge bath with cool water will usually terminate a febrile convulsion.

It is important to distinguish between these benign convulsions and a seizure due to overwhelming infection or a neurological disease. Consultation with a physician is imperative to clarify whether the episode represents a reaction to fever or indicates a serious condition. Examination of cerebral spinal fluid, blood count, and electroencephalographic studies may be necessary to obtain a definitive diagnosis. Also see Convulsion earlier in this guide, and **Chapter 22, What You Should Know about Fever.**

Feingold Diet

A diet that eliminates salicylate-containing foods and foods containing colorings and additives. Dr. Benjamin Feingold, the diet's originator, believes that these foods cause some children to be restless and hyperactive. Many parents report that adherence to the diet reduces a child's restlessness and enables him or her to participate in school and in play with less difficulty than when fed a regular diet. See Food Sensitivities and Behavior in **Chapter 21, Allergies,** for more information as well as a partial list of foods containing salicylates and food colorings and additives.

Fetal Alcohol Syndrome

A condition resulting from the ingestion of alcohol by the mother during pregnancy. This practice can be damaging to the fetus, leading to the birth of an infant who is smaller than average, and often presents a characteristic facial appearance consisting of decrease in width of the opening of the eyelids, underdevelopment of the upper jaw, and a thin upper lip. In some instances, development may be delayed.

Fever

For information on how to take a child's temperature and a complete discussion of fever, see **Chapter 22, What You Should Know about Fever.**

Fiberglass Dermatitis, *see* Dermatitis, Fiberglass

Fontanel, *see* Soft Spot

Fungus Infections

Inflammatory lesions of the skin and mucous membranes caused by the presence of tiny microscopic plants known as fungi. Common examples are thrush in the mouth, athlete's foot (see earlier listing), and inflamed diaper irritation due to a monilial infection (see Dermatitis, Monilia). Fungus infections are rarely serious, but prolonged treatment with antifungicide creams is often necessary.

Gastroesophogeal Reflex

A dysfunction of the sphincter at the juncture of the esophagus and stomach, resulting in frequent regurgitation and vomiting of the gastric contents. This condition is common in the early months of life. The regurgitation may be minimal, or it may be so extensive that irritability, discomfort, vomiting, and weight loss occur. The regurgitated gastric contents may also spill over into the larynx, causing temporary obstruction of the airway and seizurelike behavior.

In the case of a bottle-fed infant, thickening the milk mixture by adding cereal and sitting a baby at a forty-five-degree angle during a feeding often resolves the problem. The reverse flow of the gastric contents into the esophagus usually diminishes by the end of the first year of life as the muscular and neurologic functions of the sphincter at the entrance to the stomach become more efficient along with maturation of the nervous system. In rare instances, surgical intervention is necessary.

Genetic Counseling

A consultation concerning the incidence and cause of diseases of a hereditary nature. Parents who have a family history of inherited diseases or who have an infant with a disease of genetic origin often seek consultation with physicians with special training and interest in human genetics to discuss the risks of occurrence of such conditions in future children they might conceive. Most medical schools offer consultation in this field.

Geographic Tongue

A term used to describe harmless lesions of the tongue consisting of sharply demarcated, irregular, smooth, red, elevated plaques. The lesions are asymptomatic and disappear within a few weeks. This condition does not indicate the presence of any known disease, and the cause is unknown.

German Measles, *see* Rubella

Giardia

A parasite commonly found in the intestinal tract, causing abdominal cramps and, in rare instances, chronic malabsorption and growth failure. Contaminated water supplies as well as contact with feces provide the source of this infection. Appropriate treatment with antiparasitic medications is advised.

Glaucoma, *see under* Eyes, Irritation and/or Inflammation

Growing Pains

A common childhood complaint consisting of recurring pain usually in the thighs and lower legs. Pain is usually in the area of the muscles rather than in the joints. It often occurs with sufficient intensity at night to cause a child to awaken. These repeated episodes are poorly understood. Occasionally painful episodes occur in the daytime, causing a child to limit his or her physical activities. Examination usually reveals no abnormal findings. The possibility of the discomfort being caused by rheumatic disease is eliminated if there is no fever and labratory studies are normal. The pains usually disappear by the time a child reaches adolescence.

Hay Fever

Seasonal irritation of the nose and eyes, accompanied by nasal discharge, sneezing, and headache, occurring as a result of sensitivity to dust, pollens, or molds in the air. Antihistamines administered orally usually minimize these symptoms. In severe cases, desensitization by weekly injections of diluted concentrations of the offending substance (allergy shots) are necessary. Your doctor or an allergist should be consulted for either type of treatment. For more information, see Allergic Rhinitis in **Chapter 21, Allergies.**

Headaches

Young children frequently complain of headaches when they are in the initial phases of an acute illness, are tired and exhausted, or have fallen. A child suffering from a continuous headache or whose episodes are recurrent and interfere with enjoyment of play should be carefully evaluated by his or her physician. When your child's doctor cannot find any cause for the headache, it is important to consider whether the demands that are being put on the child in school or any other setting are too much for his or her age. Postponing activities such as music, gymnastics, or ballet dancing may be wise at this moment in a child's life. See also Migraine Headaches.

Hearing Impairment

A problem with hearing, ranging from the mild to the severe. Severe and profound hearing deficit is usually observed by parents because of an infant's or toddler's failure to turn toward sounds and the absence of significant language development by the third year of life. A two-year-old child should have a spoken vocabulary of at least fifty words and should be able to understand many hundred. Moderate hearing loss is often unrecognized because the infant or toddler's hearing acuity is sufficient to respond to a bell or a loud noise, but he is unable to hear much of the words spoken among family members, and, therefore, his language skills are impaired.

Hearing deficit can be due to congenital abnormalities, infection during fetal life or in the neonatal period, meningitis, encephalitis, recurring ear infections, or toxic reaction to medications. Early detection and treatment of a hearing problem are imperative since delay results not only in slowed language development, but also in a delay in the development of cognitive skills. See Ear Infections and other Hearing listings in this guide, and Hearing Problems in **Chapter 9, Developmental Concerns.**

Hearing Loss, Conduction

An auditory deficit due to several possible causes, sometimes malfunctioning of the eustachian tube leading from the middle ear to the throat. It can also be caused by fluid in the middle ear, which interferes with the movement of the tympanic membrane in response to sound stimuli. (This problem frequently occurs after repeated ear infections.) In addition, it can be due to an allergic swelling of the tissue of the middle ear, or of the lining of the walls of the eustachian tube.

Frequently oral administration of antibiotics and antihistamine preparations or removal of specific foods are effective means of treating this condition. When this fails, the insertion of plastic tubes in the eardrums, which allow the fluid to drain spontaneously, may be necessary.

Conduction hearing loss is distinguished from sensory hearing loss (see following listing). Also see Ear Infections in this guide, and Hearing Problems in **Chapter 9, Developmental Concerns.**

Hearing Loss, Sensory

Hearing loss due to abnormality in the *inner* ear. Sounds reach the inner ear, but are not transmitted to the brain because of abnormal functioning of the nervous system. This may be due to a congenital deficit, the result of a viral infection, or a toxic reaction to medications. Also see Ear Infections and Hearing Loss, Conduction in this guide.

Heart Disease, *see* Cardiac Catheterization; Cardiac Murmur; Congenital Heart Disease; Electrocardiogram (EKG)

Hemangioma (Strawberry Mark)

A raised, red lesion consisting of myriads of tiny capillaries protruding above the skin and resembling a strawberry cut in half. These lesions are not present at birth, but appear in the second or third month of life. The size increases until the end of the first year when growth ceases and regression occurs. The appearance of white fuzzy material on the outer area of the lesion is a sign that it is beginning to go away.

Occasionally there is an underlying component composed of many veins below the surface of the skin. This may be connected with the capillary hemangioma or may be a separate lesion, known as a cavernous hemangioma. It also will disappear as a child grows older.

Very rarely a toddler will fall and incur an abrasion on the surface of the hemangioma. This densely vascularized tissue may bleed profusely. Firm prolonged pressure with cold compresses will usually stop the bleeding within fifteen to twenty minutes.

Hemangiomata

A proliferation of tiny capillaries commonly present over the bridge of the nose, nape of the neck, or over the eyelids. These lesions are the result of dilation of tiny capillaries, which produce a flarelike lesion. The vast majority of all babies have them. These marks usually disappear during the first month of life. In rare instances, the lesions on the back of the neck, and occasionally those on the forehead, remain into adult life.

Hemoglobin

The oxygen-bearing iron compound in red blood cells. Low hemoglobin is the most common form of anemia in children. It is generally the result of inadequate dietary intake of iron, poor absorption of iron, or excessive blood loss. A simple test on a drop of blood can determine a child's hemoglobin level. Oral administration of iron is usually the appropriate treatment when a child is anemic.

Henoch-Schonlein's Purpura

A clinical condition in which a distinctive red rash and abdominal joint pain occur due to an inflammatory reaction in the capillaries supplying the skin, gastrointestinal tract, and joint tissues. The cause of the condition is unclear. It usually follows a mild bacterial or viral infection.

The skin rash is characterized by distinctive papules (pimples), which appear in a symmetrical fashion over the buttocks, arms, knees, and legs. Individual lesions appear in crops, then fade and are replaced by brownish pigmented areas, which may last for a week or more. Rarely, the face and mucous membranes of the mouth and nose may be involved. Children under three often have a puffy appearance of the scalp and the area around the eyes as well as the hands and feet.

Approximately two-thirds of the children with Henoch Schonlein's Purpura experience gastrointestinal and joint discomfort. Occasionally kidney involvement occurs, which leads to the presence of red blood cells in the urine.

There is no specific therapy. Full recovery is usually within a few weeks.

Hepatitis

A viral infection causing inflammation of the liver, general discomfort, diarrhea, cramps, and jaundice. In early infancy this condition is usually contracted during fetal life or at the time of passage through the birth canal. In later childhood, the disease usually occurs from contact with saliva, urine, blood, or feces of an infected person. Contaminated food, such as shellfish, or polluted water can also be a source of the infection.

A pregnant woman who has had hepatitis, or is a carrier of the virus causing this disease, should discuss with her obstetrician and pediatrician whether her baby should receive gamma globulin and hepatitis vaccine shortly after birth. Whenever an older child is exposed to a person suffering with hepatitis, you should also discuss with your doctor whether there is need for the administration of gamma globulin or other specific vaccine.

Mothers who have had hepatitis B (usually contracted through drugs or sexual contact) can pass it on to their babies during birth, and a significant number of these infants develop serious liver disease in adulthood. These babies should receive appropriate shots immediately after birth. Check with your doctor.

Hernia, *see* Hernia, Inguinal, *and* Hernia, Umbilical

Hernia, Inguinal

A defect in the musculature of the lower abdominal wall, which allows a bit of intestine in a boy or an ovary in a girl to move out of the normal position into the inguinal canal in the muscular layers of the abdominal wall. This protrusion into the hernial sac is painful and may appear as a tender swelling in the groin. Helping a baby or toddler relax in a warm tub bath often results in the intestine or ovary sliding back into its proper position. Gentle pressure applied by the fingers is often helpful.

If the intestine or ovary cannot be slipped back in place, surgical intervention is necessary. A child with a hernia that does not disappear in a few hours should be seen promptly by a physician. Prolonged displacement of a section of the intestine or ovary can lead to serious damage to that organ due to a decrease in blood supply. Immediate surgery may be imperative.

Hernia, Umbilical

A weakness in the abdominal muscles near the navel through which internal organs protrude. Umbilical hernias are common, and they usually disappear spontaneously in the first few years of life. However, if the size of the protrusion increases or shows no sign of spontaneously disappearing during these years, surgical treatment is indicated. The condition is more common in girls than in boys.

Hip Dislocation, *see* Dislocation of the Hip

Hirschprung's Disease

A congenital condition involving constipation in newborns. It is caused by an incomplete nerve supply to the rectal segment of the colon. Definitive diagnosis is made by biopsy of the inner lining of the rectum, which reveals an absence of the nerve cells that control the muscular contractions necessary for defecation. Once the diagnosis is established, surgical intervention is imperative.

Histoplasmosis

A fungus infection acquired through inhalation of airborne spores carried in soil, dust, barnyards, and other locations contaminated by bat and bird droppings. Asymptomatic infection is common and recognized by blood studies and skin tests. An acute form of the disease may produce weakness, cough, enlargement of the lymph nodes, and typical X ray findings in the lungs. Although a chronic form of the disease occurs in adults, it is rare in childhood. The disease is not transmitted from one human to another.

Hives (Urticaria)

A common vascular reaction of the skin characterized by blotchy welts that come and go. Hives can appear anywhere on the body. This condition often appears in association with the ingestion of certain foods. Common offenders are strawberries, chocolate, shellfish, nuts, pork, and tomatoes. In a sensitive individual, almost any drug can also be associated with hives. Insect stings are a common cause. Usually the administration of antihistaminic preparations relieves the itching, and the condition improves. Rarely, hives are associated with respiratory difficulties due to swelling in the larynx. When this happens, immediate medical care is imperative.

House Plant Dermatitis, *see* Dermatitis, House Plant

Hydrocele

A painless collection of fluid around the testicle in male infants. This may disappear as the baby grows, or it may continue. Surgical repair is indicated if the collection of fluid does not disappear within the first year of life.

Hydrocephalus

An increase in fluid in the intracranial cavity, associated with brain damage and enlargement of the head. It may be caused by a congenital defect, obstruction following an infection, or a brain tumor. Appropriate surgical intervention involving the placement of a small catheter to serve as a drainage path for the fluid is the usual treatment. This procedure often reduces the extent of damage to the brain.

Hydronephrosis

An abnormality of the kidney due to a congenital defect that leads to inadequate function and drainage of urine. In many instances a kidney of this nature is chronically infected. When the infection cannot be controlled with appropriate antibiotics, surgical intervention may be necessary. If a child is suffering recurrent urinary tract infections, a physician may suspect a hydronephrotic kidney.

Hyperactivity, *see* Attention Deficit Disorder

Hypospadias

A common congenital abnormality in which the penis is curved and the urinary stream is deflected toward the back of the body. Early surgical repair is necessary since a delay may cause difficulty for a boy when urinating in the standing position. If untreated, it could also interfere with sexual activity in adult life.

Hypothyroid

A metabolic defect in which the thyroid gland produces insufficient amounts of hormone to maintain normal growth and development. An infant with this deficit is known as a cretin. Early detection of the hypothyroidism and replacement therapy with thyroid medication can reverse the delay in development. Public health departments in many states provide routine blood testing of thyroid function during the early weeks of life.

Idiopathic Thrombocytopenic Purpura (ITP)

A generalized hemorrhagic tendency due to a marked reduction in the number of circulating blood platelets. This condition may follow a minor viral infection, such as German measles, chickenpox, mumps, or infectious mononucleosis. Petichiae, tiny red spots, may be found anywhere on the skin. Black-and-blue areas are often present over the anterior surfaces of the lower extremities and over bony prominences such as the ribs, shoulders, legs, and pelvic areas. Examination of the blood reveals a marked reduction in the number of circulating platelets.

The course of acute idiopathic thrombocytopenic purpura is usually a few weeks. Rarely, when the disease becomes chronic, surgical removal of the spleen may be indicated.

Impetigo

A bacterial infection of the skin in childhood due to streptococci or staphylococci. Lesions can appear anywhere on the body, but occur most frequently on the face, hands, neck, and extremities. Topical antibiotic preparations usually clear the lesions promptly. When the infection is prolonged, oral administration of appropriate antibiotics is indicated.

Infections, *see* Bacterial Infections, Congenital Infections, Fungus Infections

Infectious Mononucleosis

An acute viral disease in children, adolescents, and young adults manifest by sore throat, general weakness, lethargy, and loss of appetite. Commonly the lymph glands of the neck, armpits, and groin are enlarged, as well as the spleen.

Fever elevation may persist for more than a week before definitive signs are present. Many patients with mononucleosis also have an associated streptococcal infection of the throat, which should be treated with appropriate antibiotics.

The course of the disease varies from being quite mild —often unrecognized by patient or doctor—to moderate severity lasting for several weeks. Occasionally there is involvement of the liver with clinical jaundice. The main discomfort is due to swelling of the pharyngeal tissues and tonsils. Often a large amount of white exudate is present in the throat, which interferes significantly with breathing and swallowing. In such instances, oral administration of steroids, such as prednisone, may be relieving.

The diagnosis is supported by the presence of a specific kind of lymphocyte, known as Downey cells, in the blood, and also by a specific serological test, which becomes positive in the second or third week of the illness. A child or adolescent may be quite miserable. Recuperation to previous health status may take several weeks.

Insect Bites, *see* Bites, Insect

Insect Sensitivity

A unique tendency of an individual to experience moderate to severe systemic reactions when stung by a bee, yellow jacket, hornet, or wasp. A "normal" reaction to a sting consists of a small area of redness associated with intense pain at the site of the wound. However, about one percent of the population experiences generalized swelling or other reactions in other parts of the body, completely removed from the site of the original sting. Systemic reactions such as gagging, difficulty in swallowing, spasm of the larnyx, bronchial disease, dizziness or fainting are serious and merit immediate medical attention, since severe reactions can be life-threatening.

Individuals who experience moderate or severe reactions may need prolonged desensitization consisting of a series of injections over a period of months. Also see Bites, Insect earlier in this guide.

Intussusception

A rare condition in which the intestine doubles back inside itself so that the passageway to the bowel is obstructed. The irritation and constriction of blood supply to the affected portion produce significant swelling of the wall of the intestine. Characteristically, a child with this problem suffers severe episodic pain during which he is inconsolable. Then he relaxes and is fairly comfortable for a few minutes, only to begin to scream again at repeated intervals. A baby with intussusception looks frightened and pale. Usual methods of comforting, such as walking, rocking, and application of a heating pad or hot water bottle to the stomach, offer little relief.

Vomiting usually occurs repeatedly. After a number of

hours, a baby may pass a stool containing mucus and dark blood with an appearance of currant jelly.

Intussusception requires prompt medical attention. Careful examination and X-ray of the lower intestinal tract are important. Frequently, the injection of barium into the colon through the rectum while taking the X ray reduces the intussusception. If this does not happen, surgical intervention is necessary.

Jaundice

A yellowish discoloration of the skin and whites of the eyes due to an accumulation of bile pigments in the body. Jaundice is a normal physiologic event beginning on the second or third day of life due to the excess destruction of red blood cells as an infant adjusts to life outside the womb. The excess pigment, bilirubin, is released into the blood stream and excreted by the liver. The yellow tinge to the skin and whites of the eyes usually disappears in a few days, although the condition may be prolonged in premature babies. If jaundice persists and an unnaturally high level of bilirubin occurs, the baby may receive phototherapy, a treatment in which the baby is exposed to ultraviolet light by being placed under fluorescent lights for a few days.

Another cause of jaundice in early infancy is an incompatability between the mother's blood and the baby's red blood cells known as hemolytic disease of the newborn. Phototherapy is the appropriate treatment for this condition also. In rare instances an exchange transfusion may be necessary to remove the bilirubin completely from the body of the baby.

In older children, jaundice may result from hepatitis, a viral infection which causes inflammation of the liver and a reduction of its ability to remove bilirubin. A child suffering from hepatitis would probably be quite ill, suffering from diarrhea, malaise, and weight loss. There is no specific treatment for hepatitis other than bed rest.

Juvenile Rheumatoid Arthritis

A chronic inflammatory arthritis involving ankles, wrists, fingers, or toes. Stiffness and tenderness accompany the joint swelling. One or several joints may be involved in the initial episode. Permanent remission may take place in a few weeks or months in some patients; in others, recurrent episodes involving multiple joints occur.

Characteristically, a salmon-pink, flat rash on the chest, thighs, and upper arms is present in the initial phase of the disease. Intermittent fever is common, often preceding by several weeks the appearance of definitive joint symptoms.

Heat, physical therapy, and continuous administration of aspirin relieve the pain and promote movement of the joints. In selected cases, other medications are used to relieve the progress of the disease.

Keloid

A scar formation occurring after an operation, a burn, acne, or a minor abrasion such as the piercing of an earlobe. Initially the scar appears normal, but it continues to grow for a prolonged period of time. These lesions are harmless, but they itch and may be unsightly. Radiation and injection of steroids are the usual treatment.

Kidney Disease, *see* Hydronephrosis *and* Nephritis

Knock Knee

A common postural phenomenon in which the young child's knees meet medially and the ankles deviate laterally. The alignment usually improves as the child grows and becomes active. When the feet are exceptionally far apart, splinting may be necessary.

Kawasaki Disease (Mucocutaneous Lymph Node Syndrome)

An acute illness lasting several weeks and occurring predominantly in children under the age of five. The cause is unknown. The common symptoms are fever, sore throat, swelling of the tongue, lips, cheeks, hands and feet, conjunctivitis, generalized enlargement of the lymph nodes, a widespread red rash, and extreme irritability. Peeling of the fingertips is often present early in the disease. Definitive laboratory findings can confirm the diagnosis.

Inflammation of the heart vessels and other arteries is one of the complications that may occur. Hospitalization is usually necessary when a child contracts Kawasaki disease.

Labial Adhesions

A thin membrane or strands of tissue connecting the labia in infants and young girls. When this condition is present, your doctor will separate the labia with gentle pressure and advise application of petrolatum, zinc oxide ointment, or other benign creams. This usually corrects the problem and prevents recurrence.

Lacrimal Duct Stenosis

Obstruction of the tear duct connecting the eye with the nose. Normally tears and mucous material drain from the surface of the eye through this duct to the inside of the nose. In the newborn, this duct is frequently obstructed due to mucous adhesions that interfere with adequate drainage from the eye. This material backs up and accumulates on the surface of the eye and the inner surface of the eyelids, often spilling over and staining the area around the eye. Antibiotic eye drops and gentle massaging of the lacrimal duct with a clean finger often remove the mucous plug, and normal drainage is restored. In rare instances, it is necessary to surgically probe the obstructed duct.

Lactose Intolerance

A common condition in which the ingestion of moderate amounts of milk or milk products produces abdominal pain of varying degrees of severity. This problem is caused by a deficiency of the enzyme lactase, which is necessary to digest the sugar lactose present in these foods. Lactose intolerance often appears in early childhood in a youngster who was previously able to consume milk without difficulty. It may remain throughout life. However, there is wide variation in the amount of milk various individuals with lactose intolerance can ingest, suggesting that the cause is a relative deficiency rather than a complete absence of this enzyme. Many people who experience lactose intolerance are able to ingest yogurt and acidophilus milk (available at many supermarkets) without the discomfort that results when whole milk and other milk products are consumed. See also Milk Allergy in this guide.

Language Development, Delayed

A child who speaks no single words at eighteen months, less than ten words at twenty-four months, or whose speech is largely unintelligible at three years of age is manifesting a significant delay in the ability to achieve normal communication skills. A hearing evaluation is imperative. If a child is not hearing well, she cannot achieve the normal capacity to speak. When an auditory deficit is present, appropriate medical treatment, including hearing aids if necessary, should be instituted promptly.

Some children who possess normal hearing have the ability to understand what they hear, but have difficulty in verbally expressing their thoughts. This learning disability usually responds to appropriate stimulation and speech therapy, which should be arranged as soon as the difficulty is recognized.

Your doctor or local superintendent of schools can help you arrange appropriate evaluation and treatment for a child experiencing a delay in developing communication skills.

Lanugo Hair

Very fuzzy hair present on various parts of some newborns. This hair falls out within a few weeks, leaving the baby's skin soft and pink.

Lead Poisoning

An undue accumulation of lead in the body, which can cause anemia, irritability, slowing of thought processes, mental retardation, learning disabilities, seizures, blindness, cerebral palsy, and even death. It is a completely preventable disease.

Ingestion of lead-containing paint chips is a common cause of this disease. Although federal law prohibits use of paints containing significant quantities of lead for indoor painting, many children living in old houses or apartment buildings continue to be exposed to paint chips from paint applied when lead-based mixtures were commonly used. In addition, living in an old house with lead-based paint on the walls during restoration procedures can cause a problem. The air is filled with fine particles of lead scraped off the walls and woodwork. The absorption of this material elevates the body level of this substance, and lead poisoning can occur. Mouthing of toys, twigs, and leaves in play areas where the air and ground contain large amounts of lead is another common pathway through which lead enters the body.

Symptoms of lead poisoning are irritability, restlessness, lethargy, and anemia. If you have any concerns as to whether your child is suffering from this condition, ask your child's doctor or your public health official to obtain appropriate blood studies. Diagnosis of lead poisoning is established by chemical analysis of a blood sample. The Center for Disease Control of the United States Department of Health and Human Services states that the presence of 25 micrograms of lead per 100 cubic centimeters of blood indicates that a child is absorbing more lead than the body can excrete and is in serious danger of developing significant symptoms of lead poisoning.

Treatment of a minimal amount of lead poisoning consists of removing the child from contaminated areas, thus eliminating the source. A more severe form of the disease is treated by chelation, injection of medications that promote elimination of lead from the body. A child who has absorbed sufficient lead into his body to cause a rise in concentration of this substance should not return to the same living quarters until there has been careful evaluation of the presence of lead and the removal of the source. Recurrence of lead poisoning is common without these precautionary steps.

Learning Disabilities

Children with learning disabilities often have normal vision and hearing, yet exhibit a disorder in one or more of the basic psychologic processes involved in understanding or in using spoken or written language. These children are usually of average intellectual capacity, but have difficulty in listening, thinking, talking, reading, writing, spelling, arithmetic, or in understanding what they hear or what they read.

The basis for the difficulties may be due to congenital factors, stress during the fetal, delivery, or perinatal moments, or due to injury or illness in infancy or toddler years. It is imperative to realize that children with learning disabilities are not lazy, poorly motivated, or disturbed. They need special educational help in order to aid them in mastering age-appropriate skills and thus be able to proceed with their educational tasks.

Early recognition of these handicaps is also imperative, since specialized educational programs should be instituted before a child lags behind in achievements. Public Law 94-142, known as the Education for All Handicapped Children Act, passed by Congress in 1975, mandates special education programs for any child suffering a handicap that interferes with learning. Further information about how to obtain evaluation and remedial services can be obtained from your local superintendent of schools, state commissioner of education, or the United States Office of Education Information Center, Washington, DC 20003. Also see Public Law 94-142 in this guide, as well as **Chapter 9, Developmental Concerns, and Chapter 25, Chronic Illness.**

Leukemia

A malignant disease marked by an increased production of white blood cells that interfere seriously with the production of red blood cells. Leukemia causes anemia, pallor, and general malaise. Lymph glands are enlarged throughout the body. Chemotherapy available for treating this disease may result in remissions lasting for months or years, and the prognosis for survival is improving steadily. The disease is not contagious.

Lice

Small six-legged, wingless insects, four millimeters in size and barely visible to the naked eye. Head lice are common in school-age children, and girls are more susceptible than boys. Having them is no disgrace and is not a sign of lack of hygiene in the home.

The eggs, called nits, are oval grayish- or yellowish-white and are seen as tiny specks usually attached to hairs, although they may also be found in seams of clothing worn by an infected individual. They look a bit like dandruff flakes, but they will not brush off because they attach

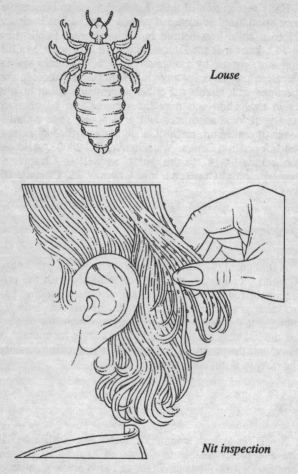

Louse

Nit inspection

themselves so firmly to the hair shafts. Removal is quite difficult. The process may be facilitated by soaking the hair with a weak solution of vinegar, which loosens the mucoid material holding the nits to the hairs. The hair should then be combed with a fine-toothed comb.

Head lice are treated with special shampoo or lotion, which your doctor will recommend. The scalp and hair should be thoroughly shampooed. The hair should be thoroughly combed. A second treatment five to eight days later is necessary in order to remove the new generation of lice that may have hatched since the initial treatment.

If your child is in school or a day-care center, you can take preventive measures by teaching your youngster not to share headgear or combs with friends—or even with other family members in order to reduce the risk of ever spreading the lice.

If your child comes home with lice, treat as recommended above and do a complete laundry of bedding and recently worn clothing and hats. Sterilize by boiling or discard all combs used by the child, and be sure to check that the lice have not spread to other members of the family.

Lisping

The inability to produce "s" or "th" sounds distinctly. Lisping is very common during preschool and elementary school years. The difficulty in articulation usually disappears by the age of seven. If it persists, speech therapy can be very helpful.

Tongue tie, that is, a shortened frenulum (the membranous attachment under the tongue) inhibiting full motion of the tongue, is related only rarely to speech difficulties. If a child can articulate "t," "d," "n," "l," or can say *no, ta-ta, and dada*, or can stick out his tongue as he makes faces, any speech problem is probably unrelated to any inhibition of tongue movements.

Liver Abnormalities, *see* Hepatitis *and* Infectious Mononucleosis

Lockjaw, *see* Tetanus

Lumbar Puncture (Spinal Tap)

The removal of a few drops of fluid from the spinal canal to determine the presence of cells and concentration of protein and sugar in the cerebrospinal fluid. This information aids in determining the presence of any inflammatory process or other disease in the brain or spinal canal.

Lyme Disease

A newly recognized disease in which the infective organism is transferred to humans by tick bite. One or two weeks later a red blotch forms at the site of the bite, followed by fever, chills, and general discomfort. Three to four weeks after the appearance of the rash, inflammation and pain in the joints occur. The disease will usually in time go into complete remission on its own, although antibiotics administered orally may shorten the course of it.

Lymph Glands

The lymphatic glands represent an important part of the body's defense system against disease. It is quite normal for the glands in the neck, armpits, and groin to increase in size and be easily palpable as part of a normal response to common viral and bacterial infections occurring in the early years of life. The enlargement of these glands usually subsides within a few weeks, only to recur with subsequent infections.

A child with prolonged glandular enlargement, particularly when associated with general malaise and fever, deserves thorough examination and laboratory studies.

An individualized enlargement of a gland in the areas of the elbow or armpit may occur as a result of an infection in the hand or on the arm. Likewise, an enlargement of a gland in the groin may come about as a result of an infection in the leg.

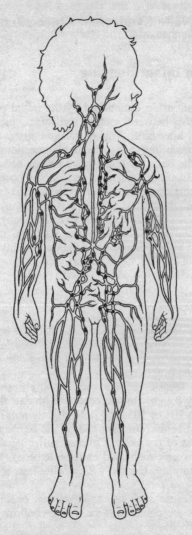

The lymphatic system

Lymph Node Syndrome, Mucocutaneous, *see* Kawasaki Disease

Maternal Infant Bonding

The relationship established by the initial physical and visual contact between mother and infant, usually occurring shortly after birth. This exchange initiates a variety of mutually rewarding and pleasurable reactions, which in part form the basis for future relationships between mother and child. Every effort should be made by hospital personnel to support opportunities for mother—and father, too—to hold their baby and initiate this important process as early in baby's life as possible. Even if a baby is sick and needs special care in a newborn intensive care unit, a mother and father should have the opportunity to observe and hold the baby as soon as is practical.

Measles

A highly contagious viral disease that may be quite serious. In recent years, the incidence of measles has been significantly reduced in the United States due to vigorous immunization programs.

Initially, measles begins with a runny nose, red eyes, and a brassy cough. On the fourth or fifth day, the temperature rises to 104 or 105, and dull, slightly red, raised spots appear, first behind the ears and on the forehead and then over the rest of the body. Children suffer headaches, discomfort, severe cough, and extreme lethargy. Bright light may be disturbing. Normally the disease lasts about nine to ten days.

Complications such as ear infections, pneumonia, and encephalitis are common. One attack confirms immunity. See also Rubella.

Measles, Three-Day, (*see* Rubella)

Meningitis

An inflammation of the covering of the brain due to the invasion of a pathogenic bacteria or virus. The source of the infectious agent may be from the bloodstream, an infected ear or sinus, or from the site of a skull fracture. Fever, headaches, nausea, vomiting, inability to tolerate bright light, and difficulty in flexing the neck are early signs of this disease. A common form of meningitis due to the meningicoccus is accompanied by a generalized blotchy red rash appearing at the outset of the disease. A viral infection such as one caused by chickenpox or mumps or a number of other viruses may also produce meningitis, which is usually quite mild, and leaves little residue.

Meningitis is a critical disease. Contact your doctor, or take your child to the nearest hospital emergency room. Immediate hospitalization and intravenous administration of antibiotics are imperative. The earlier the treatment, the less chance of residual damage.

Metaproterenol

A pharmacologic preparation that relieves the spasm of the tiny muscles of the bronchioles commonly present in asthma. The medication can be taken orally in pill or liquid form as well as by means of an inhaler. Side effects of this drug are shakiness, rapid heartbeat, nervousness, and vomiting.

Migraine Headaches

Periodic headaches, initially appearing in the frontal or temporal area and often preceded by a momentary visual disturbance. Nausea and vomiting may accompany these episodes. The discomfort may last for several hours. Quite frequently a child falls asleep and awakens refreshed. Relief of symptoms by the administration of medicine containing ergotamine supports a migraine headache diagnosis.

Milia

Tiny white raised papules appearing over the forehead, at the scalp, and on other parts of the face. These papules disappear after the first few months of life. The cause is believed to be retained sebaceous material in the sweat duct.

Milk Allergy

Allergy to cow's milk is common in infancy and childhood. In the early months, an infant sensitive to cow's milk may develop cramps, diarrhea, and vomiting after ingesting milk. A moderate congestion of the respiratory tract may also occur as an allergic reaction in the early months. Milk sensitivity with gastrointestinal symptoms usually disappears in infancy. Toddlers and preschool children are more likely to experience congestion of the respiratory tract or eczema as an expression of milk allergy. Substitution of soybean preparations or synthetic milk mixtures provide relief. Also see Lactose Intolerance in this guide, and Early Allergies: Milk and Various Foods in **Chapter 21.**

Mispronounced Words

Preschool children mispronounce many words because their physical control of the many muscles of the mouth, tongue, lips, and palate are immature and coordinate poorly during these years. When a child speaks, he must coordinate precisely his breathing, larynx, nose, lips, teeth, jaw, palate, and tongue. And also he has to think of what he wants to say. No wonder *sun porch* becomes *pun sorch* or *spaghetti* becomes *pasghetti*. Just ask your child to slow down a minute, so that you can demonstrate the correct word for him, and soon he will leave these immature patterns of speech behind.

Molluscum Contagiousum

A viral skin disorder observed in young children, characterized by small papules commonly located on the trunk, neck, and face. They are like warts. The lesions, which are discrete and globular, may last several months and then disappear spontaneously. Lesions that are bothersome or unsightly are best removed or cauterized by a physician.

Mongolian Spots

Blue or slate-gray benign lesions of the skin commonly appearing over the lower back and buttocks in early infancy. The lesions tend to disappear during the first year. There is no known relationship of these lesions to any disease or pathological process.

Monilia Dermatitis, *see* Dermatitis, Monilia

Moro Reflex (Startle Reflex)

A normal reflex movement in which a young infant, in response to sudden noise, sudden movement, or loss of support, extends her hands, arms, and legs into midair and often emits a sharp cry. This reflex usually disappears in the first half year of life as the baby's neurologic system matures.

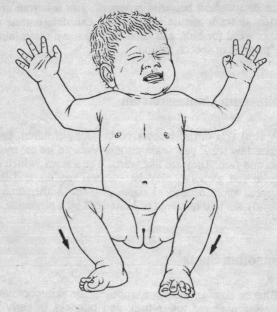

Moro reflex

Motion Sickness

Nausea, dizziness, and vomiting experienced when riding in a car, bus, train, plane, or on a boat for a prolonged period. These symptoms are due to the movement of fluid in the semicircular canals located in the inner ear. These canals ordinarily maintain an individual's balance; however, the constant movement of the fluid in the canals, caused by the motion of travel, can cause this sickness.

The administration of small amounts of antihistamine preparations half an hour before starting on a trip will usually prevent the symptoms from occurring. If a full day of travel is planned, the medication should be taken as directed throughout the day.

Mumps

A highly contagious generalized viral disease; swelling of the parotid salivary glands on either side of the jaw is the most prominent symptom. Fever, generalized achiness, nausea, headache, decrease in appetite, and sore throat are common additional findings. Pancreatitis, orchitis (inflammation of the testicles), mastitis, and encephalitis are rare complications.

The disease lasts seven to ten days, longer if some of the complications occur. An individual with mumps is contagious during the active phase of the disease and as long as ten days after symptoms have disappeared. The incubation period is twelve to twenty-five days.

Most of the complications of mumps are short-lived, although occasionally an adolescent boy with mumps orchitis may suffer sterility in later life.

Widespread use of mumps vaccination in toddler years will probably eradicate this disease in the near future.

Myositis

Significant and painful inflammation of the muscles of the body, particularly those of the thighs and lower legs. A child suffering any viral infection may often experience this. The discomfort may be so intense that a child refuses to walk. It usually subsides within seven to ten days. Bed rest and administration of aspirin offer relief.

Nephritis (Glomerulonephritis)

A rare complication of a streptococcal infection manifest by abnormal kidney function, puffiness of the face and other parts of the body, elevated blood pressure and red cells, and significant amounts of protein in the urine. Occasionally, the elevation of the blood pressure reaches serious proportions, necessitating the administration of antihypertensive drugs. Children who have this illness usually recover completely; however, prompt diagnosis and treatment are imperative.

Nightmares

Many preschool children awaken during the night having experienced a scary dream and needing the comforting presence of a parent or known adult. Quite frequently, a child will be half-asleep, but screaming with terror because of her dream. It is usually impossible to comfort a child in this state until she awakens completely so she can realize that what was frightening her was a dream and that she is really safe in her own bed with a parent or other trusted adult close by. As a child gains increasing language skills, she can be helped to understand what is a "pretend dream" and what is real. Encouraging a youngster to talk about her dreams in the daytime will often relieve the intensity of the discomfort at night.

During the night, cuddling, talking about the dream, and reassuring her that it is safe to go back to sleep are usually effective. Taking a child into one's own bed may be comforting and soothing at the time; however, it may not be advisable in the long run. The real goal is to help a child realize that her *own* bed is a safe place. Taking her into your bed may only convince her that she was right in wanting to leave her own bed. Helping a child to have the strength to feel safe on her own is the best comfort you can give at this time.

Nosebleeds

Sudden bleeding from one or both nostrils is fairly common in childhood. This is usually due to the presence of a superficial blood vessel that is ulcerated due to an upper respiratory infection, dry air, or picking at the nose.

To stop a nosebleed, squeeze the nostrils with your

fingers or apply firm pressure to the nose with ice wrapped in a handkerchief or washcloth. To prevent the blood from running into the stomach and causing nausea and vomiting, have the child sit up so that the blood runs out. If the bleeding continues for more than twenty minutes, call your physician.

Nosebleeds associated with other episodes of bleeding or with generalized black-and-blue spots suggest the possibility of a systemic hematological condition, which merits careful medical evaluation.

Nursing Bottle Syndrome

The decay of the upper first teeth, and occasionally the lower ones, in toddlers and preschool children. It is caused by a baby using a bottle at bedtime and during sleep. Since the flow of saliva, which rinses the mouth during waking hours, is reduced during sleep, the milk mixture or sweetened fruit juice or sugar mixture adheres to the teeth. This encourages the growth of oral bacteria and the formation of dental plaque, leading to decay of the enamel in cavity-prone children.

If a baby has a need to suck at bedtime and during sleep, substituting a bottle with plain water or utilizing a pacifier offers a solution without risking the possibility of contributing to dental decay and cavity formation.

Pacifier

A specially designed rubber nipple with ventilation holes and a large handle, which offers an infant the comfort of sucking at other than mealtimes. A fretful baby who has yet to find his thumb may gain considerable comfort by sucking a pacifier. I believe that the use of a pacifier can provide enormous comfort for the baby who is tired or in distress. Usually a baby will discard the pacifier toward the end of the first year, or early in the second year. You can often encourage a baby to give up the pacifier by substituting a favorite doll or blanket as a comforting item.

Parotitis

An inflammatory process in the parotid salivary gland, which is located just anterior and below the ear. The commonest cause is mumps. However, other viruses and bacteria can cause inflammatory reactions that are indistinguishable from mumps. Treatment consists of analgesics to relieve pain. The usual episode lasts from four to six days. In rare instances, an obstruction to the parotid duct (known as Stenson's duct) interrupts normal passage of saliva from the gland to the mouth. If recurrent episodes occur, evaluation of the passageway in the duct is in order.

Perforated Eardrum

A perforation in the eardrum, usually resulting from pressure caused by bacterial infection in the middle ear. Your doctor should always be consulted if you suspect your child's eardrum is perforated; even though the child may feel better after the perforation, antibiotic treatment is necessary. The perforation can result in hearing impairment. Evaluation and treatment by a nose and throat specialist are usually recommended when a perforation fails to heal. See also Ear Infections in this guide.

Perianal Redness

Redness and irritation around the anus often produced by specific foods in the diet. Whole milk and carrots commonly cause this difficulty. Also, rectal itching accompanying pinworm infestation may be the cause.

Pertussis (Whooping Cough)

A contagious disease affecting the respiratory tract and causing the air passages to become plugged with mucus. Initially, the disease starts like an upper respiratory infection, but after seven to ten days, the coughing become intense and continuous. At the end of a paroxysm of coughing, a child takes a big breath with an inspiratory "whoop," which is why it is called whooping cough. In the United States, immunization against this disease has reduced incidence tremendously. For information about immunization against pertussis, see **Chapter 16**.

Phototherapy

The exposure of a jaundiced baby to ultraviolet light, which increases the ability of the body to eliminate the accumulated bilirubin causing the jaundice. This treatment is particularly valuable in treating jaundice related to hemolytic disease of the newborn, or associated with prematurity or stress during the neonatal period.

Pica

The eating of inedible substances, such as newspaper, tissues, dirt, paint, crayons, clay, starch, leaves, soap, and almost anything else within reach.

During infancy and the toddler years, ingestion of a certain amount of foreign substances is normal! However, to avoid potential accidental poisoning, all inedible items should be out of reach of the infant or toddler.

Persistance of pica beyond the second year is abnormal, and the reason why some children continue this habit beyond the toddler years is unclear. Your doctor should be consulted.

Pinworm

A tiny threadlike white worm, from two to thirteen millimeters in length, which frequently inhabits the intestinal tract. Children are particularly susceptible to this infestation. The infection is spread from one individual to another through the transfer of microscopic worm eggs, which commonly lodge in the anal area, causing itching. Children scratch this area, thereby getting the eggs onto their fingers and then transmitting them to toys, blankets, and other items that may later be handled by other children. Sucking of fingers or mouthing toys or other contaminated items results in the ingestion of the eggs, which hatch into larval and adult worms in the intestinal tract. The worms then settle in the large intestine. There are no symptoms from the worms in the colon, but live worms may crawl out of the rectum (and are visible), particularly after a hot bath, causing severe itching. The inevitable scratching results in excoriation of the skin and, at times, secondary infections. Frequently, several members of a family are infected.

Occasionally, vaginitis in young girls is a result of the invasion of these worms into the genital tract.

There are several medications available for treating this condition. Recurrence is common, and repeated treatment is likely to be necessary.

Pityriasis Rosea

An acute, self-limiting skin disorder occurring in children and adults. The eruption follows a distinctive pattern, starting with a single isolated lesion called a herald patch, which usually consists of an oval area of scaly dermatitis two to five centimeters in diameter. This patch usually has a flat pink or brown center with a red, finely scaled and slightly elevated border. Five to ten days after the appearance of the initial patch, a secondary crop of lesions appear on the chest, abdomen, and back. The rash lasts for six to twelve weeks, and then gradually fades. Following the regression of the lesions, areas of hyperpigmentation may remain for many months.

Occasionally, a child may experience headache, sore throat, swollen glands, and general discomfort prior to the appearance of the skin lesions. Exposure to sunshine or ultraviolet light hastens the disappearance of the lesions.

PKU Disease

PKU is an abbreviation for phenylketonuria, an inherited metabolic disorder in which certain food proteins cannot be digested. As a result, toxic substances accumulate in the body and damage the brain, causing retardation. Early recognition of this metabolic condition and the limitation of protein intake in the diet are important. Many state health departments require blood or urine tests in the first month of life to detect the presence of this condition. The early institution of an appropriate low-protein diet reduces the possibility of significant retardation in later life.

Pneumonia

An inflammation in the lungs due to a viral or bacterial cause. Pneumonia usually starts with an upper respiratory infection, and after a few days or more, a child develops rapid breathing, high fever, and a deep productive cough. Although frequently a physician can detect with a stethoscope the presence of abnormal breath sounds suggesting the presence of pneumonia, the diagnosis is usually confirmed by chest X ray. Viral pneumonia runs a normal course of several weeks. Antibiotics rarely influence the course of it. However, when bacterial pneumonia is present, prompt administration of appropriate antibiotics dramatically shortens the course of the illness. For more information, see **Chapter 23, How to Tell If Your Child Is Sick or Very Sick.**

Pneumothorax

A rupture of air passages of the lung, allowing air to escape into the chest cavity and causing the lung to collapse. Breathlessness and chest pain are the usual symptoms. This condition occurs in small infants who have had a difficult delivery and who needed vigorous resuscitation. In older children it may occur as a result of traumatic injuries, or rupture of abnormal blisters in the bronchial tubes. Cure is often spontaneous. In other instances a catheter is inserted between the ribs and chest space, which allows the air to flow out and the collapsed lung to expand gradually.

Poison Ivy

A widely found toxic plant, which, when in contact with the skin of sensitive individuals, produces an inflammatory reaction. Poison ivy is the most common cause of contact dermatitis in childhood. Red skin, swelling, and itchy lesions may appear within a few hours after contact. The rash is usually limited to the exposed area, although in highly sensitive individuals, toxic substance on the hands can spread the inflammation to the face and other parts of the body. The eruption and inflammation reach a peak in about a week, and then gradually get better. Cool soaks, soothing lotions, and oral administration of steroids relieve the discomfort. See Dermatitis, Contact in this guide, and Atopic and Contact Dermatitis in **Chapter 21.**

Polio (Poliomyelitis, Infantile Paralysis)

A viral infection that attacks the nerves that control the muscles. Many individuals in the past were infected with polio virus and suffered no symptoms. Those who did suffer clinical symptoms were often left with severe paralysis. In some instances, the base of the brain was affected; these individuals needed respirators to support life. Fortunately, the widespread administration of oral polio vaccine has almost eliminated this disease in the Western world.

All children should receive this vaccine in infancy and toddler years. Many individuals who had a polio infection in early life carry live virus in their intestinal tracts and may expose unimmunized individuals to the possibility of contracting the disease. For more information, see Chapter 16, Immunizations.

Pseudo Strabismus

A condition in which the position of the eyes of a baby *appear* to be crossed due to narrowing of the opening of the eyelids. Careful observation of the pupils when a light is held fourteen to eighteen inches from the midline reveals that the focusing on the light is quite normal with appropriate reflection of the light in the same spot in both pupils.

The appearance suggesting strabismus disappears within the first year of life as the bridge of the nose grows and the horizontal opening in front of the eyeball widens. See also Strabismus.

Psoriasis

A common inherited chronic skin disorder manifest by the presence of reddish scaly plaques commonly found on the elbows, knees, back, and thighs, although any part of the body may be affected. The round, well-delineated patches begin as small, reddish, pinpoint lesions, which coalesce and form plaques one to several centimeters in diameter. The condition may begin as a solitary lesion, or with countless patches distributed in a symmetrical pattern. The nails are affected in many instances. The course is prolonged and unpredictable. In many instances, the lesions disappear, without any known reason, only to reappear a few years later. Sunlight is generally beneficial.

Topical therapy with special ointments and lotions reduces the extent of the lesions.

Public Law 94–142

The Education for All Handicapped Children Act, known as Public Law 94–142, was passed by Congress in 1975 and mandates that state departments of education and local boards of education arrange specialized teaching for all children who have a handicap that interferes with their education. In most states, specialized services begin for children of three years and eight months, although in some states, services are available earlier for children with a language or hearing disability.

Federal funds under the provisions of Public Law 94–142 provide partial payment to support local remedial programs. Parents suspecting that their child has a learning difficulty or other handicap that may interfere with their education should contact their local superintendent of schools or the state commissioner of education for help in arranging an appropriate program. If you are unsuccessful in obtaining assistance locally, write to the United States Office of Education Information Center, Washington, DC 20003. Also see **Chapter 25, Chronic Illness.**

Pyuria

The presence of many white blood cells in the urine, indicating an infection in the bladder, ureter, or kidneys. Appropriate antibiotic treatment is indicated. Follow-up laboratory examination of the urine is important to assure that the infection has cleared completely. If the infection persists, further antibiotic treatment may be necessary.

Rabies

A viral disease of animals, which, when transmitted to humans by a bite, can produce a critical illness involving the central nervous system. Animals who commonly may carry rabies include skunks, bats, raccoons, foxes, and in some areas of the country, dogs and cats. The virus is transmitted in the saliva at the time of a bite. Most domesticated dogs and many household cats are immunized against rabies and cannot contract or transmit the disease.

When a person is bitten, the animal should be captured and confined for a two-week observation by a veterinarian or health officer. If the animal is found to have rabies, the individual suffering a bite should receive a course of rabies vaccine by injection.

When it is impossible to locate the animal, it is important to discuss with your physician and public health authorities whether rabies vaccine should be administered. Also see Bites, Animal in this guide, and Scratches, Cuts, Abrasions, Puncture Wounds, and Animal Bites in Chapter 20.

Red Blood Cells

Red blood cells carry inspired oxygen from the lungs to all parts of the body, and they carry carbon dioxide from the body tissues to the lungs where it is expired. The main component of the red blood cells is the iron-containing substance, hemoglobin. Anemia, the reduction in the number of red blood cells or a diminished hemoglobin concentration in the red cell, may cause weakness, loss of energy, and poor resistance against disease. Usually this condition is due to a lack of iron stores in the body, the result of low iron intake in the diet, or to unrecognized bleeding, particularly in the gastrointestinal tract. Anemia that fails to respond to oral administration of iron should be evaluated with appropriate laboratory studies. In rare instances, anemia in children is a manifestation of a generalized systemic disease.

Regression

The tendency for a toddler or young child to return to previously abandoned behavior patterns when tired, sick, or under unusual stress. This is common when a preschool child has been ill, has moved, has a new sibling, or has suffered a loss of a family member. He asks for his long-since-discarded bottle, clings to his caregivers, sucks his thumb, hangs on to his favorite blanket or doll, and although toilet trained, may experience accidents. A popular British saying states, "Children take two steps forward and one step back," which illustrates common recognition and acceptance of this very normal behavior.

Regurgitation, *see* Gastroesophageal Reflex

Respiratory Distress Syndrome

A condition occurring in some premature infants in which the immaturity of the lung tissues interferes with effective air exchange. The duration of this condition depends on the degree of immaturity of the baby and the promptness with which supportive therapy is initiated. When prompt care in a newborn intensive care unit is available, infants with this condition usually recover as the lung tissues mature.

Reye's Syndrome

A serious condition occurring as a complication of a viral infection, manifest by marked lethargy and vomiting. A child may be difficult to arouse. Elevation of blood ammonia and other signs of liver failure occur early in this condition. An increasing number of pediatricians, neurologists, and infectious disease experts believe that the disease may be due to the ingestion of aspirin in a susceptible individual when it is administered during a bout of chickenpox or the flu.

If your child is suffering from chickenpox or any other viral infection and on the fourth or fifth day suddenly demonstrates any of these symptoms, contact your doctor immediately.

Immediate hospitalization is indicated when Reye's Syndrome is suspected. Fortunately, the disease is very rare. For additional information, see **Chapter 22, What You Should Know about Fever.**

Rheumatic Fever

A multisystem disease manifest by fever, migratory arthritis (the pain travels from joint to joint), frequent episodes of crying, and inflammation of the heart muscles and valves. Permanent damage to the heart may occur. Rheumatic fever is a complication following streptococcal infection in the throat.

The incidence of rheumatic fever as a complication of streptococcus is markedly reduced when individuals suffering from the streptococcal infection receive appropriate antibiotic treatment.

Rhinitis

An acute or chronic inflammation of the tissues inside the nose due to a viral or bacterial infection, or to sensitivity to a variety of external substances, such as pollen, dust or animal hair, ingested foods or medications, or in rare instances, lipsticks or facial powders. This condition may also occur after prolonged use of nose drops.

Sneezing, itching of the nose, nasal congestion, snorting, postnasal drip, and twitching of the nostrils are common manifestations. Often a child rubs his nose with the palm or back of his hand in an "allergic salute." Symptoms due to viral infections disappear in a few days. When the cause is a bacterial infection, such as a pneumococcus or streptococcus infection, antibiotic therapy may be indicated.

In the case of an allergy, removal of offending substances from the diet or the environment offers dramatic relief. Antihistamine preparations are also of some help. Because rhinitis from allergic causes may come from a variety of sources ranging from reaction to food or to a pet, refer to **Chapter 21, Allergies.**

Ringworm

A common fungus infection of the skin characterized by one or more sharply circumscribed scaly patches with a clear center and elevated borders. Contact with infected human beings and domestic animals, particularly young kittens and puppies, is a common source of this infection.

Daily applications of antifungal medications over a period of weeks is the appropriate treatment. Occasionally, oral administration of a fungicide is necessary to get rid of the lesions.

Roseola

A mild viral illness, commonly occurring between the ages of six and twenty-four months. It is manifest by the sudden appearance of a temperature of 104 to 105, which persists for three to five days, then suddenly disappears, and is followed by the appearance of a transient, slightly elevated, pink, discrete rash. The degree of discomfort is minimal. In rare instances, a febrile convulsion occurs due to the sudden onset of the high temperature.

Rubella (German Measles)

A viral disease that in childhood is usually mild. Initially, a child presents a day or so of lethargy followed by the appearance of enlarged lymph glands behind the ears and in the neck. Within a few days a generalized rash consisting of flat blotchy lesions appears, usually first on the face and then spreading over the entire body. Adolescents and adults often suffer joint aches and pains and severe itching. The disease runs a benign course, in most instances lasting three to five days.

There is great concern when rubella occurs in a woman during pregnancy, since the virus causing this disease crosses the placenta and infects the fetus. Exposure to this virus in fetal life, particularly during the first three months, results in serious cardiac defects, hearing loss, visual deficit due to cataract formation, neurologic deficits, and intellectual impairment. Infants who have been exposed to rubella during fetal life should be considered to be contagious for the first year of life. The virus is present in the saliva, tears, nasal secretions, feces, and urine. Transmission of the disease among children and adults is chiefly by means of contact with nasal secretions or saliva.

This disease is gradually disappearing in the United States due to massive efforts to immunize all children before they enter school. However, it is wise for a woman to be tested for rubella antibodies prior to becoming pregnant. If no antibodies to this disease are present, a woman should receive immunizations before undertaking a pregnancy. See also Measles in this guide.

Salmon Patches

Tiny pink or red discoloration present in the skin of many newborns. These lesions are found over the bridge of the nose, upper eyelids, and the nape of the neck. Disappearance of the areas of discoloration is the usual course.

Salmonella

The invasion of this bacteria into the human body causes nausea, vomiting, headaches, malaise, fever, and inflammation of the intestinal tract. Watery diarrhea with occasional blood and mucus are common. The source of the infection is contact with infected domestic animals, pets, or contaminated food such as poultry, meat, eggs, and milk.

The mainstay of therapy is the administration of fluid solutions to make up for the loss due to vomiting and diarrhea. When fluid intake by mouth is inadequate, hospitalization for intravenous administration of fluids and salts is necessary.

Scabies

A highly contagious skin disorder caused by an "itch mite," which is barely visible to the naked eye. The mite tunnels under superficial layers of the skin, producing itchy papules, blisters, and linear burrows. In infants and young children, the distribution of the lesions includes the palm, head, neck, and face. In older children and adults, lesions tend to involve the webs of the fingers, armpits, flexing areas of the arms and wrists, the belt line, and the areas around the nipples, genitalia, and lower buttocks. The itchiness can be very severe. Scratching may cause serious bleeding.

Human beings can be infected by contact with infected individuals and also from infected dogs. Application of one percent lindane cream or lotion is usually sufficient to kill the mites. However, the rash and itching may continue for several weeks, due to the allergic reaction occurring in the skin. However, if no new lesions appear, you can trust that the mites are gone and that the skin will heal in a few weeks.

Scalded Skin Syndrome

A specific inflammatory, flaky skin condition due to the invasion by a specific strain of bacteria, called staphylococcus, which releases a toxin causing breakdown of the superficial skin. The disease begins with a preliminary period of discomfort, fever, and irritability, followed by a generalized redness of the skin and neck, which develops into a sandpaperlike appearance and is extremely tender. The process may spread over the entire body. Within two or three days, the upper layer of the skin becomes wrinkled and peels with the slightest touch. An occasional patient may be quite ill. Usually the condition responds promptly to the oral administration of appropriate antibiotics. Healing of the skin may take ten to fourteen days. There is usually no scarring.

Scarlet Fever

A condition characterized by sore throat, fever, and malaise with an associated scarlet-colored rash. It is caused by a streptococcal infection. Scarlet fever is common among children.

The disease includes lesions of the tonsils, pharynx, tongue, and palate with an associated bright red rash that blanches on pressure. It appears first on the upper trunk, and then within a matter of hours appears all over the body. The face is flushed but rarely shows the rash. Usually the skin presents a rough, sandpaperlike texture—more intensely in the skin folds. The rash lasts for four to five days. Following its disappearance, the skin often peels, particularly on the hands, palms, fingertips, and soles of the feet.

The administration of penicillin or an antibiotic is the appropriate treatment.

Scoliosis

A lateral curvature of the spine causing the rib cage to be asymmetrical with elevation of the shoulder on the concave side of the bend. The condition, much more common in girls than in boys, usually becomes noticeable in the early months of the adolescent growth spurt. Once detected, a minor curvature that is less than twenty-five degrees should be observed for progression at four- to six-month intervals. If the curvature progresses markedly, a special brace may be necessary until growth is completed. In severe cases, surgical intervention with the insertion of a metal rod into the spinal column is indicated.

Seasickness, *see* Motion Sickness

Seborrheic Dermatitis, *see* Dermatitis, Seborrheic

Sensory Hearing Loss, *see* Hearing Loss, Sensory

Septal Defect

A small hole in the septum dividing the right and left sides of the heart. Most babies and children who have this defect suffer no symptoms other than the presence of a distinct cardiac murmur. The hole often closes spontaneously.

When the septal defect does not spontaneously close in early childhood, consultation with a pediatric cardiologist should be arranged. Surgical repair may be necessary.

Shingles (Herpes Zoster)

An acute eruption of the skin caused by the chickenpox virus, characterized by a blistery rash appearing in a band-like distribution, extending from the midback area around the side of the body to the anterior chest wall. It is usually unilateral. Pain and skin sensitivity may precede the appearance of skin lesions, which usually last seven to fourteen days. Low-grade fever, swollen lymph glands, and malaise may be present. The disease is self-limited. Open wet compresses and topical applications of lotions relieve the discomfort. Adolescents and adults are far more likely to have shingles than children are, and the older the victim, the more severe the illness.

Silver Nitrate

A colorless crystalline compound administered in a weak solution to the eyes of newborn infants to prevent infection due to bacteria that may have invaded the eyes during the passage of the baby through the birth canal.

A colorless crystalline form of the compound is applied as a cautery to granulation tissue that may form at the site of the umbilical stump during the first few weeks of life.

Shoe Dermatitis, *see* Dermatitis, Shoe

Sinusitis

Inflammation and infection of the sinuses, the tiny, air-filled cavities located just above the upper jaw (maxillary sinus), under the eyes adjacent to the nose (ethmoid sinuses), and above the eyes (frontal sinuses). Sinusitis, particularly in the maxillary sinuses, is now observed as a common cause of chronic nasal congestion, cough, wheezing, middle ear infection, and hearing loss in nursery and elementary school years. It is more common in children with allergies because tissue swelling obstructs the normal drainage flow from the sinuses into the nose. Definitive diagnosis is based on clinical findings upon examination, and X ray studies, which usually reveal thickening of the inner lining of the sinuses. Appropriate antibiotic therapy often clears the infection.

Skin Problems, *see* Acne, Baby; listings under Dermatitis; Hives; Impetigo; Molluscum Contagiousum; Mongolian Spots; Pityriasis Rosea; Poison Ivy; Psoriasis; Ringworm; Scalded Skin Syndrome; Shingles; Swimmer's Itch

Soft Spot (Fontanel)

The area on the top of a newborn baby's head where the skull bones are still in the process of fusing. The size of the spot varies from baby to baby, as does the time of closing. Some fontanels close at eight months and others are open until well into the second year of life. The time of closure is unimportant as long as the head circumference is growing at the usual rate of approximately one centimeter per month during the first year of life.

When the baby is sitting so that the light shines on his head, you may observe the skin over the soft spot pulsate with each heartbeat. It will be more pronounced when the baby is crying.

If the fontanel is unusually prominent or appears to be bulging above the surface, it suggests an increase in intracranial pressure within the baby's head. This can be due to abnormalities in the production and drainage of the normal fluids surrounding the brain, or it can be due to increased pressure from an infection inside the head. If you notice that the fontanel is bulging, have your baby examined promptly by your physician.

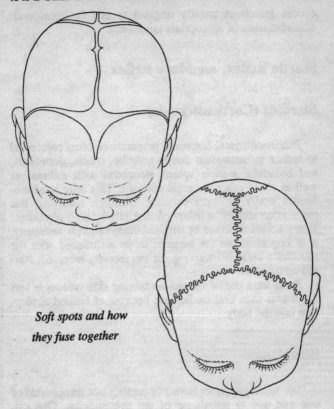

Soft spots and how
they fuse together

Spinal Tap, *see* Lumbar Puncture

Staphylococcus

A bacteria that produces abscesses anywhere on or in the body. Common in skin infections such as boils, cellulitis, impetigo, infections around the nails, or sties are often due to invasion by this organism. Pneumonia caused by infection with staphylococcus occurs rarely. Staphylococcus infections usually respond to oral or intravenous administration of appropriate antibiotics.

Startle Reflex, *see* Moro Reflex

Steroids (Corticosteroids)

Pharmacological hormonal preparations often prescribed to reduce inflammation due to arthritis, colitis, dermatitis, and bronchial muscle spasm associated with asthma, as well as many other systemic diseases. This drug is administered orally or intravenously. Children receiving this medication should be followed carefully by their physician. If any accident occurs or surgical intervention is necessary, it is important for the surgeon to be acquainted with the fact that a child is receiving, or has recently received, steroid medication.

Short-term use of steroid-containing skin creams is less hazardous than oral medication because of limited absorption into the body.

Strabismus

The turning in (esophoria) or turning out (exophoria) of one eye due to imbalance of the eye muscles. One eye focuses on what the child wishes to observe and the other eye looks elsewhere. The eye that is not used becomes "lazy" or amblyopic because of disuse. This condition should be treated as early as possible, since disuse of one eye can lead to a permanent loss in visual acuity.

Many young children appear to be suffering from strabismus because a fold of skin at the inner corner of each eye covers the pupils when the child looks inward toward the nose. When there is any question of strabismus or other eye difficulty, arrange to have your child examined by a doctor with special knowledge and training in the eye problems of infancy and childhood. Also see listings for Eyes in this guide, and Vision Difficulties in **Chapter 9.**

Strawberry Mark, *see* Hemangioma

Streptococcal Sore Throat (Strep Throat)

A throat infection due to an invasion of a specific bacteria, the hemolytic streptococcus, type B. In many children, particularly toddlers and preschoolers, the infection is low grade, manifest by slight fever, mild sore throat, and moderate enlargement of the lymph glands. This condition, known as streptococcal fever, may last several weeks.

In the school-age child, the disease is often, but not always, characterized by inflammation and pain in the throat, enlargement of the lymph glands, accompanying fever, headache, nausea, vomiting, abdominal pain, and general discomfort. The culturing of hemolytic streptococcus, type B from the throat offers laboratory confirmation of the physician's clinical findings.

Treatment with penicillin or other appropriate antibiotic orally for ten days, or by an injection of long-acting preparation is indicated. Recurrences are common, and a second course of antibiotic may be necessary. Other family members and close contacts are usually not treated unless there is some indication of illness.

Rheumatic fever and nephritis are rare complications following a streptococcal sore throat. Treatment of the initial infection with penicillin usually prevents the occurrence of rheumatic fever. However, the development of acute nephritis following a streptococcal sore throat may occur even when the initial infection has been treated with adequate antibiotics. For more information, see Nephritis and Rheumatic Fever in this guide, and refer to a discussion of strep throat in **Chapter 23, How to Tell If Your Child Is Sick or Very Sick.**

Sty

A painful infection in the eyelid at the base of an eye-lash. A white head of pus is usually present, accompanied by tenderness and redness. Within a few days a sty usually bursts, drains, and the child feels better. However, the discharge of purulent material into the eye often seeds a subsequent infection. Immediate relief of the pain is usually obtained by applying warm cloths to the eye. Reinfection can be prevented by the use of appropriate antibiotic eye drops. Call your doctor if the problem persists.

Sudden Infant Death Syndrome (SIDS, Crib Death)

Sudden Infant Death Syndrome (SIDS), often called Crib Death, describes the sudden, unexpected death of a baby who has previously shown no signs of illness. The infant just stops breathing. Although the cause is unknown, it is now believed that many infants who succumb to SIDS possess a defect in the ability to control respiratory function, which results in the baby suffering a chronic deficiency in oxygen supply to the body.

A specific type of respiratory movement has been observed in babies who have later succumbed to Sudden Infant Death Syndrome. Your pediatrician or your state health commissioner can refer you to the nearest center where your baby's respiratory patterns can be evaluated if you have any reason to be concerned about this particular syndrome (for example, if you've already lost one child to SIDS).

Additional information is available from the National Sudden Infant Death Syndrome Foundation, 2 Metro Plaza, Suite 205, 8240 Professional Place, Landover, MD 20785.

Sunscreen

A chemical substance that, when applied to the skin, absorbs ultraviolet light so that it does not penetrate through the living layers of the skin. Para-aminobenzoic (known as PABA) and its derivatives form the basis of most of the major sunscreens. PABA offers an efficient block to ultraviolet light and is safe to use on exposed areas to prevent sunburn.

All sunscreens carry a rating of their ability to provide photoprotection, which is called their "sun protective factor," or SPF. Sunscreens with higher numbers provide greater protection against the sun. Fair-skinned children should use a sunscreen with a SPF of at least fifteen.

Sunscreens are available in a wide variety of lotions, creams, and gels.

Swimmer's Ear, *see* External Otitis

Swimmer's Itch

An acute allergic skin condition due to penetration of the skin by a parasite frequently found in freshwater lakes in the northern United States. A pricking sensation is felt at the time of initial penetration. This itching, which may last for an hour or more, is associated with inflammatory lesions approximately one to two millimeters in diameter. These initial lesions may disappear in a few hours, but are followed by the appearance of larger lesions a day or so later, which cause prolonged severe itching and last several days. Often there is a residual brown pigmented area present for many months.

Treatment consists of the oral administration of antihistamine preparations and the use of soothing lotions on the skin.

Polluted waters should be treated by public health officials to remove the parasite from the bathing area.

Synovitis

A common condition occurring in young children manifest by hip pain upon walking and other types of body movements. Symptoms usually appear about one week following a significant viral illness. The child awakens with pain in one hip and refuses to walk. The cause is believed to be an inflammatory process in the hip joint initiated by the viral infection. Rest and administration of aspirin relieve the symptoms. The condition lasts seven to ten days, although in rare conditions it may last for several weeks. In that case, it is known as *Transient Synovitis*. Pain is usually mild, although rotation of the hip intensifies the discomfort. An X ray examination reveals no pathology.

Tear Duct, *see* Blocked Tear Duct

Tear Duct Stenosis, *see* Lacrimal Duct Stenosis

Teething

Inflammation of the gums and discomfort accompanying the eruption of teeth. There is considerable controversy about whether teething produces symptoms one usually associates with illness. It is my impression after thirty years in pediatric practice that many infants do suffer low-grade fever, rashes (particularly in the anal area), and alteration in bowel habits—either constipation or diarrhea—while they are teething. These symptoms often disappear dramatically when a tooth erupts. However, it is unwise to assume that teething is always the cause of these problems. If your child is suffering with any of these symptoms, call your doctor and let the physician evaluate whether an illness or teething is the basic cause of discomfort.

Testicle Torsion

Acute onset of painful swelling of the testicle, occurring as the result of spontaneous twisting, which constricts the blood supply to the organ. Prompt surgical repair is necessary in order to prevent permanent damage due to diminished blood supply.

Tetanus (Lockjaw)

Tetanus is a very serious disease caused by infection in a wound due to a toxin released by bacteria known as Clostridium tetani, which lives in the soil. This disease is quite rare in the United States due to widespread immunization programs. It is commonly seen in rural areas in underdeveloped countries.

Onset is gradual, one to seven days after exposure, and progresses to severe generalized muscle spasm and rigidity, which may last for weeks. Tetanus is potentially fatal.

Three-Day Measles, *see* Rubella

Theophyllin

A drug administered orally for the relief of coughs and breathing difficulties due to spasm of the bronchial muscles occurring in pulmonary infections and asthma.

Occasionally this drug produces restlessness and irritability. There are other comparable drugs available for treating these respiratory symptoms when side effects contraindicate the use of this medicine.

Thumb Sucking

Thumb sucking is a normal mechanism by which babies obtain comfort when they are tired, uncomfortable, or upset. Some fortunate babies are able to begin thumb sucking at the moment of birth. Other babies develop this skill in the first few weeks of life. Indeed, ultrasound studies of a baby in the mother's uterus often reveal thumb sucking long before the infant is ready to be born!

You may wonder if thumb sucking in infancy will lead to a habit that continues into the preschool years. There is no evidence to support this idea. In fact, infants whose sucking needs are met adequately in the first years of life are less likely to be thumb suckers in later years.

There is also no evidence suggesting that sucking the thumb in toddler and preschool years contributes to any dental problems later. Only when the tendency for thumb sucking continues after the permanent teeth have erupted (that is, in the kindergarten and elementary school years) is there cause for concern. In this instance, the continued thumb sucking may alter the position of the front teeth.

The vast majority of toddlers discontinue thumb sucking by their third birthday, except for occasional moments of anxiousness associated with loneliness, illness, boredom, or other discomforting experiences. When a preschool child continues to spend considerable amounts of time sucking her thumb, it is important to evaluate her daily schedule. A nursery school or other enriching activity to relieve boredom and loneliness often decreases the tendency to prolong the habit.

Tibial Torsion

A postural position of the lower legs in toddlers in which the knee faces a bit more laterally than average, and the foot tends to turn inward. This condition usually disappears spontaneously. In rare instances, corrective shoes or application of casts may be indicated.

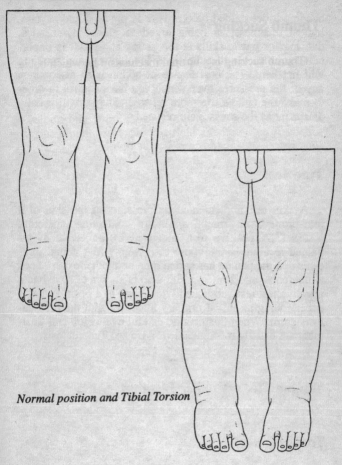

Normal position and Tibial Torsion

Tics

Nervous habits such as eye blinking, wrinkling the nose, or twisting the shoulders are commonly seen during the preschool years. These symptoms appear when a child is experiencing unusual stress in some area of life. The youngster may be feeling the effects of being pushed to become toilet trained before there is physical and psychological readiness, or being urged to master gymnastics, dancing, or music skills at too young an age. It is important to remember that the tic is involuntary, and scolding will not help. The best course of action is to discontinue any of the pressures over which you have control in order to make the child's life more relaxed. The tic will usually disappear as the stresses are reduced.

Tine Test

A skin test implemented by pressure on the skin of a four-pronged tiny metal applicator containing tuberculin material. A positive test, indicated by an elevated, inflamed reaction lasting more than twenty-four hours, indicates that the patient has at one time or another experienced a tubercular infection. A child who is known to have had a negative test and subsequently converts to a positive test is experiencing an initial primary infection with the tuberculosis germ. When this occurs, careful evaluation and treatment are usually recommended. Also see Tuberculosis.

Tongue Tie, *see under* Lisping

Tonsils

Lymphoid tissue embedded in the lateral walls of the pharynx. Normally large in early childhood, these tissues diminish in size as a child grows. In rare cases, tonsils become chronically infected and surgical removal is indicated. Whenever possible, this procedure should be postponed until the age of five or later, when a child is able to cope more easily psychologically with this procedure than in earlier years.

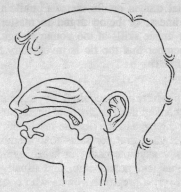

Location of tonsils

Tortocollis (Wry Neck)

A contracture of the neck muscle seen frequently in infancy, which causes the head to flex in the direction of the affected muscle and rotate in the opposite direction. A mass is often present in the center of the involved muscle, suggesting that a hemorrhage occurred in fetal life.

Rarely, this occurs as an acute condition in older children, seemingly associated with viral infections. Treatment consists of exercises to restore normal function of the muscle. Surgical intervention, in which the muscle is lengthened, may be necessary.

Tourette's Syndrome

A central nervous system disorder manifest by repeated involuntary jerking movements of the head, face, eyes, lower body, and arms and legs, accompanied by grunting, snorting or throat clearing, and repeated expressions of inappropriate words or phrases. Parents and teachers should be aware that this is an illness. The child's actions are involuntary, and he or she needs treatment.

Toxoplasmosis

A parasitic infection acquired by ingesting contaminated, undercooked meat or material contaminated with cat feces containing eggs of the disease-producing organism.

Generally, when one contracts toxoplasmosis, the disease is usually asymptomatic, or when symptoms occur they are vague and nonspecific, and usually go undiagnosed. However, a pregnant woman who contracts it may transmit the disease, which can be quite serious, to her unborn infant. Toxoplasmosis can affect the baby's nervous system, causing permanent damage or fetal death. An infected infant may have hydrocephalus, a small head, retinal damage, and seizures. X rays of the skull at birth may show calcifications within the brain. Severely affected infants may die within a few days of birth. Those surviving may experience mental retardation, learning disabilities, impaired vision, or blindness.

Blood tests specifically for the disease can establish the diagnosis in a pregnant woman or a child. Treatment with sulfonamids and other medications is in order.

Transient Synovitis, *see* Synovitis

Transitional Object

A doll, blanket, or toy to which a baby (usually in the latter part of the first year or early in the second year) is very attached, particularly at bedtime. This object is considered by the baby to be a "little bit of the mother." When a baby is separating from the mother, as at bedtime or naptime, or when she is away from home, carrying and cuddling the item will comfort the baby in the mother's absence. A baby and toddler should be supported in the use of a transitional object.

Tuberculosis

A systemic disease caused by invasion of the tubercle bacillus into the body. The usual source is respiratory droplets from an infected individual. Ingestion of contaminated milk is also a source of infection.

The primary or initial infection often observed in childhood is usually asymptomatic, the only evidence for infection being the recent finding of a positive skin test (see Tine Test in this guide). Careful evaluation, including chest X ray, is important whenever a primary infection is noted, since active involvement of the lungs and lymph nodes may occur.

A child with evidence of a primary tuberculin infection should be treated with isoniazid orally for one year.

A recurrence of active infection in adulthood is usually a more serious disease than the primary infection in childhood.

Whenever a child is found to have primary tuberculosis, determined effort should be made to find the source of the infection. Usually a family member, friend, caretaker, or teacher is unknowingly suffering from an active phase of tuberculosis.

Ultrasound

A noninvasive diagnostic tool involving the use of sound waves that are absorbed and reflected by the body and can then be transmitted to a pictorial screen or a film to reveal the size and shape of interior organs and masses. Ultrasound is commonly used to evaluate size and age of a fetus. A main advantage is that this method of obtaining images involves no radiation.

Undescended Testicle (Cryptorchidism)

The testes, the male sex glands, develop inside the abdomen and by the time of birth have usually descended through the inguinal canal into the scrotal sac. In some instances, one or both testes fails to descend. Usually spontaneous descent occurs in the first year of life. After this age, spontaneous descent is unlikely to occur. If descent fails to take place in the early preschool years, surgical intervention is necessary.

Urinalysis

A simple laboratory examination of a urine specimen performed either in a physician's office or in a medical laboratory. The specific gravity of the voided urine, the degree of acidity, and testing for the presence of albumin, sugar and ketones are the routine examinations. Usually a small portion of the urine is spun in a centrifuge and examination of the sediment under a microscope is undertaken in order to determine the abnormal presence of white or red blood cells. If white cells are present indicating the presence of an infection, the doctor may want to arrange for bacteriologic studies of the urine in order to determine the specific organism causing the infection. These findings enable the doctor to prescribe appropriate antibiotics which usually cure the infection.

Urine Culture

An examination of a sample of urine to determine the presence of pathologic bacteria indicating an infection in the bladder, ureter, or kidneys. Determination of specific organisms present in significant quantities is important in order for a physician to choose the appropriate antibiotic for the treatment of this condition.

Urticaria, *see* Hives

Urination, Painful, *see* Dysuria

Vaginitis

Irritation and inflammation of the vulval and vaginal tissues in female children. Careful physical examination and bacteriologic studies of the secretions are important. Causes of vaginitis include a foreign body in the vagina, pinworm infestation, bacterial and fungal infections, or allergic reactions to soap or nylon underwear. The finding of a gonococcus (the organism responsible for gonorrhea) in the secretions from the genital area indicates the need for careful investigation of a child's living conditions. Sexual molestation is very likely to be occurring when this organism is present.

Appropriate antibiotic or antifungal treatment is indicated when disease-causing organisms are present. When an allergic reaction is the cause, switching types of underwear or discontinuing the offending detergent or soap often results in the disappearance of symptoms.

Viral Arthritis, *see* Arthritis, Viral

Virus

Tiny, infectious agents that are responsible for many diseases in infants, children, and adults. Measles, German measles, mumps, hepatitis, chickenpox, poliomyelitis, upper respiratory infections, and gastroenteritis are examples of common viral diseases. Antibiotics are ineffective in controlling viral infections, although judicious use of these medications may prevent complications due to secondary bacterial infection.

Vision problems, *see listings under* Eyes

Vitamins

Complex substances occurring naturally in plant or animal tissues, which play an important role in maintaining normal metabolic functions in human beings. They are also available in synthetic forms. Although present to some extent in human breast milk, added vitamins A, D, and C should be offered to breast-fed infants during the first year of life. Older children usually ingest a sufficient variety of foods so that additional vitamins are unnecessary. However, a child who has a low food intake, or who has suffered a major illness or injury, benefits from the addition of multivitamin preparations to his or her diet.

Warts

A viral infection of the skin producing a small growth in the outer layers. Plantar warts occur on the sole of the foot, usually at pressure points. Other common sites are the face, neck, arms, hands, and legs.

Daily applications of lactic acid and salicylate solutions often will result in the disappearance of these lesions. Treatment may be necessary for four to six weeks. In many instances, the application of stronger medications by a physician or local treatment with liquid nitrogen is necessary. Recurrences are common.

Weaning from the Breast

Weaning from the breast to the bottle is an easy task for some infants, while for others it represents a major transition. Whenever a mother decides to wean her baby, it is important to realize that although this change in feeding is a major adjustment for the baby, mastering this hurdle represents an important step in growing up. There are several moments in the first year when weaning is likely to proceed with relative ease. One is at five to six months of age, and another at seven and one-half to nine months of age. Other babies are not weaned until well past their first birthday.

Most mothers find that discontinuing one breastfeeding for a few days, then discontinuing a second feeding, and so on works well. If a mother's milk supply remains too plentiful, reducing fluid intake and wearing a tight binder will help decrease milk production.

It is wise to wean to a prepared milk mixture or evaporated milk diluted with equal amounts of water if the baby is less than one year of age. Whole milk is poorly digested by many infants until after the first birthday.

Wheezing

A symptom of some type of blockage of the respiratory passages. While wheezing may be caused by constriction of the airways due to an infection or an allergic reaction such as asthma, a child who suddenly begins to wheeze (particularly in the absence of an allergic history) deserves a chest X ray. A foreign body such as a small toy, screw, nut, or a tooth may have been swallowed and aspirated, causing a mechanical obstruction. Such items can lodge in the larynx, trachea, or bronchus, and need to be removed by bronchoscopy as soon as possible.

White Blood Cells

The components of the blood that help to control bacterial infection. A determination of the number of circulating white blood cells in a drop of blood helps to determine the nature of a child's disease. Diseases due to invasion of pathogenic bacteria cause a marked elevation of the white blood count; in viral diseases, the number of white blood cells are usually normal, or just slightly elevated.

Whooping Cough, *see* Pertussis

Zinc Deficiency

An inadequate amount of zinc in a child's diet may result in anemia, reduced rate of growth, and in rare instances a severe chronic eczematoid rash. Oral administration of zinc preparations is the appropriate treatment for this deficiency.

Appendix: Your Child's Body

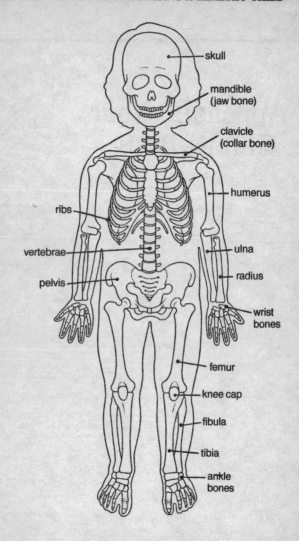

Skeletal structure

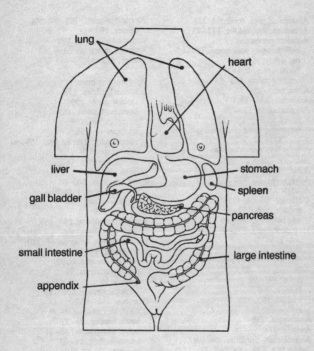

Internal organs

Index

About the Author

Dr. Morris A. Wessel has practiced pediatrics in New Haven, Connecticut for more than thirty-five years. A graduate of the Yale Medical School, Dr. Wessel received postgraduate training at the Babies Hospital in New York, the Mayo Foundation, and the Yale New Haven Medical Center. Currently he is a Clinical Professor of Pediatrics at the Yale Medical School, a member of the American Academy of Pediatrics and the Society of Adolescent Medicine, and a consulting pediatrician at Clifford Beers Child Guidance Clinic.

Dr. Wessel has been closely associated with *Parents* magazine for many years. For six years he wrote the column, "New Mothers Want to Know," and for three years, "Ask Dr. Wessel." He has also written for *Ladies Home Journal, Working Mother,* and numerous textbooks and professional journals. His own hands-on experience with children includes raising with his wife, Irmgard Wessel, a clinical social worker, three sons, David, Bruce, and Paul, and one daughter, Lois.

BRINGING UP BABY

A series of practical baby care and family living guides developed with the staff of *PARENTS™ MAGAZINE*. Explains both the whys and how-to's of infant care.